MAURICE BARING

MAURICE BARING

A Citizen of Europe

Emma Letley

CONSTABLE · LONDON

First published in Great Britain 1991
by Constable and Company Limited
3 The Lanchesters, 162 Fulham Palace Road
London W6 9ER
Copyright © 1991 by Emma Letley
The right of Emma Letley to be
identified as the author of this work
has been asserted by her in accordance
with the Copyright, Designs and Patents Act 1988
ISBN 0 09 469870 8
Set in Monophoto 11pt Sabon by
Servis Filmsetting Limited, Manchester
Printed in Great Britain by
St Edmundsbury Press Limited, Bury St Edmunds

A CIP catalogue record for this book
is available from the British Library

FOR MY MOTHER, AUDREY FINLAY (BARING)

Contents

CONTENTS

PART VI THE LAST YEARS 1936–1945

Illustrations

between pages 96 and 97

MB's parents in 1870 from Susan Baring's (later Lady Reid) albums
(*Sir Alexander Reid*)
Membland (*Mrs Helen Foster*)
A page from Susan Baring's albums (for 1874–1878) showing the
family and Chérie in 1877 (*Sir Alexander Reid*)
MB as a young actor (*Sir Alexander Reid*)
Maurice and Hugo Baring and their sisters (*Mrs Helen Foster*)
Mary Ponsonby (Aunt M'aimée), 1890s (*Sir Alexander Reid*)
Chérie (*Sir Alexander Reid*)
John Baring (later Lord Revelstoke) in 1887 (*Sir Alexander Reid*)
MB in 1885 (*Sir Alexander Reid*)
MB in 1895, at about the time he met Conrad Russell (*Sir Alexander
Reid*)

between pages 192 and 193

Count Benckendorff by John Singer Sargent (*Mrs Humphrey Brooke*)
Countess Sophie Benckendorff (*Mrs Humphrey Brooke*)
MB in St Petersburg (*Baring Brothers & Co Ltd*)
The home of the Benckendorffs at Sosnofka (*Mrs Humphrey Brooke*)
Picnic, Sosnofka 1894 (*Mrs Humphrey Brooke*)
MB in Manchuria: a) 'My sleeping quarters on the summit of Tsien
Chan' (*Mrs Humphrey Brooke*)
  b) 'The Mandarins of Mukden' (*Mrs Humphrey Brooke*)
  c) 'Buriat Cossacks at home' (*Mrs Humphrey Brooke*)
  d) 'Lama Priests' (*Mrs Humphrey Brooke*)
Constantinople, 1912. MB at San Stefano (*Sir Alexander Reid*)
Dame Ethel Smyth (*The Hulton Picture Library*)
Lady Diana Cooper, 1924 (*The Hulton Picture Library*)
Ethel Grenfell (later Lady Desborough) 'Ettie' (*Mrs Helen Foster*)
Lady Juliet Duff from a portrait by Sir John Lavery, 1925 (detail)
(*Private collection*)

9

Acknowledgements

Maurice Baring's works and letters are quoted by kind permission of A.P. Watt Ltd on behalf of the Maurice Baring Will Trust. I am grateful to them and to my agent, Anthea Morton-Saner at Curtis Brown.

The Hon Lady Maclean has been consistently enthusiastic and helpful from the outset of my work. I am extremely grateful for all her kindness. I am deeply indebted to the encouragement, help and generosity of Julian Jeffs and Louis Jebb in allowing me full access to their very substantial collection of Baring's letters and documentary material; and to Louis Jebb, in particular, for sharing his extensive and inspiring knowledge of Maurice Baring with me.

For help in finding and the loan of material for illustrations and photographs I would like to thank Mrs Humphrey Brooke, Mrs Helen Foster, Mrs Audrey Finlay, Mr and Mrs Leonard Ingrams and Sir Alexander and Lady Reid.

For allowing me to quote from manuscript sources of which they hold the copyright I thank Lady Lucas (quotations from the letters and albums of Nan Herbert, later Lady Lucas); and Viscount Norwich (quotation from a letter from Lady Diana Cooper to Conrad Russell).

For approving my use of quotation from letters of which they hold the originals I am grateful to Baring Brothers & Co. Ltd, (letters to MB from John Baring [Lord Revelstoke]; Henry W. and Albert A. Berg Collection, the New York Public Library, Asdor, Lenox and Tilden Foundations (letters from MB to Edward Marsh); the John J. Burns Library, Boston College (letters from MB to Hilaire Belloc); the British Library (letters from MB to G.K. Chesterton); the Brotherton Collection, Leeds University Library (letters from MB to Edmund Gosse); Piers Dixon; the Hertford County Record Office (letters from MB to Lady Desborough); Julian Jeffs; Louis Jebb and Sir Alexander Reid, Bt.

Quotations from *Maurice Baring* by Ethel Smyth appear with the permission of David Higham Associates; those from the Letters of Conrad Russell, edited by Georgiana Blakiston, with permission of John Murray; and those from *The Light of Common Day* and *Trumpets from the Steep* by Lady Diana Cooper with permission of Michael Russell Ltd.

Quotations from *The Letters of Virginia Woolf* are with permission of the Estate of Virginia Woolf and the Hogarth Press.

Many thanks are also due to the British Library, the London Library and the Senate House Library, University of London who have been unfailingly kind and efficient in locating material for me and answering queries.

My work has been very much helped by the following people who have provided assistance of various kinds: Alan Baer; Nicholas Baring; Mrs Muriel Barker; Marjorie Barlow; Peter Chapman; Artemis Cooper; Piers Dixon; Charlotte Gere; the late Margaret Fitzherbert; Arabella Heathcoat-Amory; Col and Mrs Hopkinson; the late Hon Mrs Daphne Pollen; the late Hon Mrs Mildmay-White; Mrs Victoria Ingrams; Diana Lethbridge; Dr John Orbell; Sue Palmer; Xenia Polunin; Nicola Pears; Michael Pye; the Lady Jean Rankin; Alex Revell and Audrey Ryan.

And, of course, many, many thanks to Peter Letley.

I cannot but believe that at the General Resurrection Maurice Baring, of all men now living, will be the most warmly greeted by the greatest number of his fellow-creatures from every country and continent, and from every walk of life. Russian peasants, German students, old women in China, all the *beaux mondes* of Europe, writers, painters, actors and musicians from all winds, men, women, and children who have known him for a week or for a life-time, will rise up and embrace him with individual affection.

(Edward Marsh, *A Number of People*, 1939)

[1]
The Enchanted Land
1874–1898

The Family
and its Houses

I N 1912 Maurice Baring set off on a round-the-world cruise; as the ship passed the coast between Bolt Head and Wembury Point, he felt a quickening recognition:

. . . having been brought up in that little corner of land. I played on those beaches as a child, picnicked on those cliffs, played at robbers and smugglers in those caves. It is like a piece of a dream to see these familiar, these intimate rocks and cliffs, after so many years.

The sea has that peculiar glitter as of a million golden scales, and the sky has something peculiar in the quality of its azure, something luminous, hazy, and radiant which seems to me to belong to the seas of South Devon, and to the seas of South Devon alone.

Is this really so? Does it, I wonder, strike other people in the same way? Or is the impression I receive due to the unfading spell and the old glamour of childhood?

There is a ruined church nestling in the rocks right down by the waves; there are the paths, and the pools, which were the playground of hundreds of games, and the battlefields of mimic warfare, and the temples of the long, long thoughts of boyhood.

There are the spots which to childhood's eye seemed one's very own, a sacred and permanent possession, part and parcel of the larger entity of home which was the centre of one's universe, and seemed to be indestructible and everlasting.[1]

In a letter to Countess Benckendorff of 22 June 1922 Baring gives his private reaction to this journey which was to take him not to his beloved Russia but eventually to New Zealand; he would, he says, give all the world to be at the Benckendorffs' house at Sosnofka, that place that was to become so important to him from his meeting with the Benckendorffs in the 1890s onwards; to see this coastline 'avec la route faite par mon père et les rochers et les plages ou je jouais comme enfant me donne un ridge (depression) terrible'.[2] It was here, near this coastline in South Devon that, at the height of Baring Brothers' success in 1870, Edward Baring (Ned) had acquired the house and 4,000 acres at Membland, about twelve miles from Plymouth. Ned (later Lord Revelstoke) was the son of a famed gambler, Henry Baring (a man believed to have won his London house at cards) and Cecilia Windham, known above all for her musical talent (she was trained by Rossini). Ned, too, had the gambler's instincts; recklessly extravagant, his financial personality also has great charm. He would collect Breguet watches, not to keep but to give as presents to people who would appreciate them, 'He had a contempt for half measures and liked people to do the big thing on a large scale'. Once, he gave Maurice a particularly poignant gift, a little path in the grounds of Membland and the iron gate at its end, a perfect present.[3] On this property, originally an eighteenth-century house, he had lavished apparently limitless funds. The architect, George Devey (a prolific, if now forgotten, adapter of country houses in an imitation of the Jacobean or Queen Anne styles), had previously worked for Baring at Coombe Cottage in Surrey in the early 1860s; and in 1877 he was commissioned to enlarge Membland. Wings were added, as were stables and a building to be used as a large laundry. A ten-mile drive was built along the cliffs so that it was possible to drive in a complete circle from the house along the coastline; and three ornamental tea pavilions and a private telegraph office were constructed on the estate. There was a special larder for 2,000 head of game and Membland became one of the first houses in England to install electricity.

This was the ideal setting for the childhood of Edward Baring's children. Later, friends were to comment that they could only begin to understand Maurice when they accepted what a very, very happy small boy he had been (Vernon Lee was one such when she spoke of the silver spoonery of his boyhood).[4] The houses on the Membland estate were all recognizable by their distinctive blue ('Revelstoke blue') doors and window frames. There was an equally distinctive gate modelled with figures of 'Bull and Bear' in honour of Revelstoke's marriage with the Bulteels. He had married Louisa Emily Bulteel, daughter of John Crocker Bulteel of Flete in Devon and Elizabeth, daughter of Charles, second Earl Grey (she was also a sister of Mary Ponsonby, and granddaughter of Lord Grey of Reform Bill fame) from nearby Pamflete. There was also another family of cousins very close by in the Mildmays of Flete. (Flete was in fact the old seat of the Bulteels and Membland the old seat of the Bulteels' cousins the Perring family from whom Ned bought the house and estate.) With the children of these families the young Barings enjoyed many picnics, swimming parties and sailing expeditions on Edward Baring's 150-ton cutter, the *Waterwitch*, moored in the river Yealm. It was from this group of people, Barings and Ponsonbys, that a very enclosed and characteristically private language, 'The Expressions' emerged, much of which is enshrined in Maurice Baring's letters (see the glossary at the end of the book). *Ridge*, for depression has already appeared. Of course, other families (the Mitfords for one) had their own familiar languages but this one is particularly private. It was used amongst relations and special intimates both in conversation and in letters and is arcane and almost impenetrable to outsiders (part of the Barings' inherent family exclusiveness, perhaps?) who tended (and tend) to be bemused to discover that *Robespierre* means shabby, *Ibsen* means ordinary and a *dentist* is a heart-to-heart talk.

Membland was a place of huge and infectious enjoyment, the appropriate home of a man who 'conformed naturally to the customs of other countries' amd whose acquaintance was varied and international. One Eton master (later to become Provost of King's) wrote in the visitors' book that everything there reminded him of the presence of fairyfolk, 'Where telegrams come by the dozen, concocted behind the door'.[5] There were a great many fashionable house parties: at Easter, at Whitsun, in the autumn for shooting, and, of course, at Christmas. Ned was an assured and discriminating patron of the arts and his wife shared his talents as well as being extremely musical. Guests at Membland included the Prince of Wales, the Empress Frederick, Madame Neruda, the violinist, and Sir Charles Hallé (founder of the well-known orchestra, and later husband of Mme Neruda). The tenor and in particular the easy, informal culture of Revelstoke's entertaining is recaptured in Maurice's *Cat's Cradle*. In this the heroine Blanche Roccapalumba and her husband Guido go to a musical party in the country given by the Roden family whose

> . . . house was the centre of everything that was most agreeable in London. There was a slightly foreign element in it and something not Bohemian, but in touch, nevertheless, with the world of art, letters, and music. There you might meet a painter or a sculptor, and almost certainly a musician, but no lion-hunters and no lions. If a celebrity

was there, it meant he or she was not only a friend but a great friend . . . .

Guido and Blanche arrive at a 'cool house with its panelled-oak rooms full of flowers, its chintz chairs, cool verandahs and shady lawns' and see a typical scene:

There, the centre of a group of fervent admirers, was tall Lady Vanbrugh in the first bloom of her dazzling beauty. There, too, was Countess Felseck . . . the centre of another group in which were Gabriel Carteret, the painter, Adrian Tyne, the diplomatist, who had translated Musset into English and wrote original verse, too; and a little way off, talking to Madame Frantz, the pianist, was young Lord Stonehenge, the Parliamentary Under-Secretary for Foreign Affairs . . . . One or two people were in a small room, like a small smoking room, waiting for Madame Frantz to play. There were sofas and chairs and a grand pianoforte. Princess Marie of Halberstadt was sitting on the sofa: appreciative and rather large. The dining-room looked out on to a verandah, but the guests in the garden were hidden from sight by the Venetian blinds, which were down. Madame Frantz, a dignified lady with grey hair, was sitting at the pianoforte. She looked at the little audience and smiled . . . She played a Chopin prelude, and then a Beethoven Sonata, Op. 112. A few more people, attracted by the sound, came as she played, and sat silently in the verandah . . . When she had finished there was no formal applause, but a spontaneous pouring out of thanks and appreciation. After a slight pause, Mrs Roden said something to Waller, the baritone, and he came forward with some music. He sang the 'Erlkönig' first, in German, and then Schubert's 'Leiermann'. By the time he had finished there was a crowd in the verandah, and they asked for an encore, and he sang Gounod's 'Maid of Athens'.

After that, Mrs Roden thought the artists had been generous enough, and said that everybody must come and have tea – they must all be so thirsty. Tea was in a large tent outside on the lawn: tea, iced coffee, and strawberries and cream; and a band began to play – not a brass band, but a Hungarian band which played Strauss' valses in so intoxicating a manner that some one suggested a dance, and presently couple after couple began dancing on the lawn.[6]

The young Maurice spent his time partly at Membland and partly in

London at 37 Charles Street, W1. This house was a very different proposition from Membland and indeed from the comfortable, rambling Coombe Cottage, upon which the fictive Rodens' country house is modelled, 'an ivy-covered red-brick house, with a tower at one end . . . an enchanted spot for us . . . a place where it was always summer and where the smell of summer and the sounds of summer evening used to make the night-nursery a fairy place . . .'[7] Charles Street was a showplace; Cubitts were employed as the contractors and Turner Lord of Mayfair as the decorators. No expense was spared, with panelling transported from Parisian houses, the columns outside the front door imported from Russia, and an elaborate Portland stone front added which cost £9,000. The vast sum of £55,000 was spent on the new house (which joined the two adjacent properties).

It was here, on the third floor, that much of Maurice's nursery life was passed.

> I can remember the peculiar roar of London in those days; the four-wheelers and hansoms rattling on the macadam pavement through the fog, except when there was straw down in the street for some sick person; and the various denizens of the streets, the lamplighter and the muffin man; often a barrel-organ, constantly in summer a band, and sometimes a Punch and Judy . . .[8]

Here he shared his life with his brother Hugo and his three elder sisters. His elder brothers, John, Cecil and Everard were at Eton. They were, like their brother Maurice, all to become known in their different ways. John, as elder brother and head of the Bank and the family after Ned's retirement and death respectively, features more prominently in this book than do Cecil and Everard. After a successful career at Eton, Cecil did very well indeed, taking a First in Greats at Balliol; he went into the family business to be sent in 1887 to New York and, after the Crash of 1890, he had a vital role in helping to rebuild the business. To the chagrin and dismay of many Barings, he was to marry Maude Lorillard Tailer, an American divorcee, and the ex-wife of his business partner. In April 1904 they bought the beautiful, isolated island of Lambay, north of Dublin which is still owned by the family and where Cecil and Maude are buried. By contrast, Everard became distinguished in the Army and as Chairman of the Southern Railways; he married Lady Ulrica Duncombe, one of the beautiful Duncombe sisters and a serious intellectual (known familiarly as 'Mouche'). Of the sisters, Elizabeth married Viscount Castlerosse (later to become Earl of Kenmare) and lived at Killarney; Margaret married the Hon. Robert Spencer, heir to Earl Spencer, and lived at Dallington; whilst Susan, the closest to Maurice of the sisters, became engaged in 1899 to Sir James Reid, physician to Queen Victoria.

The Baring family had been gradually growing more illustrious since their arrival in England from Germany. They came originally from near Bremen where Dr Franz Baring was a pastor of the Lutheran church (by and large the family retained its Protestant traditions, with one grandson of Sir Francis, Charles Thomas Baring, becoming Bishop of Durham). In 1717, Franz Baring's son Johann was sent to Exeter to become apprentice to some cloth manufacturers. He married and in 1740 had a son called Francis who, after joining the East India Company, founded the family firm of merchant bankers in London and was created a baronet in 1793. Francis's third son, Henry, from Cromer Hall in Norfolk, had ten sons, of whom Ned Baring was the fifth. Born in 1828, he became Baron Revelstoke in 1885, being offered his peerage in Gladstone's dissolution honours.[9] Ned's brother and first cousin also received peerages, those of Cromer and Northbrook. Evelyn Baring (1841-1917), famed for his statesmanship in Egypt and irreverently known in Cairo as 'Over-Baring' (Uncle Mina to his family) became Lord Cromer in 1892 and then first Earl of Cromer in 1901 whilst Thomas George Baring (1826-1904), eldest son of the first Baron Northbrook became Viceroy of India, and then in 1876 the first Earl Northbrook. He was Viceroy of India in 1872 and then served at the Admiralty during Gladstone's administration. Alexander Baring (1774-1848) had also acquired a title, that of first Baron Ashburton. Under Robert Peel's brief Tory administration, he was President of the Board of Trade and also (regrettably, he felt) Treasurer of the Navy; he acquired his title in the dissolution honours of the administration.

The family into which Maurice Baring was born at 37 Charles Street on 27 April 1874 was thus well established in the City, at court and in European high society. The image of the Barings at the time was, however, mainly that of the bankers at 8 Bishopsgate. Here they were seen, variously, as: 'strong, sensible, self-reliant men', giving an 'impression of solidity and squareness'; very enclosed and clannish, 'Their attitude towards the rest of humanity was detached and cool, at its best manifested in a balanced objectivity, at its worst disdainful and indifferent'; and intensely loyal in their business relationships. More generally, and away from the bank, Barings were not expected to be warm and forthcoming, were found to have a streak of indolence, and an invincible dullness (Thackeray is one for whom a Baring dinner is a dull dinner). Extremely public spirited the family also had (and retains) a trait of equally invincible Rising Above It, a tendency to hear only the good news. Overall, they were eminently distinguished but could suffer from 'the family coldness'.[10]

Ned and Emily were not typical Barings; they were not typical bankers either; they and their children were *clever*, at times very clever and they were in no way philistine or suspicious of the intellect, but cultured, articulate and European. Their son, Maurice, some say their favourite child with whom they could not bear to part even for a short journey, inherited much of their charm, their love of music and the theatre, their talent for languages and (from his father) an anarchic spirit that made the Bank quite the wrong place for him.

Like Paradise?
Schooltime

> . . . my first half at Eton was like Paradise,
> and I came back to Membland for the holidays quite radiant.[1]

A LL his life Maurice was to insist that the time until he went away
to private school was 'like fairyland'. This was, he would say, no
false illusion, no rosy retrospective light; countless visitors who
came to the Barings' house in the country agreed that they, too, had
arrived in a 'place of rare and radiant happiness'.[2] Both at Membland and
in London, in the Charles Street house, 'the days went by in a crescendo of
happiness'.

But there had to be an end to this magical chapter and in 1884 he went
away to private school, never again to 'be a free and lawful citizen of that
enchanted country' of childhood. A little before he went to Ascot a
phrenologist, whom he had visited with his beloved governess Chérie,
had predicted his future: 'He said I had a professional and mathematical
head, and would make a good civil engineer in after-life'.[3] There could
have been few less appropriate predictions.

St George's, Ascot came as something of a rude shock. It was not that
the school was spartan or even particularly strict; the atmosphere was
rather more sinister than that: 'There were no bullies – at least not among
the boys; the masters did the bullying. They exercised a reign of terror;
they ruled by mysterious hints and vague threats.'[4] It was a very uneasy
place where 'the boys lived for the greater part in complete uncertainty,
never knowing whether they had or not committed some terrible crime'.
Some of these crimes seem, at best, idiosyncratic, such as spoken or
implied criticism of the food, 'to speak to another boy if you met him
outside the school during school hours . . . to turn on the electric light, to
eat any food, even a grape, if brought by your parents'.[5] One boy was

suddenly beaten for cutting off a piece of his hair and keeping it in a drawer. Odder still, when the boys reached the Second Division they were punished by electricity. The Division was made to join hands and a strong electric shock was passed through them. This dubious, not to say dangerous, form of control continued until one day a boy 'smarting from an overcharge of electricity, took the battery and threw it at the master's head, inflicting a sharp wound.' There were no repercussions on the boys following this incident; they simply thought the master had been 'jolly . . . not to sneak'.[6]

The system of treats was equally arbitrary: sometimes a whole Division would be taken to a play or a group of boys would go to London to visit the Tower or the Mint. Nevertheless, in spite of the treats and Maurice's enthusiasm for football, music and drawing lessons, the school was not a comfortable place to be. The Barings as a family were staunch Liberals, the Headmaster an extremely committed not to say a violent Tory. On polling day the Conservatives were taken to the booths wearing blue ribbons; the seven young Liberals were obliged to stay at the school. On 5 November an effigy of Gladstone was burned in the grounds and the Headmaster made his feelings public in the school's *Gazette*, recording that apart from the seven Liberals 'the rest of the boys are supporters of the Church and the State'.[7]

Maurice experienced some problems both with the other boys and with the masters. The latter laughed at his pronunciation (particularly his old-fashioned habit of saying 'yallow' for 'yellow' and the boys ragged him for having a sister called Susan; 'Sisters should be warned never to let their Christian names come to the knowledge of their brother's schoolfellows'.[8] More important, his background did not always stand Maurice in good stead; the Barings' noble connections seemed to have enraged the Headmaster, a situation that may well have been exacerbated by Edward Baring's being created Baron Revelstoke in 1885.

One day Maurice was summoned to the Headmaster's study. A telegram had come from London with the message that Maurice had been invited to a children's party at Marlborough House given by the Princess of Wales. The Headmaster was acid, asking if Baring was a special friend of the Princess's. Finally it was agreed that Maurice should go to London for the party and return to Ascot that evening. All went well, the party was much enjoyed by Maurice and his younger brother Hugo but then there was a problem. He missed the train back to Ascot. Lord Revelstoke in Devon could not be asked to intervene and Emily decided that Maurice should spend the night in London. A telegram was sent to the school but the Headmaster replied that if Maurice did not return that night he need never return. So, accompanied by Emily's maid, D., he went to Ascot on a very late train arriving at 12.30 in the morning. There were no flys at that time so they walked from the station to the school.

Always very sensitive to others' opinion of him, Maurice thought he would never live this down. As it happened, however, he heard nothing further of it (his father had written a very stern letter to the Headmaster and the incident had been firmly closed). It died hard though. In his autobiography, not published until he was nearing fifty, Maurice makes the plea that, if only parents knew the distress such happenings caused their children, they would not insist on a school granting such favours 'nor ever forward invitations of that kind, not even at the bidding of the King'.[9]

In spite of difficulties like this Maurice's letters of this time sound basically happy. The tone of those to his mother is nearly always enthusiastic as he writes of his lessons, of games of Prisoners' Base and, especially, of making his own garden with 'four rose trees, several geraniums, some cherry pie, and a border of lobelias'.[10] His letters, too, show an early talent for sketching and are filled with charming, small drawings and pen-and-ink sketches of places he has been, matches he has watched, school buildings and, of course, the layout of his garden.

His parents may have failed Maurice in the matter of inappropriate invitations from the Court but, in other ways, they were extraordinarily enlightened and sympathetic about their children's education. Emily, in particular, was very much aware of her son's sensitivities. Later on Hugo was sent to join his brother at school where they shared a room and were able to continue their habitual games of Spankaboo. This was a game that had been invented in the nursery by Maurice and Hugo and it involved telling and acting the story of an imaginary continent whose countries were almost always at war. An important personage was Lady Spankaboo herself 'a prominent lady at the court of Doodahn. She was a charming character, not beautiful nor clever, and sometimes a little foolish, but most good-natured and easily taken in.'[11] The Spankaboos (he was a country gentleman) had no children but there were a great many other people in the game's cast and it grew with its inventors.

However, the presence of Hugo and games of Spankaboo could not alter the fact that Maurice could not seem to do right in the eyes either of the Headmaster or of the Second Division master and when two other masters, much more friendly towards the young Barings, went off to set up their own school, St Vincent's in Eastbourne, Maurice suggested to his parents that he and Hugo should move there. Believing this to be a fanciful and, in grown-up eyes, an impossible request, he did not expect it to be taken seriously. It was. He and Hugo moved to Eastbourne to be followed shortly by Maurice's friend Broadwood, who had also been at the Ascot school.

It must have been a relief to leave the erratic atmosphere and the sense of ill-defined unease. St Vincent's was 'a new life . . . everything was different. We played Soccer with another school; we went to the swimming bath and I learned to swim; to a gymnasium, and were drilled by a volunteer sargeant.'[12] There were also enjoyable theatrical performances, among others *She Stoops to Conquer* in which Maurice was cast as Mr Hardcastle and Hugo as Miss Hastings; Marlow was played by Broadwood. Instead of a birthday present for 1880 Maurice wrote to his mother asking for three costumes – for Marlow, Hastings and Miss Hardcastle – and, by the way, could she let him have all the white seventeenth-century wigs at Membland. Membland must have had an extensive wardrobe for such occasions judging by the easy tone in which Maurice makes this request. Indeed, theatrical events were very much part of life there where a French play, organized by Chérie was performed every year by the family. For a schoolboy production, *She Stoops*, as played at St Vincent's, sounds a most professional affair. After a number of rehearsals it was agreed that the play should be performed on a real stage, and that parents and other guests should be invited. Costumes were made for the cast in London; the scenery was painted by the school's drawing master; and many parents, including the Revel-stokes, came to see the play which went very well, with Hugo, in particular, a 'vision of beauty' as Miss Hastings.[13]

At home, both at Membland and at Charles Street, much was going on whilst Hugo and Maurice were away at school. Maurice, however, very much disliked the idea of mixing school and home, and was filled with dread if the two threatened to overlap. Once, when his mother suggested that he could bring the choir home to luncheon on a school outing, he had blanched visibly. Emily kindly reassured him that it would be a very good luncheon but he was adamant, and such an event never happened. He did meet Broadwood during the holidays in London. Broadwood would tell his parents that he was going to the Barings' house in Charles Street. Maurice would insist that he was going to Eccleston Square to the

Broadwood parents and the two boys would then go to a bun shop or do without lunch altogether as neither 'would be seen at luncheon with a friend in each other's homes'.[14] Later, Broadwood was to admit to Maurice that when his parents had asked him about 37 Charles Street he had provided a most extravagant account of the Barings' way of life.

The Jubilee year of 1887 was also the year in which two of Maurice's sisters were married – Elizabeth to Viscount Castlerosse (heir to the Earl of Kenmare) and Margaret to Robert (Bobbie) Spencer, later Earl Spencer. Hugo and Maurice attended both these weddings and also the Jubilee procession in London. From his letters, however, it seems that for Maurice one of the greatest excitements of this time was the building of an organ at Charles Street. His mother often asked his advice on this matter and his letters begin to include sketches of the organ and ideas for various modifications. The plans began modestly enough for a small organ but then became much more ambitious, developing into quite a large instrument with three manuals. At Membland, Mr Hele of Plymouth had already built an organ for Lady Revelstoke but she had instructed Maurice not to breathe a word to him about the London plans. Maurice kept his promise faithfully until one day Mr Hele came to Membland to tune the organ there. Maurice went into its entrails with him and whilst there told him about the Charles Street plans. Understandably put out, Mr Hele immediately confronted Maurice's mother saying that *he* would have been delighted to have built one for her in London as well as at Membland. She, in turn, reproached Maurice: 'I thought,' he replied, with a characteristic piece of illogic, 'that as we were right inside the organ, in the dark and in such a narrow space, that it wouldn't matter, and that he would forget'.[15]

In 1887, Maurice left Eastbourne and went to Eton. His experience there was very happy indeed. He must be one of relatively few schoolboys who would later write with absolutely no ironic intent, 'I enjoyed it all from the first to the last moment. If I had my life to live again, I should like all that piece back with nothing left out . . .' He cannot, he says, deal with the experiences of others but he was himself and remained 'a violent, an unblushing, an unrepentant partisan'.[16] His affection for Eton, the Eton of Dr Warre and Arthur Benson, is sustained throughout his life and he would habitually rush into the fray to defend his school against its detractors. This enthusiasm may seem odd to modern eyes; as alien to us, perhaps, as the unquestioned and unquestioning hero-worship of the boys (and then the adults) for each other with their whole-hearted mutual admiration. For Maurice, however, it was all in good faith when he remarked that he enjoyed Eton from the very first moment.

On his arrival his tutor commented: 'You have been taught nothing at all.'[17] Maurice had a deep-rooted habit of concealing such knowledge as he had acquired at his previous schools. He definitely has something in common with his fictional hero, Caryl Bramsley ('C' in the novel of that name) who 'was perfectly consistent in his conduct with regard to all the masters. With the French masters he pretended not to understand a word of French, and with the German master, not to understand a word of German.'[18] The whole time he had been at private school Maurice had contrived to hide the fact that he spoke very good French (thanks to his mother's wise educational policy and the efforts of Chérie). All his life he was to wear his knowledge very lightly indeed, often hiding his real learning. Reports suggest that he was, academically, very like C. with 'little aptitude for mathematics, and, although he had not in him the makings of a scholar, his mind responded to classical subjects, and he had been well grounded in French at home.'[19]

Eton at this time was a school that valued athletic success above all:

They toil at games, they play with books:
They love the winner of the race[20]

These lines, written by an Eton poet and quoted by Maurice are much to the point. The standard of value throughout the school had always tended, Maurice thought, to be athletic rather than intellectual or aesthetic. Oddly, at first sight, Maurice claims to think this a good thing. Clumsy and rather inept at sports, and strangely ill at ease physically, he was much happier with such standards than with the intellectual alternative which he was to loathe all his life: 'The tyranny of the intellect is the worst of all. The rule of intellectuals is far severer than that of athletes.' In any case the system had one overriding advantage; he liked being part of the 'obscure majority' who would never distinguish themselves on the playing fields.[21] The importance attached to games gave those who were inclined towards study every opportunity to pursue their interests undisturbed and to develop their own tastes. At this time he would not have known the comments of Renan but these were to become very important to him and to be used in the face of the (somewhat humourless) intellectual ire of such as Vernon Lee who accused his fictive characters of regrettable frivolity: in reply to her, Maurice invoked Renan when he said that 'if there were not a multitude of people going to the Auteuil races he would not be sitting in his *cabinet de travail* at work; that 10,000 idle people are necessary in order that one savant may work.'²² In part, Eton was responsible for this, one of Maurice's lifelong attitudes.

Eton too offered a much wider life; at last he felt as if he were being treated as an adult and it was a relief to know that there was no one who knew or cared that his sister was called Susan. Fagging was, of course, very much part of the way of life but for Maurice it was a 'light operation'. He had to take his fag-master toast, boil the occasional egg, show that he had clean hands and that was the end of it; 'Then one was free to cook buttered eggs or fry sausages for one's own tea.'²³ Food was always an important preoccupation of Maurice's. Alternately very fastidious and somewhat greedy, his letters from school tend to contain elaborate descriptions of meals or requests for a cake or some other special item (usually accompanied by the plea that his mother shouldn't think him grasping).

From his first half onwards Sundays were spent at the Norman Tower, Windsor with his Ponsonby cousins, the family of Queen Victoria's Private Secretary, Sir Henry Ponsonby and his wife, Maurice's Aunt M'aimée. These were days to which Maurice looked forward all week. Sometimes his cousin Maggie would take him to the Library or to the State Rooms and, if they heard approaching steps they would race away – once they were not in time and discovered the Empress Frederick looking quietly at the pictures by herself. Betty Ponsonby, another cousin at Windsor, was also a great ally and came to share many of Maurice's literary enthusiasms, particularly towards the end of his time at Eton. And, most importantly, there was his affection for Aunt M'aimée – a remarkable woman with a special fondness for Maurice, who was later to describe her as 'a lady of infinite wit, wisdom, tradition and English-ness'²⁴ and one of the first and most perceptive critics of his literary efforts.

His first half at Eton was, unlike that of some of his contemporaries, 'like Paradise'. His academic work was under the supervision of one Mr Heygate, a man who has become enshrined in the Baring family language (a *Heygate* is, regrettably and very possibly unfairly, someone who dislikes all odd or new things, someone dull and drily academic, second-rate). Despite starting with Heygate, Maurice did quite well at Eton. In 1888 he won the Trials Prize, attained a distinction in Trials, and was awarded the Brinkman Divinity Prize (value £5). Hitherto he had fostered the fiction that he could barely write so that the most he was ever expected to produce was a completely illegible script. In this year, the Lower Master's report reads: 'Had I known what I discovered at the end of the half that he could write perfectly well, I would have torn up every scrap of his work during the half.'[25] His careful strategy of academic concealment had come to an end.

Eton in the 1880s and 1890s offered a primarily classical education and Maurice was well aware, when he wrote of his school, of the criticisms levelled against it. He came especially to deplore the tendency to judge an education by its practical value, and its relevance: 'It is said that boys are taught nothing at Eton, and that the reason for this is that the education is classical. It is said that if boys were taught Pitman's shorthand, book-keeping by double entry, how to mend a motor-bicycle and how to break a watch, business Chinese and modern commercial Greek, they would learn more.'[26] Maurice had serious doubts on this score and pointed out that in any case the education was not purely classical but was mixed with Mathematics, Science, French and Classical French. He also insisted that it was quite wrong to say that the boys learned nothing. In *Lost Lectures* (talks given to imaginary audiences and published in 1932) he recalls some of the things he was taught at Eton:

Alcohol is in solution, but castor oil is in suspension.
A diamond is really only a piece of charcoal.
Troy was captured in 1184 B.C. and King Magnus was drowned in 1184 A.D.
    A guinea and a feather take exactly the same time to reach the ground in a vacuum (or *in vacuo*).
    . . . If you had a bamboo house and the pressure of air were taken away from it the house would swell, or smell – I forget which.[27]

Apart from his work and the accumulation of such characteristic pieces of miscellaneous learning, Maurice's activities at Eton included learning more music for the organ, looking after a pug puppy (some pets were allowed), going on the river (in 1888 he asks his mother for a lock-up gig), learning to stuff birds, and of course reading. His list of books read in 1889 is remarkable for its range; it includes works of now-forgotten pulp writers such as Edna Lyall, together with books by authors as diverse as Haggard, Daudet, Dumas, Lord Lytton, Stevenson, Charlotte Brontë and Charles Reade. Always a tolerant critic Maurice's comments in the final column of his list vary from 'perfect book' to 'worth reading'; only two are dismissed as 'trash' – Haggard's *Mr. Meeson's Will* and *Mawaia's Revenge*.[28]

Sharing his reading and also his current enthusiasm for learning to stuff birds was his friend, Dunglass; gradually, too, Maurice made friends with Arthur Benson, through one of Benson's pupils named Willie Coventry. Maurice had twice been in Benson's division but had never really got to know him or to feel entirely at ease in his company. Thought by some to be dry and dull, Benson tended to miss the point of the more quirky of his pupils. Maurice, however, felt he owed him a great debt and appreciated him as 'the most natural and unconventionally-minded of all the masters, incapable of saying anything he did not think, and never giving the impression of being paradoxical'. He was thought much more sympathetic out of school and was very willing to encourage his pupils' aspirations, 'quiet, firm and friendly, like a large St Bernard'.[29] On Sunday afternoons a group of boys met in Benson's rooms and read poetry. These included Arnold, the son of the novelist Mrs Humphry Ward as well as Dunglass and Maurice himself. These meetings offered a good audience for some of his earlier literary efforts, such as a libretto (on which Maurice was working in 1889) with a problematic Fairies' Chorus. 'I don't like these galloping metres, but I see you have got a good vocabulary' was Benson's comment. Next Maurice tried an 'Ode on Eton's Tercentenary'. In the verse he alluded confidently to Fielding as 'the great wielder of the painting pen'. Benson judiciously asked whether he had in fact read any Fielding. Maurice had not. 'I see,' said Benson, 'you take him on trust.'[30]

Benson, too, was a strong influence on Maurice's reading. The master startled some of his charges by his 'frank heresies'. He thought little of Milton's *Lycidas*, wished that Shakespeare had been a modern and a novelist, was indifferent to Shelley, loathed Byron and disliked Carlyle and Ruskin – a strange set of prejudices for an academic at the turn of the century. But Benson also introduced his pupils to the work of Arnold, Rossetti and to Fitzgerald. As a family, the Barings all read a large number of novels, in particular, Thackeray and Scott. They considered the Waverley novels a treat, something to which they were promoted at an appropriate age and an event to which they looked forward with considerable anticipation. In 1889 Maurice asks for an 'old edition' of Scott for his Christmas present. He had by this time also read a great deal of poetry. Betty Ponsonby gave him Swinburne's *Atalanta in Calydon* but, lest there should be any scruples about its lack of godliness, she explained carefully to her cousin that 'the denunciations of God in it applied only to the Greek gods'.[31] *Poems and Ballads*, however, was a much touchier matter. When Maurice mentioned them both Betty Ponsonby and Aunt M'aimée changed the subject, a moment that remained with Maurice when he wrote *C*.:

> They were both of them unaware of the existence of *Poems and Ballads*, which was not on the shelves of the school library, until C. happened to find the volume in question, which had belonged to his brother Edward, at home. Lady Hengrave saw him looking at it and she promptly burnt the book.[32]

The enthusiasm for Swinburne also finds its way into *C*. as Maurice describes how the hero and his friend, Calmady, set out to visit the poet: unfortunately, due to an error over his initials (they confuse A.C. with C.A.), they end up face to face with the wrong Mr Swinburne who was agreeable enough but not the poet. It was, to use the family's phrase for an embarrassing, blushing incident, a bad case of *curling toes*, and both boys dreaded their parents finding out: ' "Those are just the sort of things that leak out years afterwards when one has forgotten all about them," said C., remembering dramatic belated disclosures in novels . . . like in a Greek tragedy or Hall Caine.'[33]

By November 1889, although he was very happy indeed at Eton, the time had come for Maurice to think about what he was going to do next. His talent for languages was by now obvious and his literary leanings were also more than apparent. It seemed as if he was brimful of talent and creativity that was as yet unchannelled (there are those who would say that he never really gave vent to the true artist in himself). His total inability to cope with mathematics was also all too evident. In November he told his mother that he was working for the Junior Prince Consort Prize (for languages) and asked her whether there was any examination to enter a Government Office. If so, it was vital that it should not include compulsory mathematics.

By the following autumn, however, an event had happened that superseded such immediate considerations, one which changed the lives of all the Barings. Up until this time, the holidays had been spent by Maurice in London and at Membland; there were cruises on the *Waterwitch*, off the Devon coast and to the Scilly Isles; and there were visits to Paris with Chérie and sister Susan – in particular, one most memorable occasion in 1889 when they saw the preparations for the Exhibition and the just-completed Eiffel Tower. Such visits were a matter of course; but in November 1890 this began to change. Maurice describes in *Puppet Show* how:

> In the autumn of 1890 Hugo and I went up to London for long leave. My father and mother were staying at my sister Elizabeth's [Kenmare] house in Grosvenor Place, and there we heard about the financial crisis in Baring Brothers, which had nearly ended in great disaster. When we went back to Membland at Christmas everything was different. There was no Christmas party, and the household was going through a gradual process of dissolution. Chérie was leaving us, the stables were empty and the old glory of Membland had gone for ever.[34]

Maurice was very conscious of this sad dissolution (he was to deal with similar situations in C. when the family home, Bramsley, is repeatedly threatened by financial crises). This particular crisis was largely the result of the extensive involvement of Baring Brothers in South American business. Known at the time as specialists in that area, the bank, under the guidance of Maurice's father, had subscribed heavily to South American securities. Dealing with South American governments and institutions (among others, the National Bank of Uruguay, the Buenos Ayres Railways, and the Buenos Ayres Water and Drainage Company) Barings had underwritten a large portfolio of investments which it then found impossible to sell to the public.

By 1890 it was becoming apparent that Barings' zest for South American business had not always taken due account of the situation. Within the bank there had been criticism of Ned Revelstoke's strategy and at least one family member withdrew his personal assets. In early October there were rumours in the City that Barings was in a precarious position. By 8 November matters had reached such a pass at Number 8 as it was known (8 Bishopsgate, then and now home of the bank) the word came to the Governor of the Bank of England, William Lidderdale, that Revelstoke had said, 'I shall be able to tell you on Monday whether we can go on or whether we have to stop.'[35]

The last major City crisis had been in 1866 but some experts thought that 1866 was a mere ripple compared with the potentially grand storm that might result from the failure of such a well-established house as Barings. Such a collapse had to be averted to avoid a large scale panic throughout the financial community. In the event, City institutions, the Bank of England and the Government itself all intervened; the Prime Minister was consulted on 10 November; gold was bought from the Bank of France and the Russian Government; and a full rescue scheme was mounted so that Barings was able to meet its bills as they began to pour in after 14 November by which date news of the bank's difficulties had begun to reach the press. Eventually a fund of £17,105,000 was guaranteed for Barings. The historian of the Bank of England in his official history holds that, 'everything was so quick, so decisive, and so highly centralised that there was no true panic, on the Stock Exchange or anywhere else, no run on banks or internal drain of gold' and he insists that the vast majority of the country's business was little troubled by the near-failure at Number 8.[36]

In the history of the City of London, intervention on this scale was unprecedented (although it would be required again in later twentieth-century crises). It indicates just how influential Barings had become and it shows the fragility of that great Victorian commercial banking structure – there is a strong feeling that if one link failed the whole edifice might come tumbling down, Humpty-Dumpty-like. It is an episode that is perhaps closer to the monetary reversals in Dickens and Trollope than financial historians would have us believe.

Barings was saved but the family was affected as a result of 1890. Some still shudder today about the 'crisis'. John Baring took over from his father. He was only twenty-seven at the time but under his leadership the bank was reconstructed as Baring Bros and Co. Ltd. Private family fortunes had to be thrown into the breach and it took four years to complete the liquidation process before the new operation could get underway. The family were now relatively poor. At the height of his wealth, Edward Baring was believed to have had the enormous annual income of £100,000. He was much depressed by the state of affairs and then embarked on a spate of activity. 'Such a Metamorphosis in the space of one month it is impossible to conceive,' Lady Revelstoke told Everard. 'Tearing spirits – and at the sight of the sideboard with nothing on it, exclaiming "By heaven, I cannot be starved! Let's have enough to eat!" So things *must* be better.'[37] As Maurice had said, Membland was much reduced, and there are indications in letters of 1891 that there was a threat to Charles Street, valued at £75,000 with £50,000 for Lord Revelstoke's collection of French furniture, pictures and *objets d'art*.[38] Some of the relations suggested that it was inadvisable to be seen to be living in a house where £9,000 had recently been spent on the façade alone at a time when retrenchment, to put it mildly, was more than necessary. The nuance of being seen in such opulence just would not do – as Aunt M'aimée, among others, suggested to Maurice.

Maurice was not affected as immediately by the crisis as his brothers; his relationship with the financial world was always tenuous (although, as he was extremely extravagant and not particularly adept at making money, banking was indirectly the source of some of his income); he made only one foray into this world when in St Petersburg he was involved in some negotiations for a tramway loan. But in 1890 he was more engrossed with his adventures in English literature than he was with merchant banking. Back at Eton for his last term he was a member of the House Debating Society in which there were discussions on such topics as whether or not sports were brutalizing, or whether conscription was justified. He was particularly happy during the summer of 1891; and it was then that he was introduced to the Cornish family by Aunt M'aimée. Mr Cornish was to become Vice-Provost of Eton and the Cornish children (Gerald, Hubert and Cecilia) all became close friends of Maurice's. Hubert was with him in Germany shortly after they left Eton; and Cecilia was to join him in a number of literary enterprises (including an unpublished but promising novel, La Chose).

Maurice's prime ambition at this time was to win the Prince Consort Prize, an ambition with which Chérie was understandably very sympathetic. Although she had left Membland at the time of the crisis, Maurice kept up his connection with her. She had gone to live with her friend, a Miss Charlesworth, at a house called Waterlooville, near Cosham in Hampshire. There she was able 'to realise the dream of her life, namely, to have a large garden of her own full of hollyhocks and sunflowers and sweet peas.'[39] She was one of the few people at this time who seem to have had a deep understanding of Maurice and of his talents. She realized that he would very much want to distinguish himself in some way and that his pride would not allow him to do otherwise.

Back at Eton after the summer holidays of 1892, he worked very hard for the Prince Consort Prize. The examination, consisting of papers on several texts, an essay in French and unseen translations, took five days. There was then a delay until the results were published. Maurice however got his in advance when he was summoned to see his Uncle Henry at Windsor Castle. This time their meeting was inside the castle and not, as usual, in the Norman Tower. Ponsonby told him that he had won the

Prize; the Queen had informed her Private Secretary immediately and he had lost no time in passing the news on to his nephew. Delighted, Maurice at once sent a telegram to his mother and then one to Chérie (she was overjoyed). When the news became official, his parents came to Eton to see him and his father with his characteristic generosity gave Maurice one of his Breguet watches.

It was arranged then that Maurice should not return to Eton in the autumn but should go to Germany to learn the language; and, after that, he would prepare for the Diplomatic Service examinations. His last half passed 'like a dream' and he did not fully realize that he was to leave Eton. It was goodbye to his friends (his main friends in that last year were Dunglass, Leslie Hamilton and Gerald Cornish, he tells us; and, among the masters, Arthur Benson and Henry Luxmoore). Eton was to remain an important influence throughout his life; later he was to bring his experiences into a novel (C.) and to draw on Eton's characters for, among others, the novel *Friday's Business* where the fictional Mr Ducros is modelled quite clearly on one James Bourchier who was 'mercilessly ragged . . . was deaf, and afterwards a famous *Times* correspondent at Sofia – a man who could do what he liked with the Bulgars, but who could not manage a division of Eton boys . . . When he died at Sofia he was canonized as a national hero, and his head now [1924] appears on some of the Bulgarian postage stamps.'[40]

Maurice's Eton past was to continue to pay good dividends but it was not until the hour of leaving that he 'realized in that last fleeting glimpse of the trees, the river, and the grey Castle all that Eton life had meant, and what it was that in leaving Eton I was saying goodbye to.'[41] It was an experience he was to recreate in a novel some thirty years later:

How often C. had wondered what it would feel like when the well-known words

> Let Thy father-hand be shielding
> All who here shall meet no more;

would apply to him. They had always given a feeling of sadness, but, on the whole, it was a pleasurable sadness; and, now, for the first time in his life, he learnt the difference between the tears that are luxuriously shed in tasting an emotion that does not belong to you and the tears of recognition that respond to the call of actual experience.[42]

Hildesheim. Oxford-and-Cambridge.
The Way to the Diplomatic

IF Eton had been a dream, a paradise from which it was very difficult to retreat, Baring's first post-Eton experiences were still similarly dream-like. From leaving school until 1899, the years were centrally occupied with his efforts to get into the Diplomatic Service and the necessary languages had to be acquired and examinations negotiated. It was a pleasurable interlude: the Baring parents found a family, the Timmes, living in Hildesheim, near Hanover, where Maurice could spend time to learn German. For the next five years Hildesheim became an important place in his life. 'A charming old little town. One part of it was really old, and straight out of a fairy tale, with houses with high gabled roofs, and mediaeval carvings on them, and there were quaint and interesting churches, including the old cathedral with its ravishingly beautiful cloister behind it, and a rose-tree said to be a thousand years old.'[1] Maurice loved the place, found the life engaging, even when not understanding the language at all, came to read and love the German poets, and with Hubert Cornish, then resident in nearby Dresden, spent much time reading such authors as Swinburne, Kipling, Hardy and Meredith and debating theories of life. Hildesheim was a place that represented the ultimate in *gemütlichkeit*, one of Maurice's favourite words. 'There was a wrapping of cosiness and warmth . . . and one had the same sense of utter simplicity and intimate comfort that a fairy tale of Grimm gives one.'[2] It is this simplicity that, later, we meet in Baring's tales and occasional stories, tales like those published in *The Glass Mender*. Another great source of solace at this time was Maurice's growing acquaintance with the work of Wagner, an enthusiasm that he shared with his brother, John. He had gone one night to hear *Tannhauser* expecting 'something vaguely noisy' (this was the most usual response of the Mozart-loving previous generation) but was overwhelmed by it all: 'I did not know music was capable of so tremendous an effect . . . and I was so excited afterwards that I could not sleep a wink.'[3]

In spite of his affection for Hildesheim, its amusing charm and the congenial domestic life with the Timmes family, Maurice missed Eton: 'I would sell my soul for the "Eton Chronicle" at this moment. Give my love to Coventry and G. Cornish. Tell them to write to me. I really have, on the average, two letters to write a day, which is I consider a great deal, considering I receive on average, one a week!'[4] It was, as he suggests here to Arnold Ward, isolating to be without letters and the sense of being abandoned would have been strong if he had not been kept in constant touch by his friends' correspondence.

In the autumn of this year, back at Hildesheim after a long holiday travelling around Europe, Maurice received a telegram telling him that his mother was ill. He arrived just in time to see her, 'A specialist came down from London, but there was nothing to be done.'[5] Worn out by childbirth and the anxieties of the 'crisis', Emily died almost at once. It was a loss too great to write about; the absence in Maurice's autobiography continues throughout both his fiction and his non-fiction and, in the novels, there are either part-portraits or direct inversions of the shadowy, if sympathetic, presence of Emily Baring.

Christmas 1892 was spent at Membland after a short stay in Berlin. Then there were the usual family visits to the Ponsonbys and also meetings with the Benson family. At this time, Maurice heard a great deal about Ethel Smyth, a long-standing friend of the Bensons, a more recent acquaintance of the Ponsonbys. He had heard of 'her wonderful singing, her energy, her vitality, her talk'[6] and when they met they became immediate friends and continued to be so throughout Maurice's life despite some stormy patches (an *Ethel* in the family language came to mean an undue display of temper). Although a wonderful musician, Ethel could be a great bore but Maurice was extremely loyal to her, as she was to him, for the forty-odd years of their friendship. At this time she found him at 'a stage of youthful effervescence which those who have only known him since he came relatively to years of discretion may have difficulty in realizing.'[7]

Once he had learned German, it was settled that Maurice should study Italian. When in Florence for this purpose he made the acquaintance, among others, of Violet Paget (otherwise Vernon Lee), 'by far the cleverest person I ever met in my life and the person possessed with the widest range of the rarest culture'.[8] Vernon lived in a villa, Il Palmerino, on the Fiesole side of Florence and asked Maurice to visit her there whenever he liked.

At the end of June, Maurice was back in England. The plan was that he should go to either Oxford or Cambridge but there was a problem: either university required an exam 'in which sums had to be done'.[9] At first, Oxford seemed the best idea but then the exams (called Smalls) turned out to be insuperable so it was decided he should go to Cambridge but first he needed to brush up his Latin and Greek and make at least some inroads into Arithmetic. In August, therefore, Maurice went to Mr Tatham who lived near Abingdon and was willing to tutor him. Tatham did not even try to teach Maurice maths, thinking it an utterly impossible task. He did, however, teach him Greek and Latin; they read the *Plutus* of Aristophanes, some Catullus and, thanks to Tatham, Maurice was led into new areas of English literature. It was altogether an enjoyable time. Clearly a convivial soul, Tatham would laugh at dinner until he cried and once laughed so much he was almost ill and had to retire to his bedroom to recover. Together they composed triolets and in this eight-line form, with its rhymes, they continued to communicate until Tatham's death in 1937. Some of the triolets were printed in *Northcourt Nonsense* including this, the first from Maurice to Tatham:

> May I wear a silk tie
> To-night at the table?
> I've been stung by a fly,
> May I wear a silk tie?
> I will bind it as high
>   And as low as I'm able
> May I wear a silk tie
>   To-night at the table?

Tatham replied at once:

> The tie that you wear
> May be wholly of silk
> Or of stuff or mohair,
> The tie that you wear;
> If the pain you can't bear,
> Better bathe it with milk,
> The tie that you wear
> May be wholly of silk.[10]

The triolets continued in telegrams once Maurice was safely installed in Cambridge where he passed into Trinity in October 1893, took rooms in Trinity Street and intended to read for the Modern Language Tripos. His relationship with the university, however, was, to say the least, unorthodox. By accident, as he puts it himself, he was, in fact, resident at both the universities in turn, taking part in the undergraduate life in each without actually being fully integrated into either. His university career can make light-hearted nonsense of the idea of alma mater as, with some disingenuousness, he writes in his *Lost Lecture* entitled 'Oxford-and-Cambridge' that time has so affected his memory 'the two universities are indistinguishable' and:

> Sometimes in a dream we see a composite street: a street which we know is Regent Street, and yet in which there are many houses that unmistakably belong to Paris or Berlin. It does not bother us; the dream street remains Regent Street.

This is how it is with Maurice's memories of Oxford-and-Cambridge (the teasing hyphens come in after the introductory disclaiming paragraphs of the Lost Lecture):

> When I think of Oxford-and-Cambridge the vision of a city arises before me made up of both the places, in which a street called King Edward and Trinity Street lies somewhere between the Broad and King's Parade. I spell Magdalen, Cambridge without an 'e', and the President gets letters that are meant for the Master.[11]

The confusion and conflation continue: the exam is the Small-Go, the Hall is at Trino-Balliol, and the well-known bookshop is named Basil-Elijah-Blackwell-Johnson.

At Cambridge, since that is, in fact, where Maurice went first, he belonged to two debating societies, speaking publicly quite frequently. He was also a member of the ADC, the dramatic society, and, in the summer term of 1894, he edited a newspaper, retrospectively self-styled 'ephemeral' and called the *Cambridge ABC*. It lasted for four numbers and contained, among other sections, some typically anarchic fairy-tales by Maurice called *Immoral Tales for Children* in which selfless children are punished, naughty children are rewarded and cheats come out on top.

At Cambridge Maurice was on the edge of the small intellectual world of the Society of the Apostles. In his autobiography he tells us that this arcane society discussed philosophy in secret and numbered among its members Bertrand Russell and the poet, Robert Trevelyan. These men, among the intellectual elite of Cambridge in the 1890s, told Maurice that he should not go to chapel; to do so was, they said, to set a bad example and he surely knew, by now, that Christianity was an outmoded and superstitious aberration. Maurice recalled:

> I remember thinking that although I was much younger in years than these intellectuals, and far inferior in knowledge, brains, and wits, no match for them in argument or in achievement, I was none the less older than they were in a particular kind of experience – the experience that has nothing to do either with the mind, or with knowledge, and that is independent of age, but takes place in the heart, and in which a child may sometimes be more rich than a grown-up person. I do not mean anything sentimental. I am speaking of the experience that comes from having been suddenly constrained to turn round and look at life from a different point of view.

This viewpoint prompted Maurice to feel, when listening to the talk of these intellectual men that he was 'an old person listening to young people'. He did not in fact attend church at this time of his life having shed his childhood religious habits 'as easily as a child loses a first tooth'. In 1893 he commented that he did not believe in the Christian faith and that were he ever again to go to church it would be as a Roman Catholic. In the event it was not until 1909 that this came about.

Baring's friends at this time were thus not the intellectuals of his day; they were men like Hubert Cornish and Raymond Abbott, a man who had something fundamental in common with Maurice, 'Shy and fastidious beyond words. He could not endure being shaved at Cambridge, and used to go to London twice a week for that purpose.'[12] Maurice developed his own brand of originality amongst his acquaintances at Cambridge. Of many anecdotes from this time, one is particularly characteristic. Crossing the quadrangle one evening a man clapped Maurice on the back with a hearty, 'Hullo, old chap!' Maurice turned round and found himself face to face with an unknown Indian undergraduate who apologized for his error: 'I mistook you for Mr Godavery.' 'But I am Mr Godavery', replied Baring with considerable calm. Maurice's appearance at this time must have made such incidents especially distinctive. Ethel Smyth remarked that he was a little awkward, rather lanky and 'though powerfully built, must have been very flexible judging by his passion for sitting on the floor rather than on chairs and sofas'. This habit remained with him. Some seven years later Vernon Lee commented, 'One loves him all the more because there are little things to forgive; a nervous laugh, a tendency to lie on the carpet and suck his boot etcetera.'[14] Maurice always had a distinctive, if at times awkward, demeanour. Conrad Russell, a life-long friend of Maurice and his circle, described his first meeting with him like this: 'He stood under the gas jet in the hall of Audley Square and Claud [Conrad's brother] introduced us. It must have been '96 or '97. When he had gone I said something in dispraise of his personal appearance and Claud said: "Well, he certainly hasn't got the *bel air*." You must remember he had a very big brown moustache and rather long brown hair. I at once became a greater friend than Claud was and so remained.'[15]

Towards the end of July 1893, Maurice met another figure who was to become very important to him – that ageing but influential man of letters, Edmund Gosse. Gosse, at this stage of his life, was 'an unrivalled counsellor in literary matters' to a younger generation, full of tact, sensibility and appropriate encouragement. Maurice met him whilst staying with the Cornish family when, one evening, he was invited to call round at Arthur Benson's after dinner. Gosse talked a little of Cambridge where he had been like a father to 'a little band of what he called mild decadents – the word then in vogue for the ultra-modern literary'. Their conversation moved to Verlaine and French poetry. Maurice said that he found Racine's verse enchanting, 'and Gosse gave me a look of piercing benignity through his spectacles and said "enchanting" that's just the word':

> And here you had the whole secret of his manner and fascination to the young. He was subtly flattering to them by giving them to understand that they understood as much as he did, that they were in the secret, while it was patent to them that he was intoxicated with the fun of appreciation and that there was nothing he didn't understand, no point of view that eluded him, no joke at which he couldn't laugh.

Maurice thought it was 'like having the gates of fairy-land opened to hear

Swinburne and others of that calibre, Morris and Tennyson for instance, mentioned as casual acquaintances'. At the end of the evening he had never 'heard such intoxicating talk' and was 'amazed at the dexterity and ease of his diction, his fund of amusing illustration and episode, and his deft descriptions and living thumb-nail portraits.'[16] Very shortly after this Maurice sent Gosse his *Northcourt Nonsense* triolets, a gift to which Gosse responded well, starting a correspondence lasting until his death in 1928. Always a perceptive critic of Baring's work, Gosse was one of the most important commentators on his earlier literary efforts, his opinion held to be vital by Maurice. On 27 August, 1897, he wrote to Eddie Marsh: 'I took *Entr'actes* to Edmund Gosse the day I went to Wrest & said I would come and rel with him "on the Thursday". On the Thursday I couldn't get away from Etty in time. Then I wrote to him & he hasn't answered or sent back *Entr'actes*. But the quest. is this. Shall I try and publish *Entr'actes* against Edmund's will?' It was not only Gosse who had read this early fictional attempt; it's circulation extended to Lady Lytton, who had written a 'delicious letter' commenting that there were plenty of other persons with opinions besides Gosse; to Kathie Karmarthen (otherwise Kathie Leeds) who had liked it very much (and, she, Maurice remarked 'is not only *esprit supérieur* but also *âme noble*'); and also to the older generation of 'Souls', to persons such as Lady Cowper.[17] Despite this, he wrote, again to Eddie on 23 January 1897:

> Edmund blocked Entr'actes yest', but I washed it with a smile & he was much relieved.
> I really think it had much better be washed. It's had a nice circulation already.[18]

Although abandoned, this novel had clearly given Maurice great pleasure and it had won considerable private acclaim. He compares this private approval of *Entr'actes* with the reception of Benson's *Dodo* when people said it read very well in manuscript but would not make a book.[19]

Gosse, too, gave Maurice an entrée into the literary world at many supper parties at Gosse's house in Delamere Terace. It was there that he met many of the literary stars of the day – George Moore, Rider Haggard, Henry Harland and Max Beerbohm. Sometimes there would be serious conversations on literary matters with Moore, Gosse and Arthur Symons; at others, Gosse would tell stories of his youth, when he worked at the British Museum, and of the early days of his friendship with Swinburne.

All these events happened in the nineties. Baring's view of this time was retrospectively brisk: 'When people write about the nineties now, which they often do, they seem to me to weave a baseless legend and to create a fantastic world of their own creation.'[20] He is even more definite in his *Lost Lecture*: 'books written now represent the 90s as peculiar, exciting and exotic'[21]. They themselves had, he says, no idea whatever that they belonged to an epoch or that some day people would talk of the 'naughty' nineties. They who were young in the nineties 'were unconscious of any romance, nor did the times seem very gay, and if we were being crammed, as I was, we did not find the process very inspiriting'.

Maurice may disclaim any great gaiety but his records give the era a most distinctive flavour. In London he notes that top hats were worn every day and

. . . on occasions of gloom, such as weddings, garden parties and funerals, we wore frock coats. No body under 40 wore a white hat at a race meeting; nobody wore a short coat and a black tie in the evening. Our collars were straight and ties could be sailor's knots, bows or four-in-hand with frock coats, silk with a cut-away coat or cotton with a lounge suit; and in the country we wore straw hats.

In the daytime, Maurice attended the crammers run by Mr Scoones in Garrick Chambers. 'Short, electric, vivacious' and a 'fascinating talker' Scoones 'gave his pupils a compendium of all the out of the way words in the French language'. In the evenings there were balls at all the large houses – Maurice singles out those at Stafford, Grosvenor, Montagu, Dorchester, Devonshire and Bridgewater Houses. He notes that only *valses* were danced except for, sometimes, the lancers. The women dressed in satin, mostly in white, pink or light blue; it was only the old women and, occasionally, the hostesses who wore tiaras. Except on rare occasions, cotillions had died out. At the theatre, Mrs Patrick Campbell made a sensation with *The Second Mrs Tanqueray* in the summer of 1893 and both Sarah Bernhardt and Duse had seasons in London, 'and then there was the opera, which was very much like it was now [1932], except that in those days the young high Brows were indifferent to Mozart and couldn't abide anything but Wagner, and snorted when Verdi or Italian opera was mentioned.'

Literary taste, meanwhile, neglected Byron, found Kipling 'a real

45

excitement' and hailed Stevenson as 'probably the favourite author of the literary majority'. Oscar Wilde's brief career was passing, 'He was despised by the Brows as a writer but acknowledged as a wit.' Baring preserves one Wildean moment in particular. Osgood, Wilde's publisher, has just died. His new publisher, John Lane, asks if he is going to the funeral:

> 'I don't know where to go', said Wilde.
> 'What do you mean?' asked Lane.
> 'Well,' said Wilde, 'he is going to be buried simultaneously in London and New York.'

Best-selling books included those by Marie Corelli and Hall Caine, Sarah Grand's *Heavenly Twins*, 'the first book to be what is called frank about certain illnesses [syphilis]', and E.F. Benson's *Dodo* (Maurice's comment on this was 'No book was ever more talked about.') Then, there was *The Yellow Book*. In the Lost Lecture on the nineties Baring almost neglects to mention this. Later historians and students of the period had, wrongly he thought, taken it as a symbol of the epoch whereas, in fact, it had played 'a quite insignificant part' and, once the novelty of its colour was diminished, was rapidly forgotten.

The Yellow Book was, however, important to Maurice as the place where he published, in the volume of April 1895, an article on Anatole France. In it he concentrates on France's writings about children, his ability to write a 'real fairytale' and his preoccupation with 'the melancholy sunset of Paganism and the troubled moonrise of Christianity'. Ironically, these are characteristics that became the hallmark of the more mature Maurice Baring:

> ... It is very rare that a man of letters can look back through the prison-bars of middle-age with eyes undimmed by the mists of his culture and philosophy, and see the ingenuous phases, the gradual process from thrill to thrill of awakening, that take place in the soul of a child.[22]

This article, originally suggested to Maurice by Henry Harland one evening over dinner at Gosse's, was the first criticism of France that had appeared in England and the same issue of *The Yellow Book* also included a story by France himself, 'L'Evêché de Tourcoing'. When the proofs arrived, Maurice took them to Gosse and read the piece to him in his office at the Board of Trade in Whitehall:

> He was pleased with it, and his meed of generous and discriminating praise and encouragement was extremely welcome and exhilarating. He said there was a unique opportunity for anyone who should make it his aim and business to write gracefully and delicately about beautiful and distinguished things, and that I could not do better than try to continue as I had begun.[23]

This encouragement was crucial; it was all too easy for Maurice to disclaim his literary talent. Cambridge had not proved a 'stimulating place for aspiring writers'. The dons had seen it all before and 'undergraduates are so terribly in earnest and uncompromisingly severe about the efforts of their fellow-undergraduates.' Thus it was 'at Cambridge I hid my literary aspirations, and when I left it I had partially renounced all such ambitions.' Gosse's praise 'kindled the smouldering ashes and prevented them from being extinguished'.[24]

Towards the end of the summer of 1895, after the appearance of the *Yellow Book* piece, Maurice returned to Germany, this time to be joined by Eddie Marsh. Even at this young age, Marsh was an excellent scholar, the most impressive that Professor Timme had ever had. Eddie could, however, be extraordinarily tactless, gossipy and insensitive and it was his misfortune to offend the 'easily ruffled susceptibilities of the Timme family' on such occasions as the one when he remarked roundly that the town's river, the Innerstyle, was dirty. Profesor Timme, with some considerable irritation, replied that it was much cleaner than many a river that comes from a big town and might *look* quite clean. After some slight unpleasantnesses of this kind, Maurice and Eddie left for Heidelberg.

Here they invented a game which Maurice enjoyed more than any other game he had ever played with the exception of his boyhood games of Spankaboo. It was called simply 'The Game' and was played like this:

> One player gave the other player two lines or more of poetry, or a sentence of prose, in any language. The other player was allowed two guesses at the authorship of the quotation, and, if he said it immediately after the second guess, breathlessly so to speak, a third guess; but there must not be a second's pause between the second and the third. They had to be 'double leads'. The third had to come, if at all, helter-skelter after the second guess. If you guessed right you got a

mark, and if you guessed wrong you got a nought; the noughts and crosses were entered into a small book, which went on getting fuller and fuller. They were added up at the bottom of every page; but as The Game is eternal, we shall never know who won it, until the Last Day, and then perhaps there won't be time.[25]

Eddie and Maurice played very well so they thought, with some lapses. Maurice could never guess a line from Milton's Lycidas and Eddie always missed his point if the quotation was from Adonais. In Hildesheim, Maurice tried these lines out on his friend: 'Sank in great calm, as dreaming unison, /Of darkness and midsummer sound must die/ Before the daily duty of the sun.' 'It's magnificent – Shakespeare', responded Eddie without hesitation. It was, however, as Maurice informed him 'not by Shakespeare; it is the end of a sonnet by Maurice Baring, written at Hildesheim in 1892.' The sonnet, 'After seeing Romeo and Juliet', was included in a privately printed edition of sonnets and short poems in 1897. With Eddie, it convinced him that mistakes in his favour were more than possible and proved something of a further encouragement particularly as, when he had tried out this sonnet on some undergraduate friends at Cambridge it had met with a most dismal response.

Back in London at the end of the year, the time was approaching for the First Examination for the Diplomatic and a period of very intensive cramming with 'scores of teachers' and 'hour after hour taking private lessons in Latin, German, short-hand, and arithmetic'. He went up for the examination in January 1896, failing in both Geography and Arithmetic and so he had to begin the dreary routine of cramming all over again: 'All the next year I rang the changes on Florence, Hildesheim, and Scoones.'[26]

The exams over, Maurice went with Claud Russell (also to become a diplomat and later, to acquire the reputation of being the cleverest man in the Diplomatic Service) to visit Paris and Monte Carlo and, then, on his own to Florence. Here, staying at Vernon Lee's villa he met her brother, the enigmatic Eugene Lee-Hamilton, a man who was, arguably, to provide part of the inspiration for one of the most chillingly memorable of his fictive male characters, Prince Guido Roccapalumba in Cat's Cradle. In Puppet Show, Lee-Hamilton is described as a man 'who had been a helpless invalid for over twenty years, had suddenly, in a marvellous manner, recovered, and his first act had been to climb up Mount Vesuvius.'[27] To Gosse, however, Maurice is more expansive:

[Lee-Hamilton] is indeed a trying person. He is a robust egotist with all the exigence and none of the excuse of an invalid. He, as you remember, went to bed for 24 years while nothing was the matter with him – now he looks back upon that time with a wistful longing and behaves as if he was still there: that is on his back he could not bear people to talk to him and on his feet he won't let them, so much does he talk himself. He takes everything with a funereal solemnity till something occurs which makes him bubble over in nervous floods of impassioned Tuscan – and he says every sentence twice over like the thrush from the fear that someone is going to interrupt him.

Despite the trying presence of Eugene, Maurice found Vernon a great source of inspiration:

She knows every inch of Tuscany and took me to see white early Renaissance farm-houses with delicate loggias and miniature chapels, and late Renaissance sumptuous villas with broad grass terraces behind them and avenues of cypresses and elaborate fountains.[28]

After this happy interlude in Florence and its dream world ('A place that belongs to a fairy tale' is one of his most characteristic comments) came the summer term at Scoones and more cramming, 'distracted and dislocated by many amusements' such as the Derby, the first performance of *Magda*, with Mrs Patrick Campbell, Duse at Drury Lane and Sarah Bernhardt at Daly's. Maurice went to Ascot; he went to balls; he stayed at Panshanger, home of the Cowper family and later to be inherited by Lady Desborough in 1913, and, at the end of the summer, at the de Grey house, Wrest Park

... where a constellation of beauty moved in muslin and straw hats and yellow roses on the lawns of gardens designed by Lenôtre, delicious with ripe peaches on old brick walls, with the smell of verbena, and sweet geranium; and stately with large avenues, artificial lakes and white temples; and we bicycled in the warm night past ghostly cornfields by the light of a large full moon.[29]

On 14 November (1896) Baring again took the Diplomatic Examinations and, as soon as that 'long nightmare' was over, set off, once more with Claud Russell, to Egypt. They took the train to Marseilles, then the Messagerie steamer on which he spent his time reading *War and Peace* (his intense involvement with Russian literature was to come a little later). On board ship the other passengers were almost all French and treated Claud and Maurice with some contempt, 'but Fate avenged us, for when we arrived at Alexandria, we were, in obedience to the orders of my uncle, Lord Cromer, allowed to proceed at once, while the rest of the passengers had to wait in quarantine.' Evelyn Cromer was at this time in Cairo as British Agent and Consul General and was to remain in this position until 1907. In the evenings of their visit Cromer would delight in reading passages of abuse about himself to Claud and Maurice. He was particularly pleased with one comment which singled him out as 'combining the oiliness of a Chadband with the malignity of a fiend'.[30] He was in the process of writing his book *Modern Egypt* and the evenings were also partly taken up with reading this aloud. A cultured man with wide literary tastes, including the Classics, eighteenth-century English poets and French novels, Cromer shared with his nephew an admiration for French prose and for the 'French gifts of expression in general, their newspaper articles, their speeches, and, above all, their acting'.[31]

Maurice and Claud journeyed up the Nile and, on M.S. *Cleopatra*, travelled to Luxor and saw the tombs of the kings, the temple of Carnac and the statue of Memnon; they bathed in the Nile and smoked hashish. But this happy time could not go on indefinitely. When staying with Cromer Maurice had learned that he had again failed the exams and, once more, in Geography and Arithmetic. Three attempts only were allowed and he had already used up two. What could be done? Maurice was told that this time he must pass. The problem was, as always, the arithmetic. He knew that he just could not acquire any more proficiency in the subject than he had already achieved with the most intensive cramming. Professional opinion at Scoones suggested that Baring's work had been of quite the wrong kind. He had wasted time reading French and German authors. It was simply no good having a scholarly knowledge of Renan and Mommsen. Candidates who knew the languages far less well had passed merely by learning long lists of words, 'but not knowing the German for belligerent, I was beaten by others who knew the language less well.'[32]

The solution as to what Maurice should do next came almost by accident. In the Winter of 1896-1897 he met Auberon Herbert, son of the eccentric 'Auberon the Anarchist'. Bron became one of Maurice's dearest friends. Wounded when War Correspondent in South Africa, he was appointed Under-Secretary for War and for the Colonies and, later,

President of the Board of Agriculture and a member of the Cabinet. He served with the Flying Corps in World War I and, renowned for his wild daring, died in action in 1916. In 1897, the meeting with Bron prompted Maurice to go to Oxford. He found rooms in King Edward Street, went to tutors in Latin and Arithmetic and, for two terms, lived exactly like an undergraduate except that he was outside the jurisdiction of College authorities, so there was 'no Head-bowing or *gate* rows. I am as free as a bird and I have delicious lodgings full of beautiful pictures and the works of Renan.'[33]

This was a very fortunate time for Maurice. He had been crammed and crammed and, if he did little work at Oxford, at least he had time to digest something of what he had learned. The life was most congenial and there were plenty of opportunities for making new friends, notably with Hilaire Belloc. Four years older than Baring and already married to Elodie Hogan, Belloc was working coaching students in the town. As an undergraduate he had become a familiar figure, a member of the Union, very active and, at times, violent in debate, a strong Catholic, a poet and a sailor. Maurice was clearly impressed. He refers to him in a letter to Hubert Cornish as 'the semi-Frenchman, a brilliant orator and conversationalist who . . . lives entirely by his wits.'[34] They immediately had literary concerns in common. Maurice by this time had written, in addition to the Anatole France article, a number of sonnets, which had been privately printed, two volumes of nonsense, and two unpublished novels, including *Entr'actes*. The first meeting was memorable. The one thing that Belloc said to Maurice was that he would most certainly go to hell. It was not long, however, before Maurice showed his sonnets to Belloc and was gratified by his approval. Belloc even copied out one of them and hung it up in his room on the back of a picture. Maurice also showed him those parodies of French authors he had had printed under the title of *Hildesheim*; *Quatre Pastiches* – parodies of Pierre Loti, Paul Bourget, Ernest Renan and Anatole France written in French. This was later published in France on the advice of Henri de Régnier. The poet was impressed by Baring's sense of the French language and was convinced that none of the four authors could have written the pages more emphatically himself. At this time Belloc was working on a book about Danton and would also, on occasion, compose poems which became the *Bad Child's Book of Beasts*.

With Belloc soon a firm friend, Maurice would give apocryphal supper parties at King Edward Street. The musician Donald Tovey, then a music scholar at Balliol, would come and play and discuss music with a rowing blue. Belloc would hold forth on the Jewish Peril, the Catholic Church, the *Chanson de Roland*, Ronsard and the Pyrenees, with extreme 'gusto and vehemence'. People would arrive through the windows, siphons would be smashed and butter thrown, chairs piled high and songs sung. A lot was drunk and there was even a special kind of port, known as 'throwing port' just so that it could be thrown and spilt with no feelings of outraged economy. The evenings would most often end with long serious, intense talks ranging over topics from transubstantiation to toggers, and from the last row with the Junior Dean to Predestination and Free Will.[35] There really wasn't much difference between the days at Eton and those at Balliol, Cambridge *was* different, less sympathetic and much less congenial. Life at Oxford was a series of minor dramas such as the typical moment one day when Bron pulled the Master's chair round the Quad., and a college meeting was held and Bron almost sent down. Men who had previously been up at Balliol would come and stay the night at King Edward Street, especially Claud Russell and Anthony Henley.

In the Easter Vacation of 1897, Maurice went back for the last time to Hildesheim. Later he tried to sum up his ideas of what had impressed him in the five years in which he had visited Germany. In England, it was thought that in this period relations between the two countries were good. Lord Salisbury's direction of foreign policy was intended to maintain the balance of power in Europe and to emphasize good relations with both Germany and France. The Germans, however, whom Maurice met and he owns that they mainly belonged to the bourgeois, the professional class and the intelligentsia, never thought that relations between England and Germany were at all amicable, and blame was always laid at the door of the British. England, said the Germans, made the situation impossible; the English were very sly (comment here was made specifically about the cession of Heligoland to Germany). In the schools, history lessons focused on the belittlement of England. This was particularly true of those world histories which were read for pleasure by the pupils where they would find that the part played by the country was represented as 'either insignificant, baleful or mean'.[36] Earlier periods of England's history were not mentioned at all and the whole of the country's success was thought to derive from money and money making. The Timme family would reiterate, 'Sie haben den grossen Geldbutel' (You have the large purse). Clearly, thought Maurice, the Germans loathed the English nation to an extent of which the English were quite oblivious. In a typical quip of this time a boy once said to him, 'The English are not brave, but they know how to boast.' He left Germany after this visit very grateful for the experience, with an affection for many of the people whom he had met, but 'convinced that there was not the slightest chance of popular opinion in Germany ever being favourable towards England, as the feeling the Germans harboured was one of envy ...'; envy of the kind that 'a clever person feels for someone he knows to be more stupid than himself yet to be far more successful, and who succeeds without apparent effort, where he has laboriously tried and failed.'[37] Maurice was never to return to Hildesheim after this visit except when on the way to and from Russia he stayed there for occasional nights. Just before the outbreak of war in 1914 he received a letter from Kurt Timme saying his father was dead and asking Maurice to come to his wedding. Two weeks later war had broken out.

Back in Oxford for the summer term, Bron, Jack Kershaw, that 'irrepressible Irishman with a morning-face, who is always bird and laughs all day but has entirely wrecked his constitution and has no coating in his stomach'[38] and Maurice gave a dinner at the Mitre to which forty guests were invited. The menu was submitted to the caterers as follows:

June 16, 1897
Melon, Two soups, Salmon, Whitebait, Sweet-bread,
Bits of chicken, lamb, potatoes, Asparagus,
Duck, Peas, Salad,
Jelly, Ice, Strawberries, Round Things.

The caterers were not very happy about printing this menu, wishing for the more conventional safeties of *Purée à la bonne femme* and *Poulets printaniers*, but Maurice was firm and the menu stood as it was. The dinner was a repeat of the King Edward Street evenings: 'Very soon, during dinner, the musical instruments were smashed to bits, and towards the end of the meal there was a fine ice-throwing competition. After dinner the guests adjourned to Balliol Quadrangle.'[39]

The year 1897 was that of the Diamond Jubilee and London was busy with preparations for the procession and many festivities. Maurice was much looking forward to a fancy dress ball at Devonshire House and indeed had a most complicated costume for it. In the event none of the family went to it because of the death of Uncle Johnny (John Crocker

53

Bulteel, that celebrated sporting character from Devon known particularly for his wild and endearing extravagance; if he went to the theatre he would take all the stalls). It was arranged, however, that they should go and look at some of the people dressed for the ball at Lord Cowper's house in St James's Square. Maurice remembers 'a tall and blindingly beautiful Hebe, a dazzling Charlotte Corday, in grey and vermilion, a lady who looked as if she had stepped out of an Italian picture, with a long, faded, Venetian train and a silver hat tapering into a point, and another who had stepped out from an old English frame, a pale figure in faded draperies and exquisite lace, with a cluster of historic and curiously set jewels in her hair, and arms and shoulders like those of a sculpture of the finest Greek period.'[40] In the midst of this festive, Jubilee summer, Maurice's father, who had been ill for some time died. It was a great loss for all his children and it meant goodbye to the extravagances of 37 Charles Street for ever.

In the spring of 1898 there was yet another examination for the Diplomatic Service and, this time, Maurice finally qualified in all subjects, and was given half marks in Arithmetic. At the time, he was almost sure these marks must have been a gift from the examiners since, after the exam was over, he compared his answers with those of other candidates and found there was little if any resemblance. Years later he met a M. Roche who had been the examiner in French who explained what had happened. Maurice had been going to fail because of his lack of ability in arithmetic but Roche had gone to the Board of Examiners and said that the French essay he had written could have come from the pen of a Frenchman. Thus, when the results were published, Baring was not given one of the three available posts; but, when another vacancy occurred, he was sent a letter from the Civil Service Commission saying that, owing to an additional place, he had been declared a successful candidate. He was duly admitted in June to the Foreign Office and sent to work in the African Department.

Fortunately the novelty did not wear off too quickly. That first summer at the Foreign Office officials from West Africa 'would drift in and tell us interesting things' and then the whole office was enlivened by the Fashoda crisis when suddenly it seemed as if the country were on the brink of a European war and the question in many people's minds was whether or not Lord Salisbury would climb down. The situation, thought Maurice, was made a great deal worse by inflammatory speeches by MPs which, ultimately, had no effect whatsoever on Foreign Office policy which was already determined in Lord Salisbury's mind.

The internal Foreign Office arrangements were of some amusement to the young Baring: under the rule of Lord Sanderson, the clerks lived in a state of terror. A stickler for accuracy, Sanderson checked every detail even on the printed forms which the clerks were required to fill in when enclosing other communications. In the Foreign Office at this time all despatches were kept folded; all the other offices kept them, much more conveniently – flat. It was suggested that, perhaps, the F.O. should follow suit. There was a storm of protest; despatches had been folded for a century; a change was not to be thought of, perhaps a compromise. They could be half folded and kept curved. This was abandoned.

It wasn't surprising that Maurice was soon bored. Half the day passed with clerical work and it was 'most exhausting, except in the commercial department, which was a haven of gentleman-like ease'[41] The methods did not result in any great degree of efficiency. One Saturday Maurice had to send two telegrams, one to Sweden and one to Constantinople. He sent the Swedish one to Constantinople and vice versa and, as no one noticed the error nothing could be done till Monday. Then, there were problems with sending off the diplomatic bags: 'someone nearly always out of excitement used to drop the sealing-wax on the hand of the clerk who was holding the bag, and sometimes the bag used to be sent to the wrong place.'[42]

One day two senior diplomats came into one of the departments to make sure that the bag was sent to the right place: 'The excess of cooks had a fatal result on the broth, and the bag, which was destined for some not remote spot, was sent to Guatemala by mistake, whence it could not be retrieved for several months.'[43] It was, perhaps, just as well that, in January 1899, Maurice could leave this atmosphere for an appointment as Attaché to the Embassy at Paris and the beginning of his career as a diplomat.

[II]

A Really Degrading Profession?

– 4 –

Unpaid Attaché:
Paris

I N January 1899, Maurice's short-lived career in the diplomatic began
in earnest as he took up his duties as unpaid attaché. Arriving at the
Embassy he was given rooms over the Chancery looking on to the
Faubourg St Honoré, and was, what was then called, Resident Clerk,
with the job of dealing with any news that arrived at odd moments. There
was a large staff. The ambassador was Sir Edward Monson, 'a large,
grey-headed, swaying, majestic man, a fluent speaker and a still more
fluent writer'. The Councillor was Michael Herbert, distinguished for his
'economy of phrase' which was 'sharp, short and to the point, expressed
in a high, rather steely voice'. The Head of the Chancery was Reggie
Lister, brother of Lord Ribblesdale, 'sensible, a rapid worker and a
buoyant and gay companion', a most popular man in Paris and a very
competent diplomat.[1]

Daily life for the Resident Clerk consisted of writing out dispatches on
a typewriter, registering them and deciphering telegrams. This was the
most important part of the very dull work, 'It was for that that one had to
hang about in case it might happen, and it was liable to happen at any
moment of the day, or the night.'[2] Maurice endorsed Reggie Lister's view
that diplomats were not paid for what they did 'but for hanging about in
case there should be something to do'.[3] He contrived to find, however,
some entertainment at the Paris Embassy; it was a place where people of
all nationalities would call and ask for bewildering things:

A lady would arrive and say she would like to paint a miniature of
Queen Victoria; a soldier would arrive from India who thought he had
been bitten by a mad dog and ask to see Pasteur; a man would call who
was the only legitimate King of France, Henry V, with his title and
dynasty printed on his visiting card, and ask for the intervention of the

British Government; or someone would come to say he had found the real solution of the Irish problem, or the Eastern question; or a way of introducing conscription into England without incurring any expense and without English people being aware of it.[4]

In addition there were the problems raised by British subjects in Paris who would request 'facilities to see Museums, to write books, to learn how to cure snake bites, to paddle in canoes on the Oise or the Loire, to take their pet dogs back to England without muzzles (this was always refused), or to take a book from the Bibliothèque Nationale, or a missal from some remote Museum.'[5] The more junior staff were required to interview all such people and, if suitable, forward their requests to the French Government. Sometimes there were complications. One day a man asked for permission to consult an edition of Livy which was somewhere in the French provinces in the charge of a bishop. The Ambassador wrote to the bishop; his letter was, of course, in French and he referred to Livy as *Titus Livius*. Maurice knew this to be quite wrong and that the correct form was *Tite-Live*, so he passed this fact on to the Second Secretary and, at the same time, pointed out another mistake the Ambassador had made, this time in the gender of a word. (He had made the French for *fiddle-de-dee* masculine rather than the correct feminine.) These suggestions were not wholly welcome; the Ambassador accepted and corrected the error of gender but he would not hear of calling Livy *Tite-Live* which, he thought, was at best pedantic, and even affected; and, anyway, he asked whoever had suggested such a thing? 'The Secretary mentioned me, and the Ambassador said that an unpaid attaché had no right to call Livy *Tite Live*.'[6] The position of a 'Scrub', the name given to new employees in the Service, was a little sensitive and Maurice's standing cannot have been increased by this minor pedantry nor indeed by his penchant for practical jokes and exploits.

His humour could, on occasion, dangerously misfire. Paris was, at this time, alive with *L'affaire*, the well-known Dreyfus case. It had been alleged that the document on which the evidence for convicting Dreyfus, an Alsatian Jew, of selling military secrets had been forged; its forger had been protected by reactionary military authorities, who had 'seized upon the excuse to expel Jews and Protestants from the armed forces'. Zola contributed his controversial article '*J'accuse*' setting out the charges against the army, and this became part of a heated debate on the subject, with a high degree of fevered public excitement.

The personal issue of the guilt or innocence of Dreyfus was lost sight of, and the issue became one of general principle. It was a clear issue between the military claim, that the honour and prestige of the army mattered more than injustice to any individual, and the Republican civilian claim, that individual justice must triumph over all else.[7]

After a long and concerted campaign on the part of the Dreyfusards to prove the man's innocence, the case finally closed in 1906 when the conviction was quashed. The situation 'made conversation on all other topics quite impossible', thought Maurice. 'No political fact, no social fact, no artistic fact, no play, no book, no picture, could any longer be taken at its own value and appreciated on its own merits.'[8] In March 1900, Baring points out that when Anatole France did not like Sarah Bernhardt's performance in *L'Aiglon* this was, unfortunately, linked with the fact that Rostand's piece had been adopted by the anti-Dreyfusards so that the Dreyfusards 'feel obliged to say that it is worthless'. Diplomats were, of course, cautioned to be very discreet on the subject. This should have been easy enough for Maurice who had no settled convictions on the matter. At times he expressed strong anti-Dreyfusard sentiments, at others, he states that he approves of Dreyfus's case but loathes his supporters. Diplomatic reserve was not, however, second nature to Baring:

> The form, however, his discretion took was to walk straight through a restaurant one evening – in at one door and out of another – vociferating 'Vive Dreyfus!' – an act of audacity which so paralysed everyone present that not a word of protest was uttered.[9]

Lesser but characteristic acts of audacity included the 'Battle of the Inkpots', the result of an altercation between Maurice and one of the Third Secretaries. Baring was losing an argument and threw the contents of the inkpot at his adversary who immediately returned fire with another inkpotful, and this interchange of ink continued until all the black ink was used up, and then all the red ink: 'Every single inkpot was emptied, and while grenades of ink whizzed at our heads the other secretaries ducked theirs.'[10] When all the ink in the Chancery was finished, the fight resumed in Maurice's sitting room next door; then, down the Chancery steps, through the courtyard and into the street. One shot from the sitting-room window left a black streak down the house's white walls.

Not only were all the staff involved soaked in ink so also were the Chancery carpet, staircase and walls. Worst of all was the carpet which was new and expensive, and of very thick red pile. It was very difficult to remove the black ink. They tried prussic acid, but 'The remedy was worse than the disease. The acid made a huge white hole in the carpet like a huge blister.'[11] Told of this event, the Head of Chancery merely sighed and determined that he would try to keep the matter from the Ambassador. It wasn't, though, possible to keep it from Herbert, the Councillor, who walking up the stairs to the Chancery next day was assailed by drops of ink on his top hat 'like the drops of blood in the murder scene in *Monte Cristo*'.[12] Very angry indeed, Herbert summoned his juniors and told them acidly that they were no better than dirty little schoolboys. The Chancery could clearly no longer be confused with King Edward Street, Oxford.

Though unpaid, Maurice was, even now, habitually extravagant, as careless of whole libraries as he was of Chancery carpets. It was at this time that he became addicted to 'the expensive craze of constructing anthologies for himself by the simple process of cutting favourite poems out of hundreds of books and periodicals and pasting them in admirably bound manuscript books.'[13] The books so compiled he called *gepack* (luggage) and there were two types – Heavy Luggage and Light Luggage; as soon as one volume was complete, it would be given to a (generally) delighted recipient and another one started. Best known of the *gepack* is the published anthology *Have you anything to declare?* (1936)

His own literary efforts between 1899-1990 were focused especially on the jointly written novel, *La Chose*, in collaboration with Blanche Warre-Cornish, 'a delightful bridge between Paris and Eton' as he expressed it to her in November 1899.[14] In February 1900 they busily considered different methods of collaboration and wondered if, perhaps, they should try that adopted by Stevenson and his stepson, Lloyd Osbourne, who wrote the same chapter one after the other; one drafted it and then, the other rewrote it.[15] It is not possible to ascertain which scheme they finally adopted and the manuscript of this novel does not survive.

Some idea of the novel comes, however, from letters: set at the time of the South African war. The novel concerns Mark Rivers, a very selfish young man, and his marriage plans in a social world of Duchesses and water parties. There is a very managing woman named Mrs Milden, scenes of 'ironical comedy' and serious discussions about the war and whether selfish Mark should volunteer. Thus, on 17 January 1900,

Maurice writes to Mrs Cornish: 'We must have conversations about the war in which the various characters give their appreciations of the situation: then we must have a psychological chapter about Mark's debate with himself as to whether he ought to volunteer or not; he must make up his mind that it is his duty to stay at home and Mrs Milden must change it. We might have more about the German governess.' At all costs they must avoid anything *type novel*: 'Don't let us have anything for the sake of the plot in *La Chose*.'[16]

As well as being the greatest fun, *La Chose* was also good fictional training. On 4 February 1900, Maurice is able to detect a 'great many little obscurities'; certain characters were, for instance, introduced with undue suddenness so that the reader had no idea who they were. Characteristically, he was very concerned about his characters' looks: *La Chose's* anti-hero, egocentric Mark, should have 'a square face, brindled hair, 1/2 like Andrew Lang 1/2 like Donne'.[17] He learned, too, that it was essential to trace the development of his characters' influence over one another, in particular that of Mrs Milden over Mark; and, on 2 March, he became worried about certain disproportions in the novel caused by placing a central house party too late in the narrative. He reported to Blanche on 14 October 1900 that he had shown *La Chose* to '2 very intelligent and difficile critics' both of whom were 'delighted and amused' but who made criticisms of the opening and of the vagueness of Mark's character. There was, too, a problem close to Maurice's literary heart – the too obvious identification of characters with real people. In a postscript to his letter of 14 October 1900, he comments, 'Mark is simply Arthur Benson pure and simple. He must be altered.'[18] In Baring's novels, composite characters were the closest he was prepared to go; identifiable individuals must be avoided.

La Chose was a connection with his Eton past and it was fun but there were more serious literary matters this year. In December 1899, he had written, with extreme pleasure, to Gosse about Gosse's praise of his poems: 'What you say about the poems is most encouraging & inspiriting; & makes me as proud as a pencilled peacock or a Xmas goose or a Ladyday Turkey; & swells me with Italian.' Again, Gosse's encouragement was crucial, the only thing 'which makes one do anything at all'. Twice in two years, he had given up hope of writing again, but twice in these 'years of barrenness, the lean years of waiting' there had been a 'tiny spring when I had both times given up all hope whatsoever. So I hope it may happen again. In the meantime thank *you*.'

Literary life and junior diplomacy were mixed with social events, plays, concerts and opera. In December, Maurice reports that Lady Helen Vincent, one of the beautiful Duncombes whose younger sister was later to marry Maurice's brother Everard, and her husband Edgar, an international financier, were in Paris and 'I gave a small dinner for them ... a Madame de Béarn 2 Frenchies (one a member of the Institute, one a chatterbox of 33) it was great fun and nobody stopped talking for a half second: Lady Helen looked like the lady in the Sensitive Plant:

> A lady, the wonder of her kind,
> Whose form was upborne by a lovely mind
> Which, dilating, had moulded her mien and motion
> Like a sea-flower unfolded beneath the ocean.'[19]

Of this dinner-party Mme de Béarn was very important to Maurice; she had become a great friend: to Mrs Cornish he was more expansive:

> .... I've made the acquaintance of one of the nicest people I've ever seen, a Mme de Béarn, a charming young woman with Anna Karenine eyes and the most beautiful house made of Old Louis XIV boiseries and crammed with books, and she is most charming, nice and pointful, and infinitely intelligent. A confirmed anti-Dreyfusard, which is such a good sign in France! as good as it is bad in England.[20]

In another letter, to Eddie, Maurice confides that she is likely to become one of his *amitiés amoureuses* – it was to be the most frequent kind of relationship of his life.

Sociable, even gregarious at times, Maurice soon became acquainted with a wide variety of Parisians, including 'some of those who had been famous in the days of the Second Empire: Madame de Gallifet and Madame de Pourtales'.[21] On 27 May 1899, he dined with the latter, who 'had grey hair, but time, which had taken away much from her and stamped her with his pitiless seal, had not taken, and was destined never to take, away the undefinable authority that great beauty possesses, and never loses, nor her radiant smile, which would suddenly make her look young.'[22] He also met a number of Frenchmen of letters, including the poet Henri de Régnier, the novelists Melchior de Vögué and Edouard Rod and the critic, André Chevrillon.

On 22 February 1900, he was delighted to report that he had actually met Anatole France. His house, he told Mrs Cornish, was 'like a bit of the middle ages with old doors, knockers, and high stiff chairs':

> The two new academicians were there, Hervieu and Faguet. It was most amusing. There was an extraordinary collection of people, ex Governors of Colonies and young students with beards and big ties. One of them was a very young and very violent anti-militariste. He said the Boer war was a crime just as the French expedition to Madagascar had been; and any army was a criminal thing. I told him I thought wars and armies the necessary evils and inevitable if painful results of human nature. At the end of our conversation he said, 'Je vous demande pardon de la brutalité de mes sentiments.' I said, 'pas du tout, Monsieur. Je vous demande pardon de la douceur des miens.'[23]

On 23 March he reported in another letter to Eddie that he had seen France again; Jaurès and Zola were both there, and this time, he had found his new friend 'badly bitten with the Dreyfus disease': 'However when Anatole France put Aeschylus on the block it was the greatest molasse . . . Zola sat in the corner observing the cobwebs inaccurately & thinking of obscene occurrences & not saying a word. Jaurès talked with a strong Gascon accent which gave me a fou-rire.'[24] Maurice's relationship with France would seem to have blossomed, and France obviously thought he could make some use of Baring's connections – Maurice's albums for the year 1900 contain a request that he should obtain authorization for France to visit the private apartments at Windsor whilst the Queen was away.

Much later in Maurice's life, there was a gallery of beauties displayed on the mantelpiece at Halfway House, Rottingdean, his English home until the outbreak of war. In their midst were photographs of one of the women he admired above all others, and had done since the age of six when he pencilled small drawings of her – Sarah Bernhardt. She has a chapter to herself in *Puppet Show*, a small book, a number of articles on herself and on her performances by Maurice, and vignettes in his novels – notably as Mme Lapara in *C*.

He had written excitedly to Eddie on 11 January 1899, about her performance of *Hamlet*; she hadn't acted Hamlet, she *was* Hamlet, and he had been to see her in the entr'actes, talked to her, and she had agreed to give him a ticket for *L'Aiglon*: 'She was the boilingest tea & the kindest of sobhearts.'[25] His enthusiasm, too, spills over into a letter to Gosse. He had

> . . . swelled with pride to see a vast audience swaying in a delirium under the spell of a British Rosbif Sauvage: Sarah attempted the impossible & achieved it easily: Never was there a more gentlemanly Hamlet: I thought at first it was Arthur Balfour & then for a moment that it was Lord Rosebery: the way she said Words words words: the three different intonations into which she put the whole soul of the play brought down the house & this little detail – which shows how intelligent the audience is – literally made them shout for a full minute: three whispers.

He adds that he hopes Gosse will see the play in London and that, as far as he can judge, the translation is admirable and the whole performance 'permeated by the intelligence of that wonderful woman'.[26] On 21 January 1900, also in a letter to Gosse, addressing him often as 'My dear Chermaître' he calls Sarah 'a sobheart as well as genius' and remarks that she 'sympathises passionately with the English; never having played before a Boer audience.' He'd sent her printed '*à un exemplaire* the little masterpiece of Victor Hugo' she had recited at a concert in aid of the British wounded and she had been very much touched. 'We sobbed in each others arms in her sitting room at the theatre which is like the white satin railway carriage in which Queen Victoria travels.'[27] On 17 March 1900 he went to the first night of *L'Aiglon*, 'a triumphant thunderous colossal success' and Sarah had never performed better: 'Marvellous marvellous creature, what will the world be without her!'[28] Maurice was 'intoxicated' by the whole performance, and as he comments to Mrs Cornish on the play itself: 'I think there is room in the music of the world for the band of brass instruments and fifes and drums skilfully playing inspiriting martial themes, as well as for the Schumann quintet and the Kreutzer sonata.'[29] Maurice's vindication of the place for the less highbrow in music and entertainment looks forward to his better-known and spirited interchange with the rigorous Vernon Lee on the subject of 'merely frivolous people who are bent on amusement'.[30]

The theatre was one of his deepest and most pervasive passions, and he loved great stage persons and performances. 'He admired Duse to the farthest limits of thoughts – but [that] he adored Bernhardt with both mind and heart.'[31] In 1933 Baring's short biography of Sarah appeared but, before this, he had written many reviews, letters and essays on her, and created Mme Lapara in C, bringing her also into *Cat's Cradle*. Consistently in his fiction Baring makes Sarah produce the strongest possible effect on his characters as she did on him in Paris in 1900. In C. as Mme Lapara recites, the hero, Caryl, listens to 'Obsession de Sully Prudhomme'

> ... and as she ended, her eyes were full of the sorrow of all the lovers in the world. It was as if she had laid bare a secret wound, a wound that every one had suffered and every one had concealed, and that she had touched it with a divinely magical, healing finger.

C., like Baring before him, comes to realize, through Bernhardt's work,

> ... what the whole French nation meant when they said Racine was a great poet'. [Sarah recites the terrible dream from *Athalie*]: 'She was telling the bare facts, and as she did so the fallen Queen appeared to that vast audience in all her undiminished pride. The image evoked was horrible, and great and piteous, as well as horrible; for she had come back with a painted face from the dead, and taken pains to make up even in the region of Tophet.[32]

Baring's characters respond to Sarah as if they have never before seen the *electrifying* effects of such an actress.

There were, believed Maurice, four great achievements in Sarah's career. First, her Hamlet: 'With the exception of Sir Johnston Forbes Robertson's Hamlet, it was the only intelligible Hamlet of our time'. Her second achievement was to create Rostand: 'the greatest thing an actor or actress can do is to create a poet' and she did this for 'the only really remarkable French dramatic poet of modern times.'[33] Baring was well aware that the younger generation in Rostand's time despised his plays, finding in them glitter and even vivacity but nothing or little of literary worth and seeing him as neither a great poet nor even a great artist in verse. 'He was a great poetical dramatist' for Baring and this was proved beyond reasonable doubt by the only relevant test of such matters 'that of the rapturous enthusiasm of the audience, wherever and in whatever language his plays are performed.'[34]

Perhaps an even greater achievement of the adored Sarah was her resuscitation of Racine. Those who deny this should, he suggests, see M. Emile Faguet's *Propos de Théâtre* where he shows that in the seventies when Sarah played *Andromaque* and *Phèdre*, Racine's plays were considered to be quite unsuitable for the theatre. She changed all this: 'She revealed the beauties of Racine to her contemporaries. She put new life into his plays, and by her incomparable delivery she showed off, as no one else can hope to do, the various and subtle secrets of Racine's verse.' She had done the same for Victor Hugo when she acted Dona Sol and the Queen in *Ruy Blas*; but her supreme achievement was *Phèdre*. 'It was in Phèdre that she gave the maximum of beauty, and exhibited the whole range of her highest artistic qualities.'[35]

Sarah became one of Maurice's main interests, a preoccupation that certainly rivalled, if not exceeded those *amitiés amoureuses* of this date; and when he writes of her, shortly after her death, in his essay (published in *Punch and Judy*) it is as if a very close, special person had died: '. . . when the news of her death flashed through the world it seemed an incredible thing, and the blackness and the void and the disappearance of her presence left behind were felt by the whole world.'[36]

In July 1901, Maurice went to stay with Sarah at her island home off the coast of Brittany, at the house called Fort des Poulains off the island of Belle-Ile, at the far north of the Island: 'to get there was a terrible business; it meant an all day's railway journey with many changes, two hours in the steamer, and, in pre-motor days, a three hours drive.'[37] At last he reached 'a little white square, flat-roofed building among the rocks and a stone's-throw from the sea – a great roaring grey sea, with huge breakers, leaping cataracts of foam, and beaches of grey pebbles.'[38] Sarah spent all morning working ('She was studying a Shakespeare part in English. I am not sure it was not Romeo.'[39]) and, in the afternoon, they would play tennis on a hard court; from this holiday dates one of Sarah's memorable off-stage performances:

> . . . I suspect that Sarah's idea was hygiene and that her form was not that of Wimbledon. As for Maurice I never knew he played . . . What happened that day was that Baring's first serve, delivered with maniacal violence, sped straight for Sarah and hit her on the middle of the chest . . . and now ensued the classical stage action when an assassin has attempted the life of the heroine: a piercing shriek, a swaying form caught in the arms of horrified bystanders and laid tenderly on the ground; a series of 'Ah! Ahs!' dying away into a terrifying silence . . . Then the closed eyes gradually open; a faint smile emboldens the bystanders to raise her carefully and support her off stage . . . and the curtain falls.[40]

68

It was Sarah, too, who partly inspired Maurice to make his presence felt in newspapers and magazines; one of his earliest efforts was an article on *L'Aiglon* for *The Speaker*.

'Another literary adventure' of this time became a correspondence in the *Saturday Review*. Max Beerbohm had remarked that French was a language lacking in certain powers of suggestiveness and mystery, Baring wrote a letter pointing out that 'the French language was as suggestive to a Frenchman as the English language was to an Englishman'[41]. Then a Frenchman, a professor, wrote and stated that, in his view, French was only a bastard language and that when a Frenchman wrote of a girl being *beaucoup belle* he was, in fact, speaking pidgin Latin. Other people joined in, pointing out that this professor was talking pidgin French; and, after this, encouraged by Maurice, Belloc entered the argument spiritedly saying, with some quotation from the *Chanson de Roland*, 'that an Englishman who used the phrase *beaucoup belle* in France would be treated with the courtesy due to strangers, but a Frenchman would be preparing himself for an unhappy manhood and a friendless old age.'[42]

Baring's friendship with Belloc was by now firmly established. Belloc visited Paris early in February 1900, this time 'more subdued and less truculent'. They went to the Louvre and to the Concert Rouge, to Vespers at St Sulpice and to Benediction at Notre-Dame, and 'then for a long long drive on the top of an omnibus during which Hilaire pointed out to me Danton's house, and Danton's prison, and Danton's café, and Danton's chapel, and Danton's tennis court and Danton's "Kegelbahn" and Danton's tobacconist. I daresay he didn't know anything about it: but I have the faith that swallows archaeologists'[43] (Belloc's book *The Life of Danton* was published in 1899).

A little after this visit, depression struck in the form of one of Maurice's *ridges*. With some dramatic exaggeration, he wrote to Hubert Cornish on 9 February, 'life is a ridge at this moment . . . I have been very ill; the doctor said to me "J'entend que vous avez la repuation d'être très imprudent"! But then he thinks it an imprudence ever to have a bath.' Quite well again, Maurice was nevertheless worried: "Destiny worries me. – Politics worry me. Public events and private individuals worry me. Bankers and Bakers worry me. Above all newspaper correspondents worry the life out of me. And Indians who come with plausible stories and steal one's watch while one isn't looking are a worry.' Anxious too, about his literary output, he here confessed to Hubert

69

that he had 'been foolish enough to publish an article in the National Review'![44]

Beset by worries and *ridges* and with irritating, although not serious, bouts of ill health, Baring's thoughts turned, in Paris in 1899-1900, to his religion so easily discarded as a schoolboy. In the autumn of 1899, he received a visit from Reggie Balfour, a friend from Cambridge. He had been studying French in Angers; they talked of books and of the Dreyfus case, and then, Reggie had suddenly said, quite out of the blue, that he had a strong wish to become a Catholic.

Like Godfrey Mellor in *Passing By* (1921), Maurice was 'greatly surprised. He was the last person I would expect to do such a thing.'[45] He was also, to say the least, very disconcerted. Up until this point he had known only two people who had become Catholics – his sister Elizabeth who had married the Catholic Earl of Kenmare and taken her husband's religion upon her marriage and an undergraduate who had said, simply, that 'he must have all or nothing'.[46] When Reggie confessed his intense wish to convert Maurice begged him to wait. There was, after all, 'nothing to prevent his worshipping in Catholic churches without committing himself intellectually to a step that must cramp his freedom. I advised him to live in the porch without entering the building.'[47] Maurice's own position at that time was ambivalent: 'My trouble is I cannot believe in the first proposition, the source of all dogma. If I could do that, if I could tell the first lie, I quite see that all the rest would follow.'[48]

Reggie took Maurice one morning to Low Mass at Notre-Dame des Victoires, and this impressed him very much: 'I had imagined Catholic services were always long, complicated and overlaid with ritual.' This Low Mass, on the contrary, was 'short, extremely simple, and somehow or other made me think of the catacombs and the meetings of the Early Christians'.[49] It was a key experience that almost certainly played some part in Maurice's eventual conversion in 1909. When Reggie got back to London

he sent me this epitaph, which is translated from the Latin, and is to be found at Rome in the Church of St. John Lateran, the date being about 1600:

Ci-git Robert Pechom, anglais, catholique, qui après la rupture de l'Angleterre avec l'église, a quitté l'Angleterre ne pouvant y vivre sans la foi et qui, venu à Rome y est mort ne pouvant y vivre sans patrie.[50]

Baring took this and made it the basis of his novel *Robert Peckham* to be published in 1930.

By January 1901, the thoughts of conversion seem to have become a little clearer. He refers to the plan as 'not a Leveson-Gower but a fact' (*Leveson-Gower* is the family phrase for a sudden, mad plan). It is the only course open to him, because 'I believe in [the] Divinity of Christ it is for me like a Euclid proposition that RCism is the only logical and possible conclusion to such a premise.' He could no longer believe the Anglican Church was a 'catholic church' and 'what was once the first lie has become the first truth'. But, although Maurice realized this, he was going to put off the day of entering the Catholic church: 'Don't speak of the entrance. I am going to shirk the evil day for two years.'[51] The reason for the delay, he continues, is 'sheer *cowardice* and fright of Uncle Tom'. Uncle Tom was the youngest brother of Maurice's father, and 'a large, red-faced, shrewd, irascible but lovable man' according to one of his great-nieces.[52] Maurice believed that no words would express the die-hard Protestant fury of Uncle Tom and, altogether, it seemed much more prudent to wait for a while and then present him, and other members of the family, with the fact of his conversion, with a *fait accompli*. It was not until 1909 that Baring braved the risk of family anger and entered the church.

In 1900, however, his thoughts were on his plans in the Diplomatic Service. In the summer, on leave in London, he attempted an examination in International Law after just a few weeks' preparation: 'I don't think I was able to answer a single question; my crammer told me I had not the legal mind.'[53] Despite Maurice's failure to satisfy the examiners in this necessary examination, he had not yet become seriously disenchanted with the Diplomatic Service. In fact, he objected to his cousin Arthur Ponsonby's negative views on the subject in March 1900. Writing to Aunt M'aimée Maurice insisted that he did not feel the Service was any worse than any other profession and that there was no necessity of stagnation. Arthur wouldn't allow Maurice to enter the argument because 'he says I am at Paris and when I am somewhere else I will think differently . . . But two years at Paris is so much to the credit side; so that if it is paid for by two years at Rio – a price I am only too willing to pay – the account is still square. The majority of professions seem to me all *type* Rio without the intermittent molasses.'

Reggie Lister had said he liked being in Athens quite as much as being in Paris but 'if one surrounds the profession with a halo of glory one is bound to be disappointed; but if one treats it like a bank, I don't see that it is worse than any other profession in its disadvantages and certainly better than some in its advantages.' His concluding comments on the subject to Aunt M'aimée suggested that there was plenty of opportunity for clever people to distinguish themselves in the Diplomatic and sufficient routine work for the others; and the Service was quite as good as any other profession. Arthur had replied to this, with some disparagement, "'If you are extraordinarily lucky you may be Minister at Belgrade in 35 years."' But this was surely not quite the point: people who were extraordinarily lucky gained much better prizes than Belgrade and, in any case, what was the fate of people in other professions after thirty-five years: 'Second head of a Dept. in the F.O., Head Clerk in Somerset House, a retired colonel or sailor. In fact, I think Arthur's quarrel is with human nature, and the destiny of man.'

Maurice's central interest at this point is given away in the final sentence of this letter to his aunt: 'I have written an article on the *Aiglon* which may come out in The Speaker!'[54] And, at the end of the summer, he was told that he was to go to Copenhagen; thus, at the beginning of August, he set off for Denmark as Third Secretary to Her Majesty's Legation.

− 5 −

Copenhagen, Russia, Rome

FTER the bustle and social round of Paris, August in Copenhagen seemed very quiet and restricted and there was plenty of time to begin Danish lessons at once. The diplomatic world was very enclosed. On hearing one Dane ask another Dane whether or not he received diplomats, Maurice commented that he spoke 'in the same tone of surprise as would have been appropriate had the question been "Do you receive police spies?"'[1] On 10 August he remarked to Hubert Cornish that 'It is dark & raining & the climate makes one feel as if one had no bones at all, & makes ones nerves sing so that you feel like Nietzsche and Hedda Gabbler mixed; but after a day I believe you feel gloriously well and wake up as Hereward the Wake.'[2] He recorded his early impressions of the Danes like this:

> The Danes were more difficult to get to know than the French; they disliked diplomats and to get to know them well it was necessary to learn their language. This was easy, and had the advantage of enabling one to appreciate their drama, and their acting, which was excellent. They acted Shakespeare and Ibsen, and had an extremely good ballet.[3]

The marriage arrangements and divorce proceedings were a little too relaxed and 'it was extremely difficult to know which wife belonged to which husband.' One incident was typical involving

> . . . an author whose house was furnished entirely with impressionist pictures, of cows in mists − the kind of pictures which seemed surprising in those days, though of course they are old-fashioned today [1932] − ugly still life, and a carrot painted to be cruder than Nature. The author in question was married. He had been married twice, but

73

his first wife still came to dinner every Sunday. She sat at a table by herself, to show she was less important than the second wife, and her children were not allowed to speak to her except through a third person.[4]

The staff of the British Legation in August 1900 consisted of the Minister, Sir Edward Goschen, the First Secretary, Sir Alan Johnstone, and a Chancery servant, a 'charming, simple person like a character in Hans Andersen, vaguely intoxicated sometimes, paternal, easily upset and endlessly obliging.'[5] Alan Johnstone had a small house in the country and there Maurice first met Count Benckendorff, probably the most important meeting of his short-lived diplomatic career. From this time on Benckendorff and his family were crucial influences in Baring's life. Countess Sophie Benckendorff was the inspiration for many of his letters and poems, some say the most important woman in his life: 'Till he died he kept her photograph, en profile, smoking a cigarette on his mantelpiece.' At her Suffolk home, Lime Kiln, (until recently lived in by one of her granddaughters) there are 'one or two exquisitely bound books with just one line of poetry in each – a line of love poetry of the noblest kind:'[6] and their children (Constantine, Pierre and Nathalie) all remained friends. On that first meeting at Alan Johnstone's, Maurice had a violent argument with Benck., as he was sometimes known, about the Dreyfus case: 'He was a firm believer in Dreyfus' innocence and so was I, but that did not prevent us arguing as though we held diametrically opposite opinions.'[7] He was 'the kindest and wisest of friends', and Maurice particularly appreciated his 'keenness', a quality indeed which they shared – 'The way he would throw himself into the discussion, the topic or the occupation of the moment, whether it was a book, a play, a picture, a piece of music, a political question, a wolf-hunt, a speech, a problem, even an acrostic to be guessed, or the dredging of a pond.' Benck., too, was an exceptional diplomat, one of the most delightful, one of 'those about whom there was no diplomatic style, nothing which made you think of diplomacy'.[8]

Maurice had previously encountered such a man in Michael Herbert when he was in Paris; and Benck. was also an excellent critic, 'an exhilarating and encouraging public', a man who believed that one should do more and more and who was 'for finding out what one could not do and then doing it'. In 1900 Baring began really to get to know this man whose portrait stands out so strongly in his autobiography:

He hated pessimism. He hated the Oriental, passive way of life, especially if it was preached by Occidentals. The looking forward to Nirvana and a closed door. He hated everything negative. Suicide to him was the one unpardonable sin. He hated affectation, especially cosmopolitan affectation. . . He was extremely argumentative and would put his whole soul into an argument on the most trivial point; and he was as unblushingly unscrupulous as Dr Johnson in his use of weapons for contradiction, although, unlike Dr Johnson, however heated the argument, he was never rude even for a second; he didn't know how to be rude.[9]

All friendships involving Maurice and the Benckendorffs were not, however, without problems. In October 1901 Ethel Smyth travelled to Copenhagen to meet them. Maurice did not enjoy seeing her with strangers; her tactlessness was unbearable and he was deeply embarrassed; there had been scenes that had made his blood run cold and Ethel on one occasion had made it extremely clear that she never wished to see another friend (Mrs Herbert) again. Worst of all, Ethel had got hold of the unfortunate idea that Countess Benckendorff habitually said 'des choses fortes' and so she, Ethel, 'let fly a series of the most terrible things'. She could be a serious liability: 'The terrible ugly note of coarseness which [shows] E has not got a cleansed mind and combined with a certain kind of Mrs Hunter vulgarity is the greatest loser in the universe.' Maurice was a little worried by these comments, made to George Grahame, feeling that it was, perhaps, 'dog spiteful to write all this'. It was true, however, that Benck. himself was not at all upset by Ethel: 'When she left the person who had the greatest up about her was Benck and I and Cts. B. were *wrecks*.' Luckily, too, 'Cts. B. has given her Govt. seal of real liking and thinks all her losers a necessary compliment'. Much anguished about this introduction, Maurice had had two sleepless nights while Ethel was in Copenhagen, and then feared she might 'hunt them to death'; the strain had been great. 'Write and tell me if you think me odious' he wrote to George.[10] It is one of a few letters that have odious moments.

Benck. was one of the many sympathetic characters Maurice encountered at this time; the Minister, Sir Edward Goschen was another. In a letter to Eddie, Maurice remarked that he 'looks like a sailor; like a Captain of a man-of-war. . . He reminds me when he talks in an indefinable way of Reggie Balfour and in the sort of way he laughs to himself when he says a word. . . In fact he is delightful. . . He is very type Stevenson.' Most meals were taken with the Goschens. After a morning spent at the Legation ('the work is exiguous but I do it all') lunch was eaten in the company of the Minister:

A Danish luncheon proper consists entirely of Hors d'oeuvres on a large scale. The table is littered with smoked smelt raw salmon, live trout, dead whiting, black eel, seal, potted seal, roast seal, boiled seal, flat seal, green seal, herring, herring bones, herring stitches, shrimps crayfish cucumber anchovy Norwegian anchovy, bloater, bloater paste. . . pickles leaches leeks, onions, salads, mayonnaise, sauce, jelly, slips of sausage, tinned apricot, tinned bilberries, tinned blue-berries, tinned hollyberries, tinned holly, tinned mistletoe, tinned plumpudding, tinned xmas trees. . .[11]

This, though, was a 'Danish luncheon proper', and not the usual fare at the Phoenix Restaurant where Goschen and Maurice most often had lunch and where the cook had spent forty years at the Café Anglais, and could provide an omelette, and a beefsteak, potatoes, cheese or a sweet in good English style.

In October Goschen went on leave and Maurice, from 10 October until 22 October, was acting Chargé d'affaires at the Legation. His first task was to leave cards on all members of the Diplomatic Service, a duty which always fell to Ole, the servant who was like a character from Hans Andersen. Maurice gave him some cards; some may have been left in the appropriate places but 'I think he considered that I was altogether too young to be taken seriously as Chargé d'affaires, so he left no cards on the minor diplomats who lived out of the immediate radius of the British Legation.' This was not a good start. Three days later, Count Benckendorff informed the ill-fated Chargé d'affaires that the slighted minor diplomats had held an angry meeting and that he must remedy this situation at once. Maurice this time left the cards himself. The only diplomatic interview he conducted in Goschen's absence was with the future King of Greece 'who came to see me in my room and talked about something I didn't understand'.[12]

At Christmas, Sir Edward's sons came to stay, and there was 'a Christmas tree in the house, and a treat for the church choir, and endless games of battledore and shuttlecock in the Legation ballroom'. Then, on 22 January, came the news of Queen Victoria's death. Leave had been planned but now Maurice thought it would be impossible; there would be far too much to do at the Legation. Sir Edward insisted that he go; he watched the funeral procession from a house at Marble Arch:

The only splash of colour in the greyness and gloom of the long procession was the regalia and the bright pall on the gun-carriage that bore the coffin, and everyone agreed that the most . . . impressive feature of the whole ceremony was the attitude of the crowd: its size, its silence, the universal black. London was like a dead city, and as someone said at the time: 'One went about feeling as if one had cheated at cards.'[13]

Back in Copenhagen, and after his short leave, Baring started work in earnest on his poetical dramas. On 20 February Ethel received a letter telling of the early stages of the first drama; it was to be about the Black Prince:

I do think the subject is magnificent, because this is what happened. The Black Prince after Poitiers, etc., fought a campaign in Spain and came back to Bordeaux, having got a mortal disease – a kind of plague – that slowly sapped his constitution. He lived a long time, and so drank failure to the dregs, and lived to forget himself, and lose his temper, and have the whole garrison of Limoges killed while he was carried on a sofa. When he got back to Bordeaux his son was dead. Then he went to England and got a little better.[14]

Work on this, and on the companion pieces, was an essential part of these years. In his next posting, at Rome, he produced a book of poems and four poetical dramas – *The Black Prince*, *Gaston de Foix*, *Dusk*, and *Tristram and Iseult*. He has his doubts, however, about the wisdom of committing himself too fully to this kind of writing and in December 1903, we find him writing to Henry Brewster, 'an American by birth, a Frenchman by education, an Italian by residence'[15], and a close friend of Ethel Smyth, for urgent advice. He wanted to know

. . . whether or not it is profitable and sensible for me to go on writing plays. A great many people tell me it is a mistake and nearly all are unanimous in urging me to write other things instead. What they say is this: 'If your plays could *even* be acted well and good; but if they are

77

unactable why not choose another form as apart from the commercial and practical value of plays which are a mere drug on the market there is nothing which people are so little inclined to read and people who read poems willingly stick at plays.' Again, I myself think that even if plays cannot be acted they should when read give the reader the impression that given ideal actors they could be acted; they ought to be dramatic enough for that, and if mine do not convey that impression I am perhaps following a will o' the wisp.

He wanted to go on with drama for the simple reason that 'it is the form in which my thoughts naturally express themselves.'[16] Though generally agreed to be undramatic (despite some lyrical and beautiful moments) Brewster liked Baring's plays and encouraged him to pursue his literary career in drama. It was he who suggested that *Tristram*, a 'beautiful' piece should more justly be called 'dramatic poem' rather than 'drama'. This, he felt, 'might do away with some objections that foolish people make. Definition seems to be the only intellectual amusement of the millions.'[17] The problems with the plays to some extent are summed up for us by Vernon Lee writing to Maurice from Venice in October 1903:

This much I see, that you have very remarkable poetic power, and that it has undergone a process of refining, of weeding and pruning, since the Black Prince. The progress is really great, and the value of your singular metaphorical, almost lyrical gift is tenfold since you have taught yourself to restrain it.

Gaston seems to me far away the best of the three plays, though there are very fine things in *Tristram*. I don't care much for *Dusk*. Perhaps it is my fault, but this sort of fantastic floral-fairy-nowhere-nobody land bores me. I can do with Maeterlinck's abstract grey cardboard-tower landscape, becaue it is merely negative and allows one to concentrate on the mere feeling (I am bound to say I hate Peléas and Princesse Malline for their vagueness) – but in *Dusk* there is a decorative character about the nowhere which I, personally, can't do with.

Moreover, it seems to me, that in all these plays the *play* part is exceedingly weak, and, as I don't care a *button* what happens to anyone, and I am never made to feel *how* it happens, I wish the play or story element were left out. . .

Vernon, however, also had some praise to give:

But now for the good. You have, dear Maurice, a quite peculiar, great and enchanting gift. . . It is the gift of the love-duet; of giving, in metaphors and lyric flights and pathetic snatches, the equivalent of the deepest unspoken feeling. It is the giving, *as music gives it*, a voice to the voiceless Faust-moment.

This constitutes the excellence of your three plays. Now, is it not possible, by patient incubation of this gift, to separate it from the (to me) quite dull, stale, and unprofitable vehicle, i.e., the common garden romantic play, in which you present it to us. . . Your plays at present are like a Handel opera. Three or four divine airs in pages of dull recitative. *Develop the air*, let your opera become melodic throughout; disdain the business; go for the mere culminating situation. . .[18]

Baring was not altogether happy with Vernon's reactions. On 13 November he wrote that he was ' a little perplexed' by her criticism:

The long and short of it I suppose is this:
You like plays if they are good plays, you dislike bad plays; my plays are bad plays with patches of poetry that have pleased you, and your advice is to let the patch be the whole – i.e., try and make it as full of good things and as devoid of bad things as possible. I will try. I do not expect I shall succeed, and after all one must work in one's own way, and work out one's own Salvation. . .[19]

Working out his own dramatic salvation was one thing that Baring did not entirely achieve. He never became a convincing master of dramatic form although his plays clearly gave him considerable pleasure and George Bernard Shaw, for one, thought he could have been a great dramatist.

In May 1901 Baring took his first long leave since he had passed the examinations for the Diplomatic Service. His first visit to Russia was in July, the Benckendorff family having invited him to stay at Sosnofka, their country house in the Government of Tambov, south of Moscow. Maurice did not know a single word of Russian; this caused some difficulties when his bag, containing money, ticket and passport, was stolen at Warsaw station. 'I had my first experience of the kindness and obligingness of the Russian people, for a fellow-traveller registered my luggage, bought me a ticket. . .' Arriving at Sosnofka the next day he found a 'large straggling village with thatched houses'. It was not at all as he had imagined it; all the literature he had read about Russia, notably Tolstoy and Turgenev, was not really Russian for Maurice. He had imagined *Anna Karenina* as taking place in London, feeling, too, that he knew the characters quite intimately. It was quite likely that one would meet the people out of the novels of Dickens or Thackeray but one never actually had whereas with Tolstoy it was different, and difficult, to be quite sure whether the people 'belong[ed] to bookland at all' or whether they were part of one's own past. Later on he was to describe his first imaginings like this:

> I had read translations of Russian books, but they had left no definite picture or landscape in my mind; I had read some books about Russia and got from them very definite pictures of a fantastic country, which proved to be curiously unlike Russia in every respect: a country where feudal castles, Pevenseys and Hurstmonceuxs loomed in a kind of Rhine-land covered with snow, inhabited by mute, inglorious Bismarcks, and Princesses who carried about dynamite in their cigarette cases and wore bombs in their tiaras – Princesses who owed much of their being to Ouida, and some of it to Sardou.[20]

Russia, in reality, seemed the most natural country compared with the melodramatic literary place he had conjured up in his mind, that place of 'barbaric houses, glittering and spangled bedizened Asiatic people'. On the contrary, it was 'such a natural country. Everybody seemed to be doing what they liked, without any fuss; to wear any clothes liked; to smoke when and where they wished; to live in such simplicity and without any paraphernalia at all.'[21] In *Tinker's Leave* Baring records a conversation that is clearly very close to his own experience at this time:

> Alyosha, as if he had been following Miles' train of thought, threw down his book and looked out of the window.
> 'What do you think of the country, the landscape?' he asked.
> 'I think it is rather monotonous,' said Miles.
> 'Yes, it is, and it will be like that until we reach the Urals, and more or less like that, with the exception of forests and marshes, till we reach Irkutsk. But it is what we call an "infectious" country. You can't say that in English, I suppose. Some countries are like that. They tell me Ireland is the same. You will be infected. Once the microbe gets into

one's blood – the Russian microbe, I mean – the disease never dies; it is fatal like a love-philtre, and to the end of your life you will say, "Russia, what is there between you and me?" '[22]

Alyosha then insists that Miles, like Maurice, will fall in love with Russia:

Miles looked out of the carriage window. The sun was setting; there was a pink streak under the grey layers of cloud in the west. The air was warm, but the fields and the trees were bare, and there was nothing to relieve the monotony of the brown immensity except now and then the outline of a squat village. . . He wondered whether it was true, whether there would, as Alyosha had prophesied, ever be anything between him and this grey, monotonous brownness; he thought it improbable.[23]

Maurice may, too, have thought it improbable and yet, by December 1901, he is deep in his Russian lessons, finding it 'a most fascinating language' which, he comments in a letter to Eddie, 'consists entirely of expressions'.[24] Very soon, he became as enthralled with Russia as his hero:

Russia

What can the secret link between us be?
Why does your song's unresting ebb and flow
Speak to me in a language that I know?
Why does the burden of your mystery

Call like the message of a friend to me?
Why do I love your vasts of corn or snow,
The tears and laughter of your sleepless woe,
The murmur of your brown immensity?

I cannot say, I only know that when
I hear your soldiers singing in the street,
I see your peasants reaping in the wheat,
Your children playing on the road, your men

At prayer before a shrine, I wish them well.
It is with you, with you that I would dwell.[25]

Before his Russian enthusiasm could really continue, however, there was one more diplomatic posting: 'On the 7th of January 1902 a dispatch came to say I had been transferred to [the post] of a Third secretary of His Majesty's Embassy at Rome.'

It was a posting with many compensations; the beauty of the place 'pierced [him] like an arrow' on the very first day; and it was a pleasant embassy to serve at. Diplomatic life here provided another contrast to that at Paris and Copenhagen: 'The diplomats, and there were a great number of them, were most of them an integral part of Roman society, and there were also many literary and artistic people whose circles formed part of the same system as that of the Romans and of the diplomatic world.' The Ambassador's wife, Lady Currie, was especially *sympathique* and to have luncheon or dinner with her and Lord Currie 'was one of the most enjoyable entertainments in the world'.[26]

There was time, too, for Russian lessons to continue, and Maurice made friends with a good many Russians – M. and Mme Sazonoff, Princess Bariatinsky, and Princess Ourousoff – she had known Tolstoy and been a close friend of Turgenev. She was especially kind to Maurice, contributing crucially to his education in Russian literature. Amongst the Italians in Rome his great friends were the historian Count Pasolini and his wife. Count Pasolini is often thought to be the original of Count Sciarra, the distinguished Italian who pays extravagant compliments in three languages to his hostess, in 'The Luncheon Party'. At Rome, too, he was able to get to know Henry Brewster better, often dining with him when he was on his own: 'His external attitude was one of unruffled serenity and Olympian impartiality, but I often used to tell him that this mask of suavity concealed opinions and prejudices as absolute as those of Dr Johnson.'[27]

In February 1902, Pope Leo XIII celebrated his jubilee. Maurice was deeply impressed by the Mass at the Sistine Chapel and the High Mass at St Peter's, 'Not that at that time I felt any sympathy with the Catholic Church; indeed, it might not have existed for me at Rome at that time. I thought, too, that the English Catholic inhabitants of Rome were on the look out for converts, and were busy casting their nets.'[28] This lack of interest in the Catholic Church recorded in Baring's autobiography is not entirely borne out by his personal letters of this period. In November 1902, he says to Belloc that he really must 'talk over R.C. with you', always mindful, however, of Hilaire's view that 'one *must* be born a R.C.'[29]

In May 1902 he left Rome to travel on the yacht of Mme de Béarn, his friend from his days in Paris (incidentally much disliked by Ethel who admits that she really could not stand her). She was young and pretty and her house, where Ethel stayed in Paris, was the most luxurious she had ever been received in; 'Everything in it was a priceless work of art; on the staircase, disposed at intervals, stood from morn till dewy eve, six gorgeous footmen.' On another occasion, having stayed with Martine [de Béarn] she writes that she had 'the impression of being with an invalid who can bear very little excitement, very little fatigue, and very little fresh air.' Her marriage had been disastrous and her frequent remark was that she wished people of exuberant vitality would take about with them a baize parrot-cage cover for use when in contact with weaklings such as herself.[30] In Greece, they went straight to Olympia, 'carpeted with flowers, and the fields were like Persian carpets'[31] and thence to Delphi, Corinth and Athens, and, finally, to Rhodes, Sunium and back to Rome, via Corfu.

Back in Rome, Maurice would often go for walks with Vernon Lee. Staying with the Pasolinis she would take him to see unexpected places and sights. 'Sight-seeing with Vernon Lee was sight-seeing indeed. It was the opposite of scampering through a gallery with a Baedeker, and ticking off what had been "done". For Vernon Lee and with Vernon Lee nothing was ever "done". It was there for ever in the haunted, many-corridored and echoing palace of her imagination, and, after you have seen such things with her, in yours as well.' Her company was more than exhilarating:

Commerce and conversation with Vernon Lee was to me... more than a stimulus: she lent you a magical glass, like that I read about long ago in an old fairy tale, where an astrologer gave a fairy prince a glass in which he was to look at the stars to find the one bright particular star that was to guide him to the home of an imprisoned princess. 'The stars,' said the astrologer to the prince, 'when you look at them without this glass, appear to be all the same, and all of one colour; but when you look at them through this glass, you will see them in their true colours, for they are all different – red, blue, violet and green.'[32]

Maurice went on taking Russian lessons, and made his first forays into Russian literature – Pushkin's prose stories, Alexis Tolstoy's poems, and some of Turgenev's poetry. As he looked back on that time in Rome, when writing *Puppet Show*, Baring felt it was 'all a wonderful dream-world of sunshine and flowers and beauty'; the reality was a little different – 'at the time I did not really like Rome'. And again, in a letter to Vernon Lee in January 1906, he states that Rome was a place 'which I enjoyed afterwards'[33]; furthermore, the life of a diplomat did not suit him and, when he dropped his coin into the Trevi fountain, it was with the wish that he might return to the city, but with another profession, not under the auspices of diplomacy. He felt too a cloying sense of the place, 'as if I were living in a cemetery, and I was oppressed by the army of ghosts in the air, the host of memories, so many crumbling walls and momentous ruins.'[34]

At the end of July another visit to Russia, again with the Benckendorffs at Sosnofka, hardened his decision to give up diplomacy. His heart was not in it and he 'wanted literary work'.[35] The first stage was to get back to England, so he acquired a temporary exchange into the Foreign Office. The FO, however, was not a great deal more congenial than Diplomacy, as witnessed by the only incident that he sees fit to record from this time: '. . . one day when one of those toy snakes that you squeeze and shut up in a box, and which expand when released to an enormous size, and hurtle through the air with a scream, was circulated in the Office in a redbox. Every department was taken in, in turn; and when it reached my department, I sent it up to the typists department, where it was opened by the head lady typist, a severe lady, who was so overcome that she at once applied for and received three weeks' leave, as well as a letter of abject apology from myself.'[36]

In September he reports to Gosse that John, his brother, now head of the bank, approved provided that he could find work which would offer at least adequate money; the attitude of Margaret, his sister, was that indeed he must leave the Foreign Office – 'she is convinced that if I stay in the F.O. I would never write another line – It is too *physically* exhausting', a comment that Baring echoes in his comedy *His Majesty's Embassy* when one character asks, 'why does diplomacy, which is the profession in which there's nothing to do at all, make people feel as if they were overworked?' In fact, Maurice was by now thoroughly disenchanted with his career as diplomat and the futile life of 'hanging around in case there may be work'[37]. His autobiography is cautious in its comments on the Service but retrospectively, he was able to confide to Vernon Lee that he 'had loathed the Diplomatic Service which is a really degrading profession, I think'.[38] The plan was that he should translate some of the work of Gogol or Dostoevsky into English and that, if Heinemann agreed to this, he would leave the FO without further ado.

(There were no translations of Gogol in print at this date, and his works were not translated until 1922–6 by Constance Garnett.) The publisher said there would 'be no market for such books in England'. Dostoevsky had not yet been discovered and in one of the leading London newspapers, even as late as 1905, he was spoken of in a long, serious article, as being 'a kind of Xavier de Montépin!'[39]

Despite this Maurice finally made up his mind to give up this career and to go to Russia where he arrived, once more, just after Christmas 1903, into the midst of an ever more tense political situation between Russia and Japan.

[III]

Journalist and Traveller
1904–1914

– 6 –

In Manchuria

BARING arrived in St Petersburg just after Christmas 1903 to a situation that was regarded as grave although people still did not wholly believe in the possibility of war. Throughout the autumn of 1903 the political situation in the Far East had caused some concern. 'Russia and Japan seemed to be drifting into war. The Russian Government apparently did not want to go to war, but nobody had a definite policy; and the strings were being pulled by various incompetent adventurers in the Far East.'[1] Japan, thoroughly ready to engage in imperial expansion, took advantage of this. Further, as Maurice himself comments in *The Russian People* 'The War with Japan came about owing to the sudden *volte-face* in Russia's policy with regard to the Far East, when the Government decided to adopt the aggressive policy of Bezobrazov, instead of the peaceful policy of development which had been initiated and followed by Witte.'[2]

In St Petersburg, Maurice, staying with the Countess Shuvaloff found that, despite the imminent war, the usual Court functions held at the Winter Palace just after Christmas were to take place as usual – the concert was in fact held, but the State Ball was cancelled and there was never again a State Ball held in the city. He was 'delighted by the crystal atmosphere, and the drives in open carriages; there was a little snow on the ground but not enough for sledging.'[3]

Just as in the days before the outbreak of war in August 1914, many people thought there would be no war and then, suddenly the situation changed – so on 8 February 1904, the Japanese attacked the Russian fleet at Port Arthur and torpedoed the *Retvizan*. Pierre Benckendorff, son of Maurice's friend Count Benckendorff, was on the ship. Later Maurice learned that no orders had been given by the port authorities, acting on the orders of the viceroy, Alexeyev, to put torpedo-nets ready or to take any precautions although there had been warning of an attack. This was an early sign of the problems that were to haunt the Russian campaigns in the months to come – difficulties in the chain of command, and vague relations between the military and naval chiefs were a constant feature of the war in 1904–5.

After a short time, Maurice moved to Moscow to the house of Marie Karlovna von Kotz, a lady who took pupils, mostly English pupils, to teach them Russian, 'a fine teacher, and a brilliant musician; an energetic and extremely competent woman, and an example of the best type of the *intelligentsia*'. It was here that he had his first experience of Russian life among that class, what he called their 'peculiar comfortless comfort':

> Nothing could seemingly and theoretically be more uncomfortable; the hours irregular; no door to any room ever being shut; no fireplaces, only a stove lit once every twenty-four hours; visitors drifting in, and sitting and talking for hours; but nothing in practice was more comfortable. There was an indescribable ease about the life, a complete absence of fuss, a fluid intimacy without any of the formalities, any of the small conventions and minute ritual that distinguish German bourgeois life and, indeed, are part of its charm. In Russia, everybody seemed to take everybody and everything for granted. There were no barriers, no rules, no obstacles. No explanations were ever thought necessary or were ever asked for or given. Time, too, had no meaning. One long conversation succeeded another, into which different people drifted, and from which people departed without anyone asking why or whence or whither.[4]

Altogether Moscow was a comfortable place to be in winter, with its deep snow, its evenings of tobogganing, and its many visits to the theatre, in particular to the Art Theatre, then at the height of its glory. Under Stanislavsky this had started with a company of amateurs who, according to Baring,'began by acting the *Mikado* for fun, continued acting for pleasure, and determined to spare neither trouble nor expense in making their performances as perfect as possible.' By 1904 they had the best 'all-round theatre in Russia, if not in Europe.' The acting was in an easy, naturalistic style as opposed to the very elaborate and histrionic manner then in vogue in Russia and the quality of the plays performed there was unique in Europe – it was the theatre that made Chekhov's reputation. His plays, which were only moderately successful or failed in other theatres, became grand triumphs at the Art Theatre. *The Seagull*, failing at one of the big State theatres of St Petersburg, was a resounding success at the Art Theatre:

> The reason is that Chekhov's plays demand a peculiar treatment on the stage to make their subtle points tell, and cross the footlights. In them the clash of events is subservient to the human figure: and the human figure itself to the atmosphere in which it is plunged.[5]

In 1904 the *Cherry Orchard* had just been produced and Chekhov died very soon afterwards. It was a particularly appropriate play for the time Maurice was in Moscow: 'the most symbolic play ever written', epitomizing pre-Revolutionary Russia, all its people 'dancing on the top of a volcano which is heaving and already rumbling with the faint noise of the coming convulsion'.[6] The start of this convulsion was the Russo-Japanese war. Count Benckendorff was absolutely right when in 1903 he prophesied to Maurice that as soon as war came to Russia there would be a revolution.

Pierre Benckendorff, on his way to the Front, passed through Moscow and it was he who was instrumental in the next stage of Baring's experiences in Russia – he asked why Maurice did not try to go to the War as a newspaper correspondent. He could speak good Russian by now and Pierre's father would provide the necessary letters of recommendation to the military authorities. This Maurice did, and at the end of April 1904, set off, sent by the *Morning Post*, on his way to Manchuria, 'laden with a saddle, a bridle, a camp-bed, and innumerable cooking utensils. I knew nothing about journalism, and still less about war, and I felt exactly as if I were going back to a private school again.'[7] The decision caused a certain amount of familial worry; surely this was a strange change of course for the aspiring littérateur; would he be quite safe in Manchuria? John, in particular, was worried on this score and whether it might not be just another step towards financial insecurity.

Maurice spent two nights in St Petersburg and engaged a Russian servant, 'a gigantic creature, who had served in a cavalry regiment of the Guards'. In Moscow, he met Lord Brooke, Reuter's correspondent, and they agreed to travel together. The journey began on 2 May and Maurice was surprised at its 'ease and rapidity'. In London 'the impression prevailed that the railway would certainly be blown up, that trains fell into half-frozen lakes, and that open railway trucks were the only form of accommodation.'[8] The reality was very different; as far as Irkutsk, there was an ordinary express train with 'comfortable first and second class carriages, a dining room, a pianoforte, a bath-room, and a small library of Russian literature'. The journey from Moscow to Irkutsk took nine nights and eight days, and was followed by the 'real interest' of crossing Lake Baikal. This lake was traversed by two large ice-breakers. The crossing took four hours and started at five p.m.:

As we left, the scene was one of the most strange and beautiful I have ever witnessed. It had been a glorious day, and the sun in the cold, clear atmosphere – an atmosphere that has a radiant purity which is quite indescribable – was gradually assuming the appearance of a red, fiery, arctic ball. In front of us was a silent sheet of ice, powdered with snow, white and spotless except for one long brown mark which had been made by the sledges. On the horizon westward of us a range of mountains was visible, whose summits seemed to disappear into a veil of snow made by the low-hanging clouds. It was impossible to discern where the mountains left off and where the clouds began; in fact, this low range had not the appearance of mountains at all; it seemed as if we were making for some mysterious island, some miraculous reef of sapphires, so intense was the blue of these hills, so gem-like the way they glinted in the cold air. Towards the east was another still lower and more distant range; the intense deep blue faded here into a delicate and transparent sea-green – the colour of the transparent seas in the Greek islands – and these hills seemed like the phantom continuation of the other range – unearthly and filmy as a mirage.

As we moved the steamer ploughed the ice into flakes, which leapt and scattered themselves in innumerable spiral shapes, fantastic flowers of ice and snow. As the sun sank lower the strangeness and beauty increased, for a faint pink halo pervaded the sky round the sun, which grew more and more fiery and metallic. I knew I had never seen anything like this before, and yet I felt at the same time that I was looking on something which I had already seen.[9]

This something was a recollection of Coleridge's The Rime of the Ancient Mariner and, especially:

And now there came both mist and snow,
And it grew wondrous cold:

And ice, mast-high, came floating by
As green as emerald.

Before embarking at Baikal Maurice had managed to send his first dispatch; he had made friends with the official who looked after this train, given him his pocket-knife and received his undertaking, in return, that his letter would be posted when he got back to Moscow. The official kept this promise and Maurice's dispatch to the *Morning Post* got through without being censored; it was the first dispatch from this group of correspondents but there was little or no war news in it. It contained a long and detailed account of a performance of Chekhov's *Uncle Vania* at the Art Theatre.

The next stage of the journey was considerably more uncomfortable; it resumed at 11 p.m.; the train was very full and Maurice found room only in a very busy third-class carriage (this came, however, to be his preferred means of travelling). At one point a party of Chinese coolies invaded the train, drunkenly angering the soldiers who were already on board. Eventually, after three days, they arrived at Harbin; it was not an encouraging place. Conversations with his fellow-travellers had led Maurice to expect something on the lines of 'one of those huge American cities that grow up in a night. I pictured to myself a town somewhat like Vienna, with asphalt pavement and electric light.'[10] It wasn't of course like that at all and what he found filled him with despair:

. . . the mud, the absence of vehicles, the railway station, a huge *art nouveau* edifice, the long vistas of muddy roads or swampy trails, the absence of any traces of civilisation, and then the hotel, which was dearer than any hotel I have ever stayed at before or since, with its damp, dirty room and suspicious bedstead, and its convict squinting waiters still redolent of jail life, and its millions of flies . . . At the beginning of the war Harbin was the centre of everything that was undesirable in the Russian army and in the civilian populations of the whole world.[11]

It was not a place to linger and Maurice stayed there only a week on the way out (and not at all on the way home) before proceeding to Mukden, by comparison with Harbin, 'an oriental masterpiece', a thoroughly Chinese city said to be like a miniaturized Peking:

Mukden reminded me of Hans Andersen's fairy tales; its buildings and its inhabitants, the shops, the temples, the itinerant vendors in the street, the sounding gongs, the grotesque signs, and quaint fantastic images, seem to belong to the realm of childish trolldom. Here it was, one feels, that the Emperor of China, of whom Andersen tells, sat and sighed for the song of the nightingale, when his artificial, metallic singing-bird suddenly snapped and ceased to sing.[12]

After a week of living with another correspondent, Baring moved into the town, and arrived at the Der-Lung-Den, otherwise the Inn of the Dragon, a large courtyard surrounded by rooms. He was shown one of the rooms and told it could be his but it had no floor and no paper on the walls: 'in fact, it was no more like a room than the stall of a stable'.[13] He was told, however, that all would be well and soon, with the appearance of an upholsterer, an architect and a builder the room was transformed – the Chinese did not make the room ready in any sense until they knew there would be an occupant.

Mukden, Baring reported, had there been no war, would have been a very pleasant place to spend the summer: 'Life. . . without the complicated machinery of European modern life, without any of the appliances that are devised for comfort and which so often are engines of unrest, had all the comforts one could wish. . .'[14] Nevertheless, it was an uneasy time for the new correspondent: 'I was so inexperienced that I thought it was impossible to write to the newspaper unless something startling had happened.'[15] During the course of these months Baring was often asked about the attitude of the Chinese towards the Russians and towards the war. Their relations with the Russians were, he remarked, very complicated. When he arrived at Mukden, the Chinese were making a fat profit from the war; the educated Chinese used to tell him that what they most feared was neither the Russians nor the Japanese but the possible breaking loose of the Chinese army. 'The situation was, therefore, as if Scotland had been occupied by France and invaded by Germany, and the Scotch people were vaguely hostile to the French, and guardedly friendly to the Germans, but quaking with terror at the thought of Glasgow and Edinburgh being looted by the Scots.'[16] Baring thought that the main facts about the Chinese in Manchuria were, first, 'that they are hostile to any foreign occupation, and that they regard Russian-man, English-man, German-man as one and the same – namely robber-man or *Hun-hu-ze*. That is the principal point, the rest is merely a question of detail.'[17] Second, the changed circumstances, namely that it was now wartime, altered the situation; after all, wartime occupation was a very different thing from peacetime occupation. Mostly, the Russians treated the Chinese very well and it was extraordinary that so few cases of 'friction' arose; 'I imagine this is due to the extraordinary cleverness and supple adaptability of the Chinese.' In general Baring found that the Chinese accepted the war philosophically and 'were resolved to make the best of it by letting no occasion slip of making some profit'. In terms of the future of the Chinese and the reality of the 'yellow peril', Baring had this to write:

People say airily 'the Chinese are so backward, poor things'; my advice to such people is to go and see. They will find that the Chinese arrived at a certain level of civilisation centuries ago and remained there, because they saw nothing in the progress of other countries which tempted them to imitate it. They anticipated our so-called civilisation and deliberately discarded it, since they did not consider that it would tend to greater happiness in the long run.

They are not ambitious and they are satisfied with a little. To them the important thing is not the quantity of things achieved in life, but the quality of the life lived. They are not in a hurry; for that reason they fail to see why a motor-car is a better vehicle than a rickshaw, because if no one is in a hurry, there is no disadvantage in proceeding in a leisurely fashion.

They see us spending our whole lives in hurrying after something, in aiming at being somebody, in kicking others aside in order to get somewhere. They continue the game for the sake of the game and not for the sake of winning any concrete prize. They are honest and hard-working, cultivated, intelligent, good-mannered, and good-tempered. They hate fighting, brawling, noise of all kinds, drunkenness, and bad manners. Are they so very backward?[18]

Several startling things were soon to happen; on 22 June Maurice moved to Liaoyang where he felt he was 'somewhere near a war'.[19] In July correspondents were allowed to go to the Front. Baring, with Brooke, and two Montenegrin servants left for Tashichiao, attached to a cavalry brigade of the First Siberian Army Corps; it was 'the beginning of a new life in a new world'[20], the world of war and battlefields. The landscape was particularly distinctive because, this year, unusually, the rainy season had come in fits and starts, causing the country to be either 'a baked desert or a sea of mud':

> ... on the horizon, a range of soft blue mountains. In the foreground there is a Chinese village built of mud and fenced with mud, and baked by the sun, yellow and hard. There is, perhaps, a little stream with stepping-stones in it; a delicate temple, one-storied and painted red like lacquer, on the water bank, and round it, as far as the eye can see, fields of giant millet. The women, dressed in dark blue, the blue of blue china, stand at the doorsteps, smoking their long-stemmed pipes, and there is a crowd of brown, fat, naked children with budding pig-tails.[21]

On 22 July, Maurice rode into Tashichiao and the next morning heard gunfire for the first time. On 23 July he prepared to ride towards the battle but his servant brought the news that his pony had been stolen during the night – the house was 'infested with Chinese boys and *mafoos* (grooms), who were Christians and spoke French – two bad signs'.[22] He asked what had been done to recover the stolen pony: his servant said he had been to the police and given all the details and that the necessary proceedings would go ahead in due course. This seemed likely to involve delay; it was urgent that he should have a horse or he would risk being taken prisoner by the Japanese, so a somewhat brutal expedient was adopted: 'I took every Chinese in the house by the pigtail, and said I would thrash them one after the other until the pony was brought back. I also gave a small coin to one of the *mafoos*, a certain Vasili, who was the greatest scoundrel of the lot. . . . In half an hour's time I was informed that the pony had returned of its own accord.'[23] Maurice went ahead to the major battle of Tashichiao.

This battle was a long artillery duel; he saw it around Haichen from which the retreat continued as he got back to Liaoyang, where he went down with sunstroke. At the end of the first week in August, he set off once more to find the Cavalry Brigade to which he had been attached, taking with him Dimitri,

> ... a dark-eyed Caucasian with a black beard and a nose like a beak, dressed in a long brown skirt with silver trimmings, and armed with a scimitar and several revolvers. Dimitri had lived in the saddle all his life and when I complained of my pony stumbling, he said: 'It's not the pony; the truth is, little father, that just a little you don't know how to ride.'[24]

Edward Charles Baring

L. Emily C. Baring

MB's parents in 1870 (from Susan Baring's [later Lady Reid] albums)

Membland

A page from Susan Baring's albums (for 1874–1878)
showing the family and Chérie in 1877

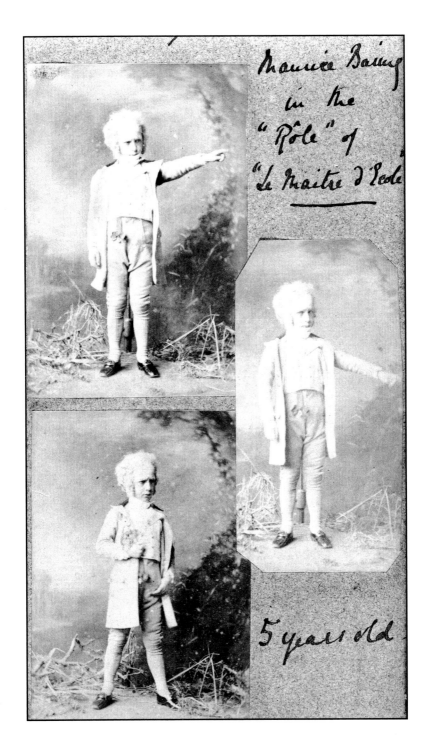

Maurice Baring
in the
"Rôle" of
"Le Maître d'École"

5 years old

MB as a young actor

Maurice and Hugo Baring and their sisters

Mary Ponsonby (Aunt M'aimée),
1890s

Chérie

John Baring (later Lord Revelstoke) in 1887

MB in 1885

MB in 1895, at about the time he met Conrad Russell (see page 43)

In search of General Kossagovsky's division, he met a volunteer at An-shan-chan who was bound for the same place. They finally found the division at Davantientung, under the command of a new general – Sichkov. Soon, however, Maurice was, most importantly, to meet up with officers of the 2nd Transbaikal Battery (Horse Artillery) of Cossacks. On the following day the battery asked him to stay with them, an offer which he accepted: 'Here a new epoch began for me – life with a battery.'[25] This was the battery with which Baring saw most of the war and with whose officers and men he became firm friends. He had the highest opinion of the Cossacks, 'the most good-natured and long-suffering of men'. He had seen them bullied by the Chinese and bearing it with great forbearance, and he found 'they were a delightful race of people, good-natured, long-suffering and ingenious. In fact, they very much resembled the Irish. They often told lies in a transparent, childish manner. They quarrelled and abused each other but never came to blows. They were extraordinarily ingenious in finding food and making themselves and others comfortable. . .' It was salutary to watch their dealings with the wounded enemy: their treatment of them was exactly what the *Times* described the Japanese treatment of the Russian prisoners and wounded as being: "namely, that they treated them not only with mercy but with tenderness'. It was worth preserving some characteristic incidents:

> The following is a story the truth of which I can vouch for. A Russian and a Japanese were found locked in a hand to hand struggle. The Japanese was taken prisoner and the Russian was severely wounded. The Russian refused to be taken to the ambulance unless the Japanese were taken with him; because the Russian said it was '*his Japanese*'. They were put together in the same hospital train and the Russian refused to be separated from the Japanese and spent his time looking after him, and fanning his head and telling all visitors that it was '*his Japanese*'.[26]

At Davantientung there followed one of those interludes or entr'actes of war. They all lived in one room of a Chinese house (that is the commander of the battery, a junior lieutenant who performed most of the gunnery work, a doctor and a vet). They got up with the sun and had dinner at noon. This was always the same – what their cook called Boeuf Strogonoff, 'huge chunks of meat, cut up and mixed with potatoes, and served in a pail'. After dinner they would relax on the K'ang ('the natural platform of every chinese house'), talk and sleep; it was very hot and there was a great languor in the air; all they thought about was eating and sleeping but both were difficult. Food was the inevitable Stroganoff and sleep was spoiled by the flies, the heat and the noise of arguments outside. There was little to read; only, perhaps, a newspaper fragment that had been read and read, whilst the military situation been discussed and discussed. When Bron read Maurice's account it reminded him of his time in South Africa and camp life during the Boer War:

> No fellow... who hasn't been through it can know what it's like. The way that everyone *says* exactly the same things that they would say if they were in London, and all the time they're *doing* most absurdly different things. The way that one drifts clean out of one's little circle, of which one has formed an integral part and in which one has been absorbingly interested, and instantaneously finds oneself in another quite new one in which one becomes in a few seconds a vastly important component part and equally absorbed. The way in which one really spends nine-tenths of one's time sitting in some beastly place without shade, brushing flies off one's face, and somehow one isn't bored with it. The way in which all things which are most boring at home become most interesting out there. The way in which everything is rather a blurr, nothing very distinct but all one's sensations funny ones, quite new and different; only the isolated little incidents stand out clear like oases. There's no general impression left. It's like tops of mountains sticking up through a fog.[27]

At the start of the battle of Liaoyang (again, an indecisive battle nominally won by the Japanese, but during which they were fought to a standstill and did not attempt to molest the Russian retreat to the line of the Shaho having suffered a loss of 23,000 to the Russian 16,000) they were at Davantientung but were driven from it by the Japanese. They were nearly cut off by the Japanese in the retreat; the battery started into action near the hills of So-Shan-Tse, and Baring was with them all the time. Here he saw the start of the terrible procession of wounded and mutilated men moving towards the Red Cross at Liaoyang: '... some men on foot, others carried on stretchers. I met one man walking quietly. He had a red bandage around the lower part of his face; his tongue and his lips had been shot away. The indifference with which the men bore their wounds was quite extraordinary.'[28]

On 1 September, the retreat was ordered from Liaoyang; by 2 September Baring was back at Mukden; he had lost touch with his battery; on 10 September he rode back south, took part in a reconnaissance patrol under fire, and was back at Mukden on 3 October. Then he was reunited with his old battery. He had a rare, peaceful interlude in a temple where there was a Chinese child:

> This child was afraid of nothing, not of boys, or horses, or men. But when he saw the Cossack on sentry-go with a drawn sword, he used to insist on being carried past him, saying 'Ping!' (which in Chinese means soldier) with an intonation which proved he shared the mistrust and contempt of his countrymen for the profession of the fighting man. A fighting man in a Chinaman's estimation ranks beneath the *Hun-hu-ze* or the hooligan; for, whereas they fear the *Hun-hu-ze*, their aversion for the soldier is mingled with contempt.[29]

In the company of his old battery Maurice saw the battle of Sha-Ho, another of the series of head-on but inconclusive battles which characterized this stage of the war (200,000 Russians in a struggle with 170,000 Japanese in this instance). Maurice was under fire for most of this battle and, again, was very nearly cut off. On 14 October they were forced to retreat at speed, Baring on a borrowed horse. Then they crossed the river Sha-Ho to attack. The 15 October was a quiet day of inaction when he spent the time discussing Russian literature with the Colonel (Maurice insisting, as was usual with him, that he preferred Dostoevsky and Gogol). Next day there was a very bloody battle, with the battery firing in support of an infantry attack. That night Maurice was involved in some terrible scenes helping the wounded: 'the Russian soldier, as a rule, bears his wounds with astounding fortitude, but the wounded of whom I am speaking were so terribly mangled that many of them were screaming in their agony. . . One seemed to be plunged into the lowest circle of the inferno of human pain.'[30]

His compassion, especially, comes through in this incident:

> I was holding up one man who had been terribly mangled in the legs by a bayonet. The doctor was bandaging him. He screamed with pain. The doctor said the screaming upset him. I asked the man to try not to scream and lit a cigarette and put it in his mouth. He immediately

stopped, smoked, and remained quite quiet – until his socks were taken off. The men do not generally have socks, their feet are swathed in a white kind of bandage. This man had socks, and when they were taken off he cried, saying he would never see them again. I promised to keep them for him and he said, 'Thank you, my protector.' A little later he died.[31]

Life as a correspondent at the front was exacting to say the least, a far cry from the rather laconic views reported in *Tinker's Leave* on the subject:

Haslam, Maurel, and Berton said that going to live with a brigade, or indeed with any unit, was sheer folly from a journalist's point of view, as they would see little, hear nothing, and not be able to dispatch any news. . . Troumestre, on the other hand, said he was determined to try life at the Front. It would at least give him copy for a descriptive article; it was better than dawdling at the railway station. . .[32]

Baring not only managed to see a great deal, and to make a great number of dispatches (they form the basis of *What I Saw in Russia*). He also comments on the peculiar and interesting position of the War Correspondent whom he found was 'regarded as a kind of Sherlock Holmes, and was credited with being aware of the plans of both armies by a process of induction'.[33] Correspondents wore a red badge on the arm; this could be something of a liability, putting the correspondent at the mercy of endless questions:

'What is that red mark on your arm?'. . .
'I'm a correspondent.'
'What country?' – 'I'm an Englishman.' (This produced a somewhat chilling effect generally.)
'What newspaper?' – 'The *Morning Post*.' (I find everybody knows the *Morning Post* by name, and considered it by far the most Russophobe newspaper.) – 'Ah!' (effect bad).[34]

Russophobe Baring most certainly was not; as he confided to Gosse in July:

The Japs are quite close if one has realised [sic] the Chinese one can have nothing but contempt for the Japs and their German ways. They flood the world with imitation soda water and imitation Bryant and May matches which explode in one's pocket. I hope devoutly they will be beaten. I suppose I ought [not] to think that but I do, and there's an end on't. I think the Russians are behaving splendidly.[35]

Like Troumestre in *Tinker's Leave* Maurice wanted to be in the thick of the fighting at the Front and, after the Battle of Liaoyang, 'neither a victory nor a defeat for either side' he rode back 'with streams of ambulances, stretchers, and wounded men walking on foot'. The awful noise of battle continued, and:

I thought of all the heroes of the past, from the Trojan War onward, and of the words which those who have not fought their country's battles, but made their country's songs, have said about these men and their deeds, and I asked myself, Is that all true? Is it true that these things become like the shining pattern on a glorious banner, the captain jewels of a great crown, which is the richest heirloom of nations? Or is this all an illusion? Is war an abominable return to barbarism, the emancipation of the beast in man, the riot of all that is bad, brutal and hideous; the suspension and destruction of civilisation by its very means and engines; and are those songs and those words which stir our blood merely the dreams of those who have been resolutely secluded from the horrible reality? And then I thought of the sublime courage of Colonel Philemonov, and of the thousands of unknown men who had fought that day in the *kowliang*, without the remotest notion of the why and wherefore, and I thought that war is to a man what motherhood is to a woman – a burden, a source of untold suffering, and yet a glory.[36]

On 17 October, Maurice was with his battery when they started for Poutilov's Hill; he was the only foreigner who was allowed to visit the hill that day. It was a horrifying spectacle with dead lying everywhere, bandages covering the road, and the corpses lying there 'in the cold dawn with their white faces and staring eyes, like hateful waxwork figures'.[37]

After a lull, Baring returned to Mukden on 31 October, remaining there until 1 December when he travelled to London, the *Morning Post* no longer wanting a correspondent in Manchuria. Such decisive action as there was was over in Manchuria and on 2 January General Stoessel surrendered the fortress at Port Arthur with 39,000 Russians. Eventually, after many setbacks, and defeats at sea far more shattering than those military defeats, Russia agreed to the mediation of the United States and peace was finally signed at Portsmouth (New Hampshire) on 23 August 1905. The lease of the Liaotung peninsula was ceded to Japan (including Port Arthur), as was the southern half of Sakhalin. Manchuria was evacuated and Korea became a Japanese protectorate. In August 1905 Maurice was once again to return to Manchuria with the intention of renewing his attachment to the 2nd Transbaikal Cossack Battery.

− 7 −

A Year in Russia

BEFORE returning to Manchuria Maurice spent some months in London writing dramatic criticism for the *Morning Post*, in particular, of productions of Duse and Sarah Bernhardt, both in London that summer. In the middle of the year, *With The Russians in Manchuria* was published and was well reviewed. In particular, it was praised as 'one of the most interesting and the most humane books issued on the present conflict in the Far East'.[1] Baring's book was welcomed also because, 'One cannot fail to warm towards the war correspondent who is ingenuous enough to devote the first chapter of his book to an analysis of the Russian stage.'[2]

Early in August Maurice returned to Russia; on 8 August he left St Petersburg for Manchuria; on 11 August he set off for Irkutsk from Moscow; everyone was asking whether or not there would be peace; on 23 August, when he was travelling through the hills of Manchuria news came of the summoning of a new duma; and on 1 September he reports that peace was officially announced; but on 7 September he comments that 'People talk about peace as if it was not yet a fact. . . express doubts as to whether the peace will be ratified, and there is talk of a revolution in Japan.'[3]

Once more Baring intended to join the 2nd Transbaikal Cossack Battery with whom he had lived in 1904 and he had telegraphed from Gunchuling for them to send horses for him. The battery was at that time in Mongolia, at Jen-tsen-Tung, about eighty miles from Godziadan. Two Cossacks arrived for him and they started on their long and exhausting ride. The first night they spent at the Chinese town of Ushitai and then proceeded the next day to a Chinese village. There a typical incident occurred. Seeing Baring's red arm-band, the sign of a correspondent, a Chinaman thought he was a doctor. He told Maurice in broken Russian that his child was ill. In the house Maurice found a brown infant with a fat stomach: 'The infant had a white tongue and had been feeding, so the Chinaman told me, on raw Indian corn. I prescribed cessation of diet, and the Chinaman seemed to be satisfied. . .' After this a concert was offered; 'Presently another Chinaman came into the room, and taking from the wall a large and twisted clarion made of brass, he blew on it one deafening blast and hung it up on the wall again. . . There was a short pause. I waited in expectation, and the Chinaman turned to me and said, "the concert is now over."'[4]

From 15 September until 1 October Baring stayed with the battery at Jen-tsen-Tung, at a pleasant place in willow trees near a broad brown river. A Chinaman lived next door preparing three students for their examination in Peking. They spent their time riding, reading, sleeping and playing patience. Jen-tsen-Tung was a large town where 'a stream of Mongols flowed in and out, wearing the most picturesque clothes – silks and velvets of deep orange and sea green that glowed like jewels.'[5] A wizard, dressed in black silk, decorated with silver moons, had situated himself at one street corner; he would answer a question for a small sum, as long as he did not need to prophesy more than a hundred days into the future.

Before travelling any farther Maurice asked this magician about his journey home. The answer was that he could return either by the west or by the east but west would be better and nevertheless he would meet with obstacles. In the event the prophecy was something of an understatement. The journey from Harbin to Moscow, starting on 17 October, was free of obstacles until they reached Samara in the Trans-Siberian express. While they were travelling peacefully the Russian Revolution of 1905 had begun: the first hint came after they had crossed the Urals and had been travelling for thirteen days and, at Samara, the attendant came into the compartment giving a heavy sigh:

> I asked him what was the matter. 'We shan't get farther than Toula,' he said. 'Why?' I asked. 'Because of the unpleasantnesses' (*niepriatnosti*). I asked 'What unpleasantnesses?' 'There is a mutiny,' he said, 'on the line.'[6]

They passed the large station of Sisran and arrived at the small town of Kuznetsk, where they were informed that the train could go no farther because of the strike. No one realized that this was not just another ordinary strike and that the train would not resume its journey within a matter of a few hours. By evening, however, the passengers, a motley crowd of 'officers, merchants, three Germans, three Americans who had returned from working a mine in Siberia, a Polish student, and some ladies'[7], were becoming restless. The following day, however, a resigned air presided, although at dinner time complaints about the disgraceful situation could be heard and on the second day the Americans left by road for Samara to journey on by water to St Petersburg. On the evening of the second day the situation began to resemble that in *Boule de Suif*. There was nothing to do except explore Kuznetsk and by the morning of the fourth day the impatience was fevered. Finally, after a ride in an unofficial train to Pensa, and then to Moscow, they arrived to find the city in darkness except for a faint glimmer of oil lamps. The next day Maurice, staying at the Hotel Dresden, 'still without lamps or light of any kind, and [where] the lift was not working'[8], learned that Russia had been given a Charter.

The reality of this was brought home to him when he went to the big Russian baths: 'Somebody came in and asked for some soap, upon which the barber's assistant, aged about ten, said with the air of a Hampden, "Give the *citizen* some soap."'[9] In the streets there was great rejoicing. Maurice went to one of the restaurants and there found old men embracing and drinking the first glass of vodka to Free Russia. The days passed off reasonably quietly apart from, among other things, the shooting of the veterinary surgeon called Baumann. In his diary for 3 November, Maurice records that: 'The outward aspect of the town during these days is strange. Moscow seems like a besieged city. Many of the shops have got great wooden shutters. Some of the doors are marked with a large red cross. . .'[10] That afternoon he went to see Baumann's funeral procession, one of the most impressive sights he had ever seen with 100,000 men taking part:

The whole of the 'Intelligentsia' (the professional and middle class) was in the streets or at the windows. The windows and balconies were crowded with people. Order was perfect. There was not a hitch nor a scuffle. The men walking in the procession consisted of students, doctors, workmen, people in various kinds of uniforms. . . As it grew dark torches were brought out, lighting up the red banners and the scarlet coffin of the unknown veterinary surgeon, who in a second, by a strange freak of chance, had become a hero, or rather a symbol, an

105

emblem and a banner, and who was being carried to his last resting-place with a simplicity which eclipsed the pomp of all royal funerals, and to the sound of a low song of tired but indefatigable sadness stronger and more formidable than the paeans which celebrate the triumphs and the pageants of kings.[11]

On 4 November, however, the tenor of life in Moscow had changed and for the next few days the time was 'marked by disorder and anarchy'[12] On 7 November, these events notwithstanding, Maurice went to see Gorky's new play at the Art Theatre, *The Children of the Sun*, in a seat given to him by M. Stanislavsky himself and on 12 November, he attended a performance of *Fidelio*. However, on 17 November the *Country Girl*, at the Opera Bouffe, was more dramatic, 'the electric light went out. The performance continued all the same; the actors holding bedroom candles in their hands, while the auditorium remained in the dimmest of twilights.'[13] Baring was still in Moscow when the strike began on 20 December. In the hotel the lifts stopped working, the electric light was switched off, and he accumulated a large store of books and cigarettes in anticipation of future events.

After two or three days in the country with Marie Karlovna von Kotz at Chernaya, Maurice returned to Moscow on 23 December to find the city eerily quiet and, on the way to his apartment, the streets were blocked by a crowd and guarded by police and dragoons. Then he learned that Fiedler's school, a large building nearby, had been the scene of a revolutionary meeting. The revolutionaries had been surrounded and had refused to surrender, 'had thrown a bomb at an officer and killed him, had been fired at by artillery, and had finally surrendered after killing one officer and five men, with 17 casualties – 15 wounded and 2 killed. All this had happened in my very street in my absence.'[14]

On Christmas Eve Maurice went to the Hotel Dresden to see his new friend from Harbin, Alexander Dimitri-Mamonov. ('He was the landlord of a small property near Kirsanov. During the war he had been employed in the Russo-Chinese Bank at Port Arthur, where he had worked during the daytime. At night he had served in the trenches. He spoke English perfectly, although he had never been to England.'[15]) He comments on how extraordinary Moscow seemed:

The streets were full of people – *flâneurs* who were either walking about or gathered together in small and large groups at street corners.

Distant, and sometimes quite near, sounds of firing were audible, and nobody seemed to care a scrap; they were everywhere talking, discussing, laughing. Imagine the difference between this and the scenes described in Paris during the street fighting in '32, '48, and '71.[16]

People seemed to go about their business as usual and cabs drove around barricades. The revolutionaries had taken up a guerrilla kind of warfare, firing or throwing bombs and then dispersing very quickly. The attitude of the man in the street was curious: 'sometimes he is indignant with the strikers, sometimes indignant with the Government'. Above all it was a feeling of 'sceptical indifference'.

On 27 December, a cabman said to Baring, 'There is an illness abroad, we are sick; it will pass.' Maurice agreed. At this time, his life consisted typically of visits to the soldiers' hospital: 'One of them asked me whether Paris was in Turkey. He said the Turks were nice. Another asked me whether there wasn't a place where it was all water. I described Venice as best I could.'[17] Despite the upheavals Maurice liked Moscow very much indeed. In a letter to Vernon Lee of 7 January 1907, he comments that he would really like to read what *she* would have to say about it; 'It has no beauty really; nothing which we enjoy anywhere else; no art, nothing stimulating intellectually either in the place or the people and yet I find it has for me an extraordinary charm. It is dirty, shabby, rather sordid, very untidy, backward, ignorant, vulgar in some parts, and ostentatious – and yet –.'[18] It was, of course, the people that accounted for the fascination. As Maurice continues in this letter, he couldn't help loving the cabman in this story, a tale that he obviously liked as he repeats it in *What I Saw in Russia*:

> A cabman who drove me home last night drove me again to-day. He said it was lucky I had taken him yesterday, because he had not had another fare; and that he had told his comrades all about it, and had said he would have been lost had not the Lord sent him a *Barin*,* and such a *Barin* too! (I had heavily overpaid him.) I said, 'I suppose you said, "God sent you a fool."' 'Oh! *Barin*, don't offend God,' he answered. The cabmen are a constant source of amusement to me here.[20]

Baring had by now had much intercourse with those who defended the revolutionaries, at times with extreme degrees of exaggeration. He was

Barin is a *'monsieur* in contradistinction to the lower class'[19]

feeling a certain reaction for he was always ill at ease with over-stated enthusiasm and, self-confessedly, could never resist the 'subtle spirit of contradiction when I am with people who belong to a party, and hear them express party feeling in unmeasured and exaggerated terms. If I am with violent Conservatives a subtle spirit of Liberalism rises within me, and *vice versa*. Besides this, I hate political *parties*.'[21]

More immediately *sympathique* was this 'characteristic story' recorded from 18 January:

A peasant was looking at a rich man's house in one of streets of Moscow. An agitator went up to him and said: 'Think of the rich man living in that great house, and think of your miserable position.'

'Yes,' said the peasant cheerfully, 'it's a big house; he's a proper *Barin*.'

'But,' said the agitator, much irritated, 'it's most unjust that he should live in such a big house and that you should live in a small house. You should turn him out of it.'

'How could that be?' answered the peasant. 'He is used to being rich. All his life he has lived in plenty. What would he do in poverty? We are used to poverty, and we must have pity on those who are not used to it.'

The agitator then gave the peasant up and went away in disgust.[22]

All this crucial winter of 1905–6 Baring was based in a small apartment in Moscow, absorbing opinions on the revolution and working for the *Morning Post*, with occasional visits to St Petersburg and the country. His counterpart in St Petersburg on this newspaper was Saki, otherwise Hector Munro, later to become correspondent in Paris and a celebrated short-story writer. Baring's opinion of him was clear; Saki was much more than just a 'funny writer', and 'had his stories reached the public from Vienna or Paris, there would have been an artistic boom round his work of a deafening nature'. He was an accomplished satirist, as well as a very witty man and his most characteristic and entertaining book was that masterpiece 'of character-drawing, irony, and pathos, *The Unbearable Bassington*.'[23]

In addition to his visits to St Petersburg, including one coinciding with the twenty-fifth anniversary of Dostoevsky's death in February, Baring spent some illuminating times in the country. Back in Moscow on 6 April, he reports that he has just spent twelve days when he had the opportunity to get some first hand information as to the attitude of the peasants who, he believed, were unquestionably 'the obscure and hidden factor which will ultimately decide the fate of Russian political life'. They were, nevertheless, difficult to get at and, especially, it was very hard to get them to speak their mind. It could be done but it was never easy, hence Baring's preference for travelling in a third-class railway carriage. He did, at this time, see and talk with peasants and with a man who had lived amongst them for many years. From these many conversations it was clear that the main attitude was one of expectation and it was uncertain whether or not anything would come of the 'levelling', the word they used for the Revolutionary Movement. 'It is,' wrote Baring, at the time, 'extremely significant that they look upon this as a process of equalization.'[24]

An interesting fact about the village where his friend lived was that the peasants had read Milton's *Paradise Lost*, and Baring's friend agreed that this was not unusual in Russia. In England this comment had been greeted with some scepticism and incredulity but Maurice found it quite easy to understand why the Russian peasant 'so backward in many things' should read this epic and enjoy it. It was, after all, popular in the same way as *Pilgrim's Progress*. The popularity of *Paradise Lost* was neither more nor less surprising than that of Bunyan or of an epic or fairy tale: 'When people laugh and say that these tastes are the inventions of essayists, they forget that the epics of the world were the supply resulting from the demand caused by the deeply-rooted desire of human nature for stories – long stories of heroic deeds in verse. . .'[25] Interestingly, too, Baring learned that the peasants in this place also liked to read *The Count of Monte Cristo* and Dostoevsky's *Letters from a Dead House*, his account of his time in a Siberian prison: 'Their taste does not to me personally seem to be so baffling. As for Dostoevsky's book, I am certain they recognize its great truth, and they feel the sweetness and simplicity of the writer's character. . .'[26]

Moving to Moscow in time for Easter, on Palm Sunday, at the Easter Fair in front of the Kremlin, Maurice was able to buy, amongst an array of booths selling, 'birds, tortoises, goldfish, grasssnakes, linoleum, carpets, toys, knives, musical instruments, books, music, cakes, lace, ikons, Easter eggs, carved woodwork, etc.', two cheap copies of *Paradise Lost* in Russian with wonderful pictures. The booths and bazaar were one aspect of the Oriental nature of Moscow and yet somehow it would not quite do simply to say that Russia was 'the most Western of Oriental nations'; it did not get any closer to the spirit of the place. On this Palm Sunday Maurice did get closer to this spirit, to a moment when he could come to the point Vernon Lee reached when she could say, 'This is Rome':[27]

> Such a moment had just occurred to me tonight, when driving home though the empty streets at 11 p.m. I passed a church as the clock struck, and I heard a voice speaking loud quite close to me. I turned round, and saw a policeman standing on the pavement, having faced about towards the church. He was saying his prayers in a loud sing-song; his whole body was swaying as he repeatedly crossed himself; in his arms he carried a twig of budding willow, which is the symbol of the palm-branches of today's festival. These branches yesterday and to-day have been sold and carried about all over Russia. Palm Sunday here is called the Feast of the Willow-branches. When I saw this policeman saying his prayers, I experienced that peculiar twinge of recognition which made me think: 'This is Russia.'[28]

Easter itself was one of the most memorable experiences of all Maurice's times in Russia, especially so in Moscow, itself 'the stronghold of old traditions and the city of Churches'. He describes the very early morning after the most solemn service at midnight on the night of Easter Saturday when the crowd begins to disperse and pour into the many churches:

> I went to the Manège – an enormous riding school, in which the Ekaterinoslav Regiment has its church. Half the building looked like a fair. Long tables, twinkling with hundreds of wax tapers, were loaded with the three articles of food which are eaten at Easter – a huge cake called *Kulich*; a kind of sweet cream made of curds and eggs, cream and sugar, called *Paskha* (Easter); and Easter eggs, dipped and dyed in many colours. . . [I] went to the Church of the Saviour, where the first service was not yet over. Here the crowd was so dense that it was almost impossible to get into the church, although it is immense. The singing in this church is ineffable, and it is worthwhile coming to Moscow simply for the sake of hearing it![29]

Easter Morning was marked by people coming with gifts and to offer greetings:

> I was writing in my sitting-room, and I heard a faint mutter in the next

room, a small voice murmuring, '*Gospodi, Gospodi*' ('Lord, Lord'). I went to see who it was, and found it was the policeman, sighing for his tip, not wishing to disturb, but at the same time anxious to indicate his presence... the policeman must, I think, have been pleased with his tip, because policemen have been coming ever since and there are not more than two who belong to my street.[30]

In May, after another brief visit to Sosnofka, Maurice went to St Petersburg for the opening of the Duma and stayed there until its dissolution in July. He spent many hours during the ensuing weeks listening to speeches in the beautiful Taurid Palace that Catherine the Second had built for her lover, Potemkin, and what he found striking was the 'extreme orderliness' compared with British parliamentary affairs. The Duma would never become turbulent because of the nature of the Russian character: 'Russians have a peculiar talent for listening to public speaking.' So Maurice wrote on 14 May, 1906:

I have noticed this constantly. I have sometimes wondered, for instance, whether it was possible for a play to be hissed off the stage in Russia just because it is tedious. A Russian audience seems to me to be capable of listening patiently to act after act of uneventful and colourless dialogue, to things which would drive an Italian audience to frenzy in five minutes, and would bore the British public into throwing a dead cat on the stage.[31]

The appearance of the Duma was fascinating: 'In the lobby, which was a large Louis XV ballroom, members and visitors used to flock in crowds, smoke cigarettes, and throw away the ashes and the ends on to the parquet floor. There were peasant members in their long black coats, some of them wearing crosses and medals; Popes, Tartars, Poles, men in every kind of dress except uniform.'[32]

This Duma was, however, to have but a brief life and on 23 July it was dissolved, and was not followed by open revolution: 'I did not think there would be another act in the revolutionary drama for another ten years.'[33] Baring put this on the record in 1906 and, in the event, he was only a year out since the revolution took place eleven years later. He was to be remembered in subsequent years as a man who, in effect, prophesied the Russian Revolution.

The Duma might have been dissolved but it was impossible, even in the country to get away from politics. On 1 August, near Moscow, Maurice writes: 'Politics filter through everywhere now; in a third-class railway carriage, at the station buffets, in the public parks, in the villages.' One day, a peasant named Feodor from a nearby village accosted him asking if Marie Alexandrovna was in his place:

> I said my hostess's name was Marie Karlovna. 'Of course,' he said. 'I don't mean here, but in your place, in your country.' I didn't understand. Then he said it again very loud, and asked if I was deaf. I said I wasn't deaf, and that I understood what he said, but I did not know to whom he was alluding. 'Talking to you,' he said, 'is like talking to a Tartar. You look at one and don't understand what one says.' Then it suddenly flashed on me that he was alluding to the Queen of England. 'You mean our Queen Alexandra,' I said. 'That's what I mean,' he answered. 'Your Queen is the sister of the Empress Marie Feodorovna.' [He meant the Duchess of Edinburgh, who had a home in the neighbourhood and was the daughter of Tsar Alexander II] It afterwards appeared that he thought that England had been semi-Russianized owing to this relationship.[34]

Later on, also in the company of Feodor, Maurice was kicked by a horse. Always anguished even by the thought of pain, he drank a lot of vodka but it didn't help at all: 'Then I went to the Wise Woman and she put some ointment on the place and spoke the pain away, saying that it was best to be cured "village fashion".' Maurice was greatly surprised: 'I knew this practice existed, but it was curious to find it so near Moscow. It was like finding witchcraft at Surbiton.'[35]

From his position as correspondent and by virtue of his temperament, Maurice had many friends in all classes of Russian society. His habit of travelling in third-class railway carriages, of hay-making with men like Feodor, and staying with ex-Government men like Mirski (an aristocrat as well) meant that he had a wide-ranging experience of the events of 1905-6. This led him to feel that there were simply two sides involved, those that had split countries throughout time – namely Russia was divided into those who supported the Government, or to be more accurate, the autocracy, and those who opposed it. The defenders held that Russia was basically an Oriental country, and that Western methods and institutions were inappropriate; although there might well be a constitution and reforms, these would remain, in reality, a 'dead letter' because they were not compatible with the spirit of the Russian people. You could not coerce Russian peasants into owning land in the way Western peasants did. Russia was like China; you could draw up a constitution but when it was carried out you would find 'that the only practical difference between the old state of affairs and the new is that the writing-table of the Minister of Foreign Affairs is to be oblong instead of round.'[36] The wish for reforms based on a European model was merely the fiction of a middle-class minority, neither Russian nor European in outlook. Russians enjoyed the form of Government they had because it was the 'result and expression of their qualities and defects'. This was Baring's view until 1904 when, after two years' contact with all sectors of Russian people, he changed his opinion and came down on the other side. The comparison with China was clearly silly given that China was a highly civilized nation with a very high proportion of literacy. Russian autocracy was not the natural outcome of the race's inherent characteristics and predilections, rather it was a '. . . fortuitous disease which has been allowed to spread without ever having been radically treated'. Neither autocracy nor bureaucracy could, with validity, be said to derive from the immemorial traditions of the Russian people. Autocracy was the product of a relatively recent change in Russian history, bureaucracy the accidental result of further changes introduced by a man of genius. The Government had set it up so that certain things, for instance the education of the peasants, were impossible; and, when the results of this were seen, said it was fruitless to give land to the uneducated and hopeless. 'This has been the proceeding of the Government: to prevent, prevent, and prevent again; and then, when the explosion resulting from the prevention occurred, to observe how right they had been in preventing, and how necessary it was to prevent more and more, because it was the only thing the people understood'.[37]

Representatives of both these schools of thought claimed to be speaking for the true Russia. Only time was to tell which was right. In 1907, Baring found that his own dealings amongst peasants and working men suggested that it was the second school of thought that would prevail.

Retrospectively, he sums up his views on the failure of the 1905 Revolution: it lost the support of public opinion:

. . . on account of the disease from which its leaders and its rank and file suffered, namely, a want of backbone and stamina, of moral discipline and moral courage. They could not create order because they would not when it came to the point, repudiate disorder. They could not set Russia free because they could not set themselves free from their own despotic and arbitrary political philosophy, which is the negation of freedom.

In the end reaction won the day because at a time when the entire country was given over to anarchy and chaos the intellectual class did not speak out against the anarchy that was maintaining its hold. In addition, although the revolutionaries fought in the name of freedom, it was a very limited freedom, confined, in fact, to one class: their morality was merely 'party morality'. Further, the movement failed not because of any outside event or outside force but because no strong leader came forward to support it and the only leader with the necessary strength opposed the revolutionary movement – that man was P.A. Stolypin (Governor of Saratov in 1903 where he gained his reputation for great firmness and courage, Stolypin became Minister of the Interior in 1906). There was no internal blow that proved fatal to the cause; the problem was an 'internal collapse' due to the nature of the leaders and members who could not gain mass support so that public opinion was, eventually, alienated to the point of disgust.[38]

Baring was able to refine some of these ideas and to see more of the Russian people in his next posting – as correspondent for the *Morning Post* again – this time in St Petersburg. He had become by now one of that rare breed of men, characterized by Chesterton, as 'the expiation of the English tripper; he may be called the English exile. . . a man of good English culture quite warmly and unaffectedly devoted to some particular foreign culture. Maurice had exactly that attitude towards Russia.' He was, in this, one of 'a microscopically small minority. . . It can only be a comic coincidence, but it is a curious fact, that they are mostly of a certain personal type; tending to slight baldness and agreeable smiles under old-fashioned moustaches.' Throughout this period of his life he became firmly established as one of Britain's 'very unofficial diplomatists' in Russia.[39]

– 8 –

Correspondent in St Petersburg

IN October 1906 Baring took up his duties for the *Morning Post* at St
Petersburg. This time John had insisted that his work for the paper
was put on a proper financial footing. On 13 November 1906 he had
had cause to comment on his younger brother's overdraft. Although he
believed that this was not due to extravagance, he wrote 'I have always
told you that I think it unwise, unnecessary and quixotic of you to
continue to [do] good work for the Morning Post. . . unless you receive
proper and sufficient remuneration.'[1] John then intervened so that an
arrangement had been made 'by which they are willing to give you £1400
a year, which sum is to include the pay you may give to an assistant, but
[they] do not, I understand, make it a *sine qua non* that he should be an
Englishman'. John also reported to his brother that, whilst the *Morning
Post* undoubtedly appreciated his work, they had been 'considerably
startled by the bill received for telegraphic messages the other day, and
were infuriated by your sending them a mass of telegraphic receipts in
roubles without any explanation'.[2] The provision of an assistant would,
perhaps, obviate the need for such censures. Nevertheless the problem
went on; and in 1907 John's tolerance had, perhaps, been pushed a little
far. It was all very well for Maurice to leave a pile of bills marked
'Account Rendered' at John's Carlton House Terrace residence but this
could not go on for ever and, strictly speaking, the 'already long-suffering
creditors' should be paid by the debtor. Further, Maurice's penchant for
the very best quality in everything was irritating. Was it really necessary
for him to 'patronise so expensive a tailor as Davies?' Could he not buy
his clothes 'from a lesser known firm?' And, although John had no wish
to read him 'a lecture on finance' he had to make his position felt.
Maurice really should be able to make ends meet now: 'Try, therefore, I
beg you, to arrange in future so that we may not have to discuss these

tiresome financial details on the few occasions I see you.'[3]

Baring soon had the opportunity of assessing the situation in Petersburg following the dissolution of the Duma; aptly, as he thought, summed up by a Japanese 'who said that in Russia an incompetent government was being opposed by an ineffectual revolution'. He points out that, although no actual revolution followed the dissolution of the Duma the situation was far from quiet:

> . . . a sporadic civil war spread all over the country, accompanied by anarchy, and an epidemic of political and social crime. Governors of provinces were blown up; Stolypin's house was blown up, his daughter injured, and he himself only narrowly escaped; banks were robbed; policemen were shot; and the political crimes of the Intellectuals were imitated on a wider scale by the discontented proletariat and the criminal class.[4]

In this cycle of anarchy and repression, whilst elections were being held for another Duma, Baring had a talk with Stolypin who struck him as a man of great character and courage who had come too late into Russian politics; 'He would have been an admirable minister in the reign of Alexander the Second, or Alexander the Third.'[5] This winter Maurice saw many Russians and was in constant touch with Russian political life but the most interesting experience he had was a journey to the North, as usual in his habitual third-class carriage. The train was full of workmen going home for the winter, peasants, merchants and mechanics. The conversation turned around Kronstadt and some of the troubles there had been there, and when it came to the topic of the Duma, someone asked 'which Duma?'. Another thought *Duma* was the name of a town. A mechanic remarked that nothing would come of the new Duma, people would not go and vote; a peasant agreed with this, saying that people would not go to vote because it would mean being put straight into prison. Then, there was a knowing chorus of '"They won't go and vote; they know better"'. At this point the mechanic came up to the painter and whispered, '"The Government-"' But, at that moment, in came the guard. The conversation stopped abruptly and that was all Baring was to hear about the Duma for the entire journey. He also made the acquaintance of two men who were dock labourers in Kronstadt who reminded him of the people whom Gorky describes. In response to Baring's question as to how he could understand an article in English a man recounted his dealings with English seamen:

> English ships come to Kronstadt, and we load them. The men on board do not speak Russian, but we understand each other. For instance, we load, and their inspector comes. We call him 'inspector' (I forget the Russian word he used, but it was something like *skipador*); they call him the 'Come on'. The 'Come on' comes, and he says, 'That's no good' ('*Niet dobro*'); and he means not right (*Niet horosho*), and then we make it right. And when their sailors come, we ask them for matches. When we have food, what we call *coshevar*, they call it 'all right'. And when we finish work, what we call *shabash* (it means 'all over'), they call 'seven o'clock'.[6]

After this followed a long discussion and comparison of the life of English and Russian workmen. Maurice went back to his berth for some sleep until a dock labourer came and fetched him telling him that he must come and see the soldiers – they were giving an exhibition of stock jokes which ended in community singing. Then a sailor came and told him how a meeting at Sveaborg had been put down. Finally, they arrived at Vologda station and Baring proceeded to Yaroslav, and then Moscow.

Travelling back to St Petersburg, he had a conversation with a young peasant whom he asked whether he thought the Government was right in relying on the inherent conservatism of the Russian people. This said the peasant is a lie, 'The war opened our eyes. You see, the Russian peasant is accustomed to be told by the authorities that a glass (taking up my tumbler) is a man, and to believe it. The Army is on the side of the Government. At least it is really on the side of the people, but it feels helpless. The Government will never yield except to force. There is nothing to be done.'[7]

After Christmas, the situation seemed to support this. The second Duma was convened but it did not make any great strides, was the result of carefully-arranged elections and, although better than nothing, was certainly not a representative body. In April 1907 Maurice had an interview with Count Witte (it was Witte who in 1905 had persuaded the Tsar to grant a Constitution and who was the author of the October Manifesto). Witte was 'a large, tall, burly figure, with slightly ravaged features, intelligent eyes, the facile opportunism and the deep-seated scepticism of those who have had a long experience of affairs, of the ruling of men, and the vicissitudes of political life.' He received Maurice tersely but then warmed somewhat and eventually was quite charming. He asked why Baring had spent so long in Russia. Maurice replied that it was because it interested him and that things appeared to be looking up. Witte responded with a look of great scepticism. The impression he gave was one of 'disillusion, indifference, fatigue, and invincible pessimism'.[8]

In May Baring went back to London and stayed there until the middle of July. Returning to St Petersburg he started on another expedition – this time, down the Volga, beginning with a train journey from St Petersburg to Ribinsk in, once more, a third-class carriage:

> The comfort of travelling third class in Russia is that there is always tea to be had. One would need the pen of Charles Lamb to sing the praises of Russian tea. The difference between our tea and Russian tea is not that Russian tea is weaker or has lemon in it. . . It is a question of kind; not of degree. You can have tea in Russia as strong as you like. The difference is not in the strength, but in the flavour and in the fact that it is always made with boiling water, and is always fresh. But if you put a piece of lemon into a strong cup of Ceylon tea and think that the result is Russian tea you are mistaken. Russian tea is an exquisitely refreshing drink, and I sometimes wonder whether tea in England in the eighteenth century, the tea sung of by Pope and of which Dr. Johnson drank thirty-six cups running, was not probably identical with Russian tea. It certainly was not Ceylon tea.[9]

Arriving at Ribinsk, Maurice then boarded a steamer down the Volga, as far as Nijni-Novgorod; he had a first-class ticket this time which entitled him to a deck cabin, with a leather sofa, a washing stand and a fountain tap. The Volga was not as he had imagined it, not 'a vast expanse of water in an illimitable plain'. It was a 'broad, brown river, with green, shelving though not steep banks, wooded with birch trees and fir trees and many kinds of shrubs; sometimes the banks consisted of sloping pastures and sometimes of cornfields.'[10] After a night at Yaroslav, he went on to Nijni-Novgorod, the city with its famous fair. He had not realized that the fair would be so huge, had not guessed that the 'Fair' was, in fact, a big town with shops, restaurants and hotels. The main commodity was fur but there were other kinds of goods – second-hand books, tea, silks from China, gems from the Urals and *art nouveau* furniture. There were also curiosity shops with such riches as church vestments, stiff copes and jewelled chasubles 'which would be found most useful by those people who like to furnish their drawing-rooms entirely with objects diverted from their proper use; that is to say, teapots made out of musical instruments and old book bindings.'[11] At the fair, Nijni was filled with every kind of merchant almost all wearing loose Russian shirts and top boots. Maurice noticed that here it did not in the least signify how untidy a person was because this did not necessarily suggest poverty, indeed a scruffy attire might well disguise a very rich man. Clothes did, however, imply nationality and soon he abandoned an English straw hat for a white yachting cap and loose silk Russian shirt.

That evening he went to a restaurant and talked with a young merchant. The merchant thought Maurice must be from the Caucasus and, if not, then definitely from the Far East. Some friends then joined in the conversation, all guessing from where Maurice could possibly be, and suggesting Archangel, Irkutsk, Warsaw and Šaghalien, until eventually one cried out triumphantly, 'I know what place you belong to; you are a native of Nijni.' A very old merchant then joined him, asking if he did not greatly wish he were twenty years younger: 'I said I did, but I did not think I should in that case be better equipped for this particular kind of entertainment, as I should be only twelve years old. "Impossible!" said the old man indignantly. "You are quite bald, and bear every sign of old age."'[12] The next stage of the journey, from Nijni to Astrakhan, by way of Kazan, Samara and Saratov, contained a similar incident. A large bearded Cossack, occupying the bunk above Maurice's, leaned down remarking:

'Thou art quite bald, little father. Is it illness that did it or nature?' 'Nature,' I answered. 'Shouldst try an ointment,' he said. 'I have tried many and strong ointments,' I said, 'including onion, tar, and paraffin, none of which were of any avail. There is nothing to be done.' 'No,' said the Cossack, with a sigh. 'There is nothing to be done. It is God's business.'[13]

The chief meal of the day was tea and every time they stopped a crowd of beggars invaded the cabin. They were never sent empty away but always given some coins, or some bread or some fruit, most likely melon. Maurice was quite certain that in no other country in the world could a beggar be so readily assured of alms; 'Here in the third class saloon it especially struck me. I did not see one single beggar turned away without a gift of some kind.'[14]

The boat proceeded from Samara to Saratov and then to Tzaritsin. Between the latter the character of the river changed and the vegetation grew much less luxuriant: 'The farther south one travels, the greater is the beauty of the river. It is a solemn, majestic river. . .' Every day on the steamer between Saratov and Astrakhan Maurice rose at dawn and went out on deck to watch the day break:

> The soft, grey sky trembled into a delicate tint of lilac, and over the far-off banks of the river, which were distant enough to have the appearance of a range of violet hills, came the first blush of dawn, and then a deeper rose, while the whole upper sky was washed with a clean daffodil colour, which was reflected in silver on the blue water. And then the sun rose – a huge ball of fire, casting golden scales beneath him on the water.[15]

There was another change in the character of the river between Tzaritsin and Astrakhan; 'both the banks were flat now – unlimited steppes with scant vegetation, culminating in steep banks of yellow sand. It was here that the river reminded me of the Nile.' Astrakhan, when it was reached, was decidedly Eastern in feel, with many booths on the quays 'and a coloured herd of people living in the dust and the dirt; splendidly squalid, noisy as parrots, and busy doing nothing, like wasps.'[16] At this date the railway to Astrakhan was not yet completed so it was necessary to return to Tzaritsin by steamer to get back to the centre of Russia. This Maurice did in order to go to Sosnofka.

Arriving there he found the country looking green after a wet summer. There was a large crowd at the station standing around a pillar of smoke and flame. It seemed at first as if there was a village fire, a common occurrence in summer in a place where almost all the houses were straw-thatched. To burn a man's house used, too, to be a common way of settling an old score. This day, however, it was not a fire, but the casting of a bell. The ceremony fixed was for four o'clock that afternoon and Maurice was given an invitation to attend the rites involved. It was a very hot day, the air and ground dry and the smoke issued thickly from the furnace opposite the church, 'a stone building with a Doric portico, four red columns, a white pediment, a circular pale green roof, and a Byzantine minaret'. Before the casting of the bell a Te Deum was sung, and the whole population of the village gathered together to take part in the ceremony. Although it was market day the market was deserted. At four o'clock two priests and a deacon began the ceremony, processing from the church; the men in charge of the furnace stood on either side of it and stirred the molten metal with long poles:

> On one side of the furnace a channel had been prepared through which the metal was to flow into the cast of the bell. The crowd assembled there was already struggling to have and to hold a good place for the release of the metal when the solemn moment should arrive. Three policemen tried to restrain the crowd; that is to say, one police officer, one police sergeant, and one common policeman. They were trying with all their might to keep back the crowd, so that when the metal was released a disaster should not happen; but their efforts were in vain, because the crowd was large, and when they pressed back a small portion of it they made a dent in it which caused the remaining part of it to bulge out; and it was the kind of crowd – so intensely typical of Russia – on which no words, whether of command, entreaty, or threat, made the smallest impression. The only way to keep it back was by pressing on it with the body and outstretched arms, and that only kept back a tiny portion of it.[17]

Throughout all this time the Te Deum went on and on and many things and persons were prayed for. The whole thing reminded one of a sacred picture or a Wagner opera. Characters from the *Nibelung* seemed to be present – Wotan in a blue shirt with a spear, Alberic meddling with the furnace, Siegfried in leather boots and sheepskin, and Mimi, whining and disagreeable. The peasants taking part in the Te Deum were more like a sacred picture, 'women with red-and-white Eastern head-dresses, bearded men listening as though expecting a miracle, and barefooted children, with straw-coloured hair and blue eyes, running about everywhere.' Watching the crowd, thinking it was like a large tough sponge upon which nothing seemed to make any impression, Maurice thought that perhaps the Russian nation was itself similarly 'indissoluble, passive, and obstinate'; it was 'certainly true of the Russian character, in which there is so much apparent weakness and softness, so much obvious elasticity and malleability, and so much hidden passive resistance.'

Suddenly the man in charge said, 'Now, let us pray to God'. This prayer was mainly for the success of the release of the molten metal, two hours having already been spent in prayer for the bell itself. At this time the excitement of the crowd reached a high pitch;

. . . then, at last, the culminating moment came; the metal was released, and it poured down the narrow channel which had been prepared for it, and over which two logs placed crosswise formed an arch, surmounted by a yachting cap, for ornament. A huge yellow sheet of flame flared up a moment in front of the iron screen facing the channel. The women in the crowd shrieked. Those who were in front made a desperate effort to get back, and those who were at the back made a desperate effort to get forward, and I was carried right through and beyond the crowd in the struggle.

Thus was the bell born; it was to be hoped that the silver rouble which Maurice had thrown into it in its making 'would sweeten its utterance, and that it might never have to sound the alarm which signifies battle, murder and sudden death. A vain hope – an idle wish.'[18]

Hitherto Maurice had come to know Northern and Central Russia but had never been to South Russia, or Little Russia as it was sometimes known. In the autumn of 1907 he paid a visit first to Kharkov and then to Gievko, a village in that area where he stayed at the home of Prince Mirski. There was a strong contrast between Central and Southern Russia, something like that between Cambridgeshire and South Devon in England:

In Central Russia there was a bite in the morning air, a smell of smoke, of damp leaves, of moist brown earth, and a haze hanging on the tattered trees, which were generously splashed with crimson and gold. In the south of Russia, little green remained in the yellow and golden woods; the landscape was hot and dry; there was no sharpness in the air and no moisture in the earth; summer, instead of being conquered by the sharp wounds of the invading cold, was dying like a decadent Roman Emperor of excess of splendour, softness, and opulence.[19]

There was a contrast in houses too. The log houses, roofed with straw, so common in Central Russia, were replaced by white or pale green houses with orchards, fruit trees and, on occasion, a glass veranda; 'There is something well-to-do and smiling about them – something which reminds one of the white-washed cottages of South Devon or the farms in Normandy.'

Prince Mirski lived in a long, low house, which recalled a 'slightly shabby Grand Trianon'. He had for a short time in 1905 been Minister of the Interior in Russia and during his period of office he had abolished all censorship of newspapers, an act which had considerable repercussions; 'Never could this censorship be restored again, and its removal let in a flood of light to Russian life. It was the opening of a small skylight into a darkened room.'

It was a most hospitable house with many guests. Mirski was a warm and welcoming host who 'spoke a beautiful, easy Russian'. He was distinguished by his 'great saltlike good sense [which] pervaded the light rippling waves, or the lambent shafts of an urbane wit, never heavy, never tedious, never lengthy, but always light, always amiable, and yet never divorced from a strong fundamental reasonableness.'[20]

After a few days at Gievko, Maurice went further south to Kiev and stayed with Count André Bobrinsky at Smielo. He lived in a compound next to a sugar-beet factory and in the same compound there were other members of the same family all presided over by the forbidding Count Lev Bobrinsky, 'an old man of astonishing vigour and activity, both of body and mind.' The Old Count knew every small detail of all that went on around him and had the reputation for being quite fearless; '. . . once when he was attacked by a huge hound he tackled and defeated the infuriated beast with his hands, and broke the animal's jaw.' Count Lev was understandably held in a certain awe by his family and acquaintances. Maurice came close to a serious confrontation with him. They had gone shooting under the precise instructions of the Count, although he himself no longer shot. They were to shoot roebuck with rifles and Maurice was told they were not to shoot a doe. Whilst he was waiting there was a noise in the undergrowth and a shout which meant don't shoot. Maurice misheard the command taking it to mean shoot. He let off his rifle; it was a doe. The whole party agreed that the old Count must not be told. In the evening when Maurice was taken to see him he went through the bag and the number of shots fired, 'and just when he was going to ask me if I had fired, Prince Yashville intervened, and said that I had not had a shot, and I by my silence gave consent to this statement.' The next day he left for the north but the following Sunday when the whole Bobrinsky clan assembled once more it became all too clear that the Count knew what had happened as he remarked with some fury, '"It is an odd thing that people can't tell the truth. Mr Baring said he had not had a shot out shooting, and one of the barrels of his gun was dirty."'[21] It was then explained that Maurice had shot a doe; with some chagrin, he felt that he could not return to Smielo.

His visit, however, had yielded one incident that later became part of his *Russian Essays and Stories*, 'Pogrom.'[22] Near the Bobrinsky estate there was a village almost entirely inhabited by Jews. One evening two men came and asked the Countess whether they might store their furniture and books in her stables because a pogrom had been arranged for the next day: '*They* were coming from Kiev by train, and from another town. The *pogrom* would take place in the morning and *they* would go back in the evening.'[23] 'They' were unspecified and nothing would elicit further details; some said it was the Tsar's orders, others said it was the Governor's orders but they had been sent to make this pogrom. The Count and Countess Bobrinsky could get no more satisfactory answers when they made enquiries – just the information that

> . . . a *pogrom* had been arranged for the next day. It was not the people of the place who would make it; they lived in peace with the Jews. *They* would come by the night train from two neighbouring towns; *they* would arrive in the morning; there would be a *pogrom*, and then *they* would go away, and all the next morning carts would arrive from the neighbouring villages, just as when there was a fair, to take away what was left after the *pogrom*. No answer was forthcoming as to who was sending *them* even when Count Bobrinsky asked the local police sergeant; he could do nothing; there was nothing to be done.
>
> The next morning, however, the cook came into Countess Bobrinsky's room saying simply, 'There will be no *pogrom* after all. It has been put off.'[24]

Baring stayed in Russia all the autumn and winter of 1907, saw the opening of the third Duma and arrived in London in the middle of December now no longer correspondent from St Petersburg but still seriously intent on earning his living from writing and from journalism.

– 9 –

A Leading Authority on Russia

BARING'S experience in Russia resulted not only in his inclusion on a visit in 1912 to Russia, a 'united expression of the desire of persons of very various political views and public interests to develop further the ties that exist between the two countries' as *The Times* described it on 23 January 1912, but also in his one foray into the world of international finance. Firmly established in St Petersburg, Maurice was asked to take part in negotiations for a tramways loan. Barings considered him eager and anxious to help but 'entirely without business knowledge' so he was put firmly under the supervision of the Bank's local representative.[1] He himself, however, dramatized the episode in a rather more characteristic light: having prepared and presented the terms he sat, so he told, silently in the Hotel Dresden in Moscow, speaking to no one, refusing contact with the outside world. There were murmurings about the transactions and, with his silence, his reputation grew. Over forty-eight hours he became an inscrutable Lord of Finance, having said nothing. Barings' somewhat stringent terms were accepted. Maurice had laid eyes on not one single member of the opposition – he would meet the Russian financiers only at the party in celebration of 'his' deal. It is the kind of joke most characteristic of the man.

The tale may well be apocryphal, not at all so were the large number of his essays, articles, critiques and books on Russia, its people, its history and particularly its literature. The country had a complete fascination for him, an overwhelming charm:

... the secret of the whole matter, that the Russian soul is filled with a human Christian charity which is warmer in kind and intenser in degree, and expressed with a greater simplicity and sincerity, than I have met with in any other people anywhere else; and it is this quality

125

behind everything else which gives charm to Russian life, however squalid the circumstances of it may be, which gives poignancy to its music, sincerity and simplicity to its religion, manners, intercourse, music, singing, verse, art, acting – in a word, to its art, its life, and its faith.[2]

The book from which this comes, *The Mainsprings of Russia*, was not published until 1914 but it contains Baring's central ideas which inform all his Russian criticism. In the dedication to H.G. Wells, he writes, 'As far as the subject of Russia is concerned, I have always, and only, had one object in view: to stimulate in others an interest which I have myself experienced.' In this book he has 'endeavoured to convey to the reader a single idea of the nature of the more important factors in Russian life.'[3] He deals with the beginnings of Russian history, moving on to a chapter on the Russian peasant. Here he claims knowledge based especially on his wartime experience: '. . . being in Manchuria during the greater part of the Russo-Japanese War, as I drifted from one part of the army to another I was thrown together with the Russian soldier, who is a peasant, often on terms of absolute equality. . .'[4] Having dealt with the nobility and the government machine, Baring comments on the causes of discontent in Russia at that date [1913–14]. He remarks on the restraints, the danger of criticism and the checks on free speech and on other kinds of freedom. At the time of writing the population was prosperous, but 'When the discontent which now exists becomes sufficiently widely and deeply felt to stir the average man to sympathy with action, and the abnormal man to violent action, then there may be an outbreak, unless it be anticipated by timely measures of reform, and the causes of discontent be removed.'[5] The great writers had given people an idea of exceptional Russians – but what was needed was a portrait of the 'average Russian'. After all, if Russians were as gloomy as they were shown to be in most novels and plays, 'the great majority of the Russian nation would have cut their throats a long time ago'. It was clear that 'there must be a great deal of cheerfulness, humour, and joy to counterbalance the gloom, the anguish, and the melancholy which is so vividly and poignantly described by so many Russian authors, or else life would not go on.' This was, of course, the case and the average Russian was well-educated, cheerful and sociable and the Russian temperament 'generous, unstinted, democratic and kind'. There were, too, surprising qualities to be met with in the most unexpected places:

One of the most contented Russians I have ever met was a man who had got the post of assistant ticket-collector on a small railway line. His duty was to check the ticket-collector. This man had once been enormously rich. He had possessed estates, where he entertained his friends on a large scale, and provided them with every kind of amusement in the way of sport. Besides this, he had a private theatre of his own and a private orchestra. He spent all his money in this way, until there was none left, and he was obliged to accept what post he could get. But as an insignificant public servant on the railway line he was just as cheerful as ever; he said he had just as much fun. 'I used to drink champagne,' he explained, 'now I drink vodka; the result is the same in the long-run. I used to have a lot of money. I've spent it; money is meant to spend. What is the good of keeping or hoarding it? One can't take it with one when one dies.'[6]

Baring also deals with education, the liberal professions, the Church, and justice, making a particular point about the peculiar and characteristic leniency of the Russian juries. But most important in this book and throughout Baring's Russian writings is the goodness of the Russian people. This belief and this attitude informs his criticism. *Landmarks in Russian Literature* aims to put its author 'into the skin of a Russian' and to see the literature through Russian eyes.[7] It is as 'an admiring and sympathetic friend' that he approaches the subject.[8] Such a friend notices the lack of hypocrisy and the great humanity of the Russians, their indulgence towards moral delinquencies, and their deep-rooted sense of pity (he stresses that in the streets of Moscow or St Petersburg one never saw a beggar beg in vain). A century behind other European nations in political terms, Russians most importantly showed a 'fundamental goodness of heart'.[9] All in all, they were a paradoxical people:

It is perhaps this blend of opposite qualities, this mixture of softness and slackness and happy-go-lucky *insouciance* (all of which qualities make a thing as pliant as putty and as yielding as dough) with the infinite capacity for taking pains, and the inspiring energy and undefeated patience in the face of seemingly insuperable obstacles, which makes the Russian character difficult to understand.[10]

A central fact about their literature was the nature of Russian realism, simply 'the natural expression of the Russian temperament and the

Russian character'.[11] Gogol, the Russian Dickens as he is conventionally considered, could be seen in terms of the 'Cheerfulness of the Russian People'. Baring's comments on *The Overcoat* are astute:

> Nearly half of modern Russian literature descends from this story. The figure of this clerk and the way he is treated by the author is the first portrait of an endless gallery of the failures of this world, the flotsam and jetsam of a social system: grotesque figures, comic, pathetic, with a touch of tragedy in them, which, since they are handled by their creator with a kindly sympathy, and never with cruelty or disdain, win our sympathy and live in our hearts and our affections.[12]

Gogol's place in Russian literature was an important one; Mérimée rated him one of the best *English* humorists but his European reputation was unjustly limited, possibly because his subject matter was remote, so quintessentially Russian. Most important of all, for Gogol's comments on Pushkin for example, as for the whole of Russian literature, was: 'This sense of pity [which] is the greatest gift that the Russian nation possesses: it is likewise the cardinal factor of Russian literature, as well as its most precious asset.'[13]

In his chapter on the work of Tolstoy and Turgenev, Baring stresses the great 'moral authority' of Tolstoy and emphasizes why it was the Turgenev at this date [1910] had been so much praised by European critics; 'it was chiefly through Turgenev's work that Europe discovered Russian literature.'[14] Baring sums up:

> . . . in modern Russian literature, in the literature of this century, leaving the poets out of the question, the two great figures, the two great columns which support the temple of Russian literature, are Tolstoy and Dostoevsky. Turgenev's place is inside the temple; there he has a shrine and an altar which are his own, which no one can dispute with him, and which are bathed in serene radiance and visited by shy visions and voices of haunting loveliness.[15]

This sentiment gave rise to a certain amount of critical opprobrium and eventually Baring was induced to add a further short chapter on Turgenev to *Landmarks*. (When the chapter on Tolstoy and Turgenev had appeared in the *Quarterly Review* he was accused of underrating Turgenev and of trying to insist that his reputation was in decline.)[16] This response showed the danger 'of trying to talk of any foreign writer from the point of view of that writer's country and not from that of your own country'.[17] Of course, Turgenev was and always would be a Russian classic but, rightly or wrongly, he was not quite so much venerated in his own country as he had been previously. In England, meanwhile, it was often the case that a reader had read *only* Turgenev and there was 'an exaggerated cult' for his work amongst educated Englishmen. Nevertheless, Turgenev was a classic and Baring no 'image-breaker'.[18]

The central and most enthusiastic essay in *Landmarks* is on Dostoevsky, for Baring the greatest of Russian writers. *Letters from a Dead House*, the 'most humanly interesting book which he ever wrote'[19] prompts this comment:

> The secret merit of this extraordinary book is also the secret of the unique quality which we find in all Dostoevsky's fiction. It is this: Dostoevsky faces the truth; he faces what is bad, what is worst, what is most revolting in human nature; he does not put on blinkers and deny the existence of evil. . . Dostoevsky analyses, not in order to experiment on the patient and to satisfy his own curiosity, but in order to cure and to comfort him.[20]

Comment on *Crime and Punishment*, 'the greatest tragedy about a murderer since Macbeth', is followed by discussion of *The Idiot*, arguably the most personal of this writer's works: '. . . for none but Dostoevsky could have invented and caused to live such a character as Prince Mwishkin, and made him positively radiate goodness and love'.[21] *The Possessed* was well ahead of its time in the same way that Wagner's music was ahead of its time. Its main idea was 'to show that the whole strength of what were then the Nihilists and what are now the Revolutionaries – let us say the Maximalists – lies, not in lofty dogmas and theories held by a vast and splendidly organized community, but simply in the strength of character of one or two men, and in the peculiar weakness of the common herd.'[22] After remarks on *The Brothers Karamazov* Baring states that his 'sole object has been to give in the broadest manner possible a rough sketch of the nature of the country [of Dostoevsky's work], so as to enable the traveller to make up his mind whether he thinks it worthwhile or not to buy a ticket and set forth. . . If one were asked to sum up briefly what was Dostoevsky's message to his generation and to the world in general, one could do so in two words:

love and pity'.[23] In *An Outline of Russian Literature* Baring insists that Dostoevsky is great 'because of the divine message he gives, not didactically, not by sermons, but by the goodness that emanates, like precious balm, from the characters he creates; because more than any other books in the world his books reflect not only the teaching and the charity, but the accent and the divine aura of love that is in the Gospels.'[24]

The final chapter [of the original version] of *Landmarks* is on the plays of Chekhov, as yet [in 1910], undiscovered in Britain. Chekhov's work was of considerable historical importance as showing 'the extreme period of stagnation in Russian life and literature.'[25] It was important, too, to see it in the context of Russian drama and its peculiarities. The reader or audience needed to appreciate that in Russia there was no such thing as the tradition of the 'well-made' French play and furthermore, the key to the issue was, once more, realism: '. . the Russian drama, like the Russian novel, has, without making any fuss about it, never done but one thing – to depict life as clearly as it saw it, and as simply as it could.'[26]

Russian poetry, too, was distinguished by a similar emphasis on realism (it is arguable that Baring learned something of his *own* talent for realism in his fiction of the 1920s in particular from his close knowledge of Russian literature). The quality of Russian realism was distinctive and unlike that of German, English or French literature:

> We. . . step into a world of quiet skies, rustling leaves, peaceful meadows, and calm woods, where the birds twitter cheerfully and are answered by the plaintive notes of pipe or reed, or interrupted by the homely melody, sometimes cheerful and sometimes sad, of the wandering fiddler.
>
> In this country it is true, we have visions and vistas of distant hills and great brooding waters, of starlit nights and magical twilights; in this country, it is also true that we hear the echoes of magic horns, the footfall of the fairies, the tinkling hammers of the sedulous Kobolds, and the champing and the neighing of the steeds of Chivalry. But there is nothing wildly fantastic, nor portentous, unbridled or extreme.

Baring comments that the region of Russian poetry is even more 'earthly' than that of German poetry; the poetic temperament of the Russian 'does not only closely cling to the solid earth, [but] it is based on and saturated with sound common sense, with a curious matter-of-fact quality.' Interestingly, too, there was, in the poetry of the earlier part of the nineteenth century very little feeling for nature:

> But what the Russian poets did, and what they did in a manner which gives them a unique place in the history of the world's literature, was to extract poetry from the daily life they saw around them, and to express it in forms of incomparable beauty. Russian poetry, like the Russian temperament, is plastic. Plasticity, adaptability, comprehensiveness, are the great qualities of Pushkin.[27]

Baring goes on to deal with Krilov, then to Zhukovsky the 'first and best translator in European literature'[28]; he twice translated Gray's *Elegy*, the second time after a visit to Stoke Poges. Pushkin, the poet most admired by the Russians themselves, was little known outside Russia because his work was untranslatable; 'It is worthwhile learning Russian simply for the sake of reading Pushkin'.[29] He was a most remarkable poet 'because he combines gifts that are rarely met with in conjunction: the common sense, the reality, the detachment, and the finish of a Miss Austen; the swiftness and masculinity of a Byron; and the form, the lofty form, easy withal and perfectly natural, of a Racine; reaching at times, and should it be necessary, the sublimity of a Milton.'[30] Without doubt he was the 'Mozart of poetry'. Baring includes a prose translation of 'The Prophet', simply in the hope of stimulating in some reader the desire to learn Russian so as to read this poem in the original:

THE PROPHET

My spirit was weary and I was athirst, and in the dark wilderness I went astray. And a seraph with six wings appeared to me at the crossing of the ways: And he touched my eyelids and his fingers were as soft as sleep: and my prophetic eyes were awakened like those of a startled eagle. And the angel touched my ears and he filled them with noise and with sound: and I heard the Heavens shuddering, and the flight of the angels in the height, and the moving of the beasts under the waters, and the noise of the growing vine in the valley. He bent down over me and he looked upon my lips; and he tore out my sinful tongue, and he took away all idle things and all evil with his right hand, and his right hand was dabbled with blood; and he set there in its stead, between my perished lips, the tongue of a wise serpent. And he clove my breast asunder with a sword, and he plucked out my trembling heart and in my stricken breast he set a live coal of fire. Like a corpse in the desert I lay. Then the voice of God called out and said unto me: 'Prophet, arise, and take heed, and hear. Be filled with My Will and go forth over the sea and over the land and set light with My Word to the hearts of the people.'[31]

Pushkin's successor was Lermontov, a Romantic influenced by Byron whose treatment of his themes was, nevertheless, that of a realist. Many of his short lyrics are included in Baring's *Oxford Book of Russian Verse*; in *Landmarks* there is a prose translation of 'The Testament'.

Lermontov left only one remarkable Russian poet to succeed him – Koltsov, a great folk-poet. Then there was a time of prose: Gogol, the Westerners and Herzen; and the Slavophils, amongst whom was one notable poet, the patriot Khomyakov. Then came the age of the great novelists, until Count Alexis Tolstoy whose work is shown in a poem in which he rises to great heights, 'Tropar' ['Hymn' in Baring's version]. Lastly, Baring deals briefly with Blok who died during the Russian Revolution; 'His most famous poem, and the masterpiece of modern Russian poetry, "The Twelve" [which] is a vision of Bolshevism and amazingly impressive. . .'[32]

Baring's *Book of Russian Verse* was compiled at the start of the First World War and since that time he had had no access to modern Russian literature. Thus, he concludes his piece on the subject by recommending those who wished to pursue it further to consult Prince Dmitri Sviatopolk-Mirsky's anthology *Russkaia Lyrika* published in Paris in 1924 where he would meet, among other material, the work of 'a remarkable poetess, Anna Akhmatova'.[33]

In 1914, for the Home University Library, Williams and Norgate published *An Outline of Russian Literature*, written just before the war at Sosnofka. The book opens with a statement about the difficulty Englishmen had hitherto experienced in writing about Russia, the 'prevailing ignorance of the English public with regard to all that concerns Russian affairs', an ignorance that was likely to remain until the English went to Russia and got to know Russian people at first-hand. It was simply not enough to know the work of a certain number of Russian writers; and it was only a certain number because 'although it is true that such writers as Tolstoy and Turgenev had long been naturalized in England, it is equally true that some of the greatest and most typical of Russian writers have not yet been translated.' Most regrettably, there was no complete translation of Pushkin (Baring was himself to have a selection of Pushkin's verse privately printed in 1931), 'much the same situation as if there were in Russia no complete translation of Shakespeare or Milton.' Similarly, there was no translation of Saltykov, a great Russian satirist, and no complete translation of Leskov, a renowned novelist; whilst Russian criticism and philosophy, 'as well as almost the whole of Russian poetry, is completely beyond the ken of England. The knowledge of what Russian civilisation, with its glorious fruit of literature, consists in, is still a sealed book as far as England is concerned.'[34]

Mirsky comments in his book *The Intelligentsia of Great Britain* that in Britain the period in which the passion for Russian literature reached its height was the war period; 'In the years of the 1914-1918 war, when the crisis of British capitalism became part of the general crisis of capitalism. . .'[35] Mirsky's comments, too, make it clear that Baring's appreciation of, for instance, Dostoevsky was well ahead of his time. According to Mirsky, the 'cult of Dostoevsky began in Great Britain among the intelligentsia during the war'. For him, the cult of Chekhov, especially amongst the Bloomsbury set, was more unexpected. It could be explained, however, by the fact that, after Tolstoy and Dostoevsky, Bloomsbury 'found a Russian writer who was completely bourgeois, completely devoid of those rough corners in which, as a result of serfdom, Russian writers used to abound, and when they read him they feel quite at home'.[36]

An Outline, which duplicates much material, though in a reduced form, from *Landmarks* ends in 1905 with the Russian Revolution of that year. The summing up reflects Baring's preoccupations throughout his work on Russian literature:

> Looking back over the record of Russian literature, the first thing which must strike us, if we think of the literature of other countries, is its comparatively short life. . . [It] begins in the nineteenth century. The second thing which will perhaps strike us is that, in spite of its being the youngest of all literatures, it seems to be spiritually the oldest. In some respects it seems to have become over-ripe before it reached maturity. But, herein, perhaps, lies the secret of its greatness, and this may be the value of its contribution to the soul of mankind. It is 'Old in grief and very wise in tears': and its chief gift to mankind is an expression, made with a naturalness and sincerity that are matchless, and a love of reality which is unique, – for all Russian literature, whether in prose or

verse, is rooted in reality – of that grief and that wisdom; the grief and the wisdom that come from a great heart; a heart that is large enough to embrace the world and to drown all the sorrows therein with the immensity of its sympathy, its fraternity, its pity, its charity, and its love.[37]

Baring's work on Russia was, on the whole, well-received: 'He knows the language, he knows the people, he is earnest, his taste is good, he reveals facts of the Russian temperament not commonly perceived, and turns them artfully to illuminate characteristics of their literature.'[38] His Russian work was welcomed because 'he has both the necessary knowledge and the necessary literary gift'.[39] The *Observer* commented that, '. . there are two ways of criticism: to attack, desiccate, to sift, to estimate; the other, and by far the rarer quality in an Englishman, to get into the soul of things, to expound, to reproduce, to recreate as it were, the atmosphere of the author or the book in question.' This was Baring's achievement and his 'splendid sympathy' meant that he was able to get beneath the veneer of the Russian and reach a rare understanding; his insights showed him 'to be a true critic'. Additionally, he was praised for his appreciation of Dostoevsky, at this date, 1910, 'Comparatively unknown even today in this country and still only partly procurable in English translations.'[40] Baring's was the only criticism in English of Dostoevsky until Middleton Murry's influential book published in 1916 (the situation was more satisfactory in France where there were a number of critical works and more translations). He wrote about his favourite Russian writer 'with discrimination and enthusiasm'. But there were reservations; in particular about Baring's stress on realism, and about his shaky grasp of some aspects of Russian history:

> But we cannot leave unremarked the extraordinary perversity of his vision when he sets himself to expound the reasons of the superiority of Russian literature, the *differentia* of Chekhov, the meaning of realism and the like. He holds foggy and impossible theories and asseverates palpable untruths in support of them with the grim earnestness of a Covenanter. . . He persists in believing that Russian tales and plays are good because they represent 'ordinary life', that the Russian goes to the theatre to see again what he sees every day outside the theatre. . .[41]

The Russian People was written

... to supply the average reader with an introduction to the course of Russian affairs; to supply him with a rough idea of those things which, it is generally assumed, the student will not have found out for himself. I wish to sketch as briefly as possible the main features of the Russian soil and race; the main episodes of history and development of the nation; to point out the chief characteristics of the country and its people; and to trace the manner in which its chief institutions grew up and developed: in fact, to put before the reader the chief landmarks in the story of the Russian People.[42]

This formidable task had its own problems at the outset: 'Even with the best will in the world it is doubtful if such a work as Mr Baring designs could really be written on any subject because the gaps in each inquirer's knowledge are different.' It is lucky, so states this reviewer, that the execution is a little different from the agenda:

... and what we get is a few really brilliant and informing sketches loosely connected by less exhilarating passages... After a first chapter devoted to a conscientious catalogue of the physical peculiarities of the country and the nature of its various soils... we come to a charming impressionistic description of certain landscapes and the sentiment that emanates from them. From that we pass, through a mercifully rigorous simplification of the confused early history, to a spirited sketch of Peter the Great and his work; this is one of the finest things in the book and shows Mr Baring at his best...

But well though he wrote the book suffered from bewildering confusions, and:

To tell the truth, Mr Baring is positively dreadful on everything ethnographic; he still holds strange early Victorian creeds about an 'Aryan race' that 'migrated' in successive waves from Asia; and seeks to prove the European affinity of the Russians by the 'Aryan type' to be seen in portraits of Tolstoy and Pushkin, though Tolstoy, as is well known, was exactly of the Hairy Ainu type and Pushkin a thick-lipped octoroon.[43]

Baring's records of the Russo-Japanese War called forth no such adverse criticism. A characteristically favourable comment appeared in the *Daily Graphic*:

> Many of the correspondents who have come back from Manchuria have complained of the curtailment of their privileges. . . but the more candid among the complainants have admitted that their chief difficulty has been that, owing to the conditions of modern warfare, there is so little that may be seen in safety. . . [Baring] does tell us what the Russian officer was like, what the Russian soldier was like, what the commissariat did, what the value was of the Russian Medical Corps, and what, to put it in a sentence, were the surroundings and conditions of the Russian Army during the war. He does this admirably, and we think that in the way he does it he has rendered a real service, not to Russia alone, but to his own country. In this war the Russian has hitherto been beaten by a better man, by a man who is directed by a greater intelligence and by a higher power of organisation. But he has fought a losing fight well, and no reasonable person can believe that he could have done half as well, or a tenth part as well, had a hundredth part of the accusations levelled against the Russian officer and the Russian Official been true.[44]

Belloc contributed a rather more vigorous but very approving review which appeared in *The Speaker*. Newspapers, said Belloc roundly, 'never, and books hardly ever tell one what one wants to know'; here was a book that told him something he 'wanted to know, and that is what the Russian soldier is like and why you hear throughout Europe that he had done a great deal better in Manchuria than a Frenchman or a German could have done'.[45] *Vanity Fair* commented that the war letters were well worth reprinting (from Baring's *Morning Post* dispatches) and *The Outlook* remarked, 'Mr Baring has a temperament. His book has a strong individual note; it is the tenth we have read on the subject, but we do not find it a page too long.'[46]

In 1917 *A Year In Russia* was reprinted and hailed as 'the best thing which has so far been written upon the Russian Revolution of 1917, though the year extends from August 1905, to August, 1906. It is, that is to say, a strictly contemporary account of the first ineffectual revolution, which ended with the dissolution of the first Duma and Stolypin's accession to power.' This reviewer remarks that it might, in November 1917 seem 'a foolhardy thing for any man to reprint to-day what he wrote of Russia at that time. But Mr Baring's confidence is justified; and, although he abstains from remarking that he told us so, his restraint is hardly worth the effort it must have cost him. It would have been impossible for anyone to have complained.'[47]

Reviewers of Baring's Manchurian books were almost unanimous in thinking that he had done a real service to the Russians, and especially to the Russian soldier and to his image; in this, he had, as Belloc put it, told the public something it wanted to know, 'what the Russian soldier [was] like'. He was to offer a comparably valuable service to the British soldier and especially to members of the Flying Corps, with his book on World War One, *Flying Corps Headquarters* in 1920; but that was much later and, first, there was his work as correspondent in the Near East and his 'Letters' from that zone.

From London to the Near East.
Fright of Uncle Tom

IN December 1907 Baring returned to London, still in the employment of the *Morning Post*, and in the spring of the following year moved into North Cottage, 6 North Street, Westminster. The address was misleading, for it was

> . . . far more countrified than anything you could find today [1938] within ten miles of Hyde Park Corner, yet huddled comfortably under the wing of the Houses of Parliament. For some unknown reason left in the lurch by modern progress, it stood on a rough plot of ground; there were grassy growths and a few unhappy-looking fruit trees. One staircase ran up the outside wall and led, I think, to rooms sometimes occupied by Mr Belloc.[1]

North Cottage also had an underground passage to Westminster Abbey, a feature that was very appealing to Maurice. It was this house, too, that was the site of the memorable party described by Chesterton in his autobiography, one of Maurice's 'moonstruck banquets':

> It were not wholly wise perhaps to tell the whole story of that great supper-party in a vast tent in a garden in Westminster; after which eggs were boiled in Sir Herbert Tree's hat (because it was the most chic and shining of the hats of the company); and I remember indulging in a wild fencing match with real swords against a gentleman who was, fortunately, more intoxicated than I.[2]

It was the perfect house for this kind of party. Incidentally, the duelling party was the one from which Bernard Shaw who had drunk nothing walked out in protest.[3]

In the summer of 1908, Maurice joined with Belloc and edited a newspaper. Printed on a press bought by Maurice and set up at North Cottage, it was called *The North Street Gazette*. The paper was written by Belloc, Baring and Raymond Asquith, and was supported entirely by subscribers but it never reached a second issue. Its epigraph was 'Out, out, brief scandal!' and it opened with a statement of policy asserting that it was 'a journal written for the rich by the poor' which 'will fearlessly expose all public scandals save those which happen to be lucrative to the proprietors, or whose exposure might in some way damage them or their more intimate friends'. There would be illustrations, poetry and prose and a special feature of the paper was 'that the Russian correspondence will be written in Russian, and the English in English'. The reader was instructed as follows: 'All communications (which should be written on one side of the paper only) will be received with consideration, and those accompanied by stamps will be confiscated.'[4] It is a publication with a 'good deal of schoolboyish charm'.[5] The leading article was constructed wholly of clichés, a long piece by Belloc advocated votes for monkeys, and the dramatic criticism consisted of a review of *Hamlet*:

> Mr William Shakespeare's effort – not his first attempt in that kind – is better in some ways than in some others which we recently noticed. . . We see unmistakable signs of power in Mr Shakespeare's verse, although too often marred by deplorable touches of coarseness. But we have not the slightest desire to condemn Mr Shakespeare as a poet because he has written a play on an unpleasant theme.[6]

The newspaper ended with Belloc's 'Sonnet Written in Dejection in the House of Commons' and a selection of correspondence written by Raymond Asquith on 'Mr Gladstone's Diction' and 'Coincidences':

> Sir, – The following may not be without interest to those of your readers who care for natural history. Yesterday as I was walking home from the city, I noticed a large flock of flamingoes (*Phoenicoptenes ingens*) hovering over Shaftesbury Avenue. This was at 6.17 p.m. On reaching home I went up to dress to my own room, which communicates with my wife's by a stained oak door. Judge of my surprise to find it tenanted by a giraffe (*Tragleaphus Asiaticus*). Surely the coincidence is a remarkable one.
> The only analogy which occurs to me at this moment (and that an

imperfect one) is a story which my father used to tell me, of how he was one day driving down Threadneedle Street and observed a middle-aged man of foreign appearance standing under a lamp-post and apparently engaged in threading a needle! On enquiry he discovered that the man's name was Street!![7]

The *North Street Gazette* died after its one number, but it was the indirect begetter of the *Eye Witness*, edited first by Belloc and then by Cecil Chesterton, and which in turn, became the *New Witness*.

Baring was by now fast friends with the other two writers, the triumvirate in Gunn's picture 'Conversation Piece' of 1932, now that he had consolidated his friendship with Chesterton whom he had met with the Bellocs some years before. From Moscow in 1908 Baring salutes him:

Dear Gilbert may I leave out the Chesterton?
(Prince, may I call you by your Christian name?)
(Your surname is so solemn & so long:-
Prince may I call you by your Christian name?)
I hope to be back in London this week.
(Prince, let us meet & swallow wine & beer.)
I hope to see you very soon on my return.
(Prince, there is no one like you in the East.)
I hope you & I & Hilaire may meet. I hated GBS's article on you &
Hilaire. I thought it rude, beastly & untrue.
(The sun is shining on the melting snow)
Prince let us drive in Winter's last fast sledge
(The sun is shining on the melting snow.)[8]

The article was the 'Chesterbelloc' in the *New Age* of 15 February 1908 in which G.B.S., among other unpleasantnesses, wrote that 'Chesterton and Belloc is a conspiracy, and a most dangerous one at that. Not a viciously intended one: quite the contrary. It is a game of make-believe of the sort which all imaginative grown-up children love to play; and, as in all such games, the first point is that they shall pretend to be somebody else.' In this game, Chesterton is cast as 'a roaring jovial Englishman' and Belloc as a Frenchman, not a stage Frenchman 'but a French peasant, greedy, narrow, individualistic, ready to fight like a rat in a corner for his scrap of land, and, above all, intensely and superstitiously Roman Catholic.' Wells and G.B.S. in contemplating the Chesterbelloc 'recognise at once a very amusing pantomime elephant'.[9]

It is impossible to say with any certainty how much influence the other two members of the triumvirate had in the central event of Baring's life in this period, namely his conversion to Roman Catholicism. What we do know is that he was in constant touch, at least with Belloc, throughout the formative years prior to the event, asking for information and eager as ever for a spiritual sparring partner. *Puppet Show* gives only a characteristically spare treatment of the matter:

> On the eve of Candlemas 1909, I was received into the Catholic Church by Father Sebastian Bowden at the Brompton Oratory: the only action in my life which I am quite certain I have never regretted.[10]

As Julian Jeffs has justly pointed out, the conversion was far from as sudden an event as this might suggest[11], having its roots at least as early in Maurice's life as Reggie Balfour's visit to Paris in 1899. Then in January 1900, he had written to Ethel:

> . . . I wish we were all born Roman Catholics. I believe in their spirit and refuse to acknowledge the Exclusive Supremacy of their Church: . . . I should be a R.C. if (1) I believed in Xtianity, (2) if I believed in the Roman Catholic Church.[12]

About a year after this Maurice confided in George Grahame that there were by then only two alternatives open to him – namely agnosticism (which he considered tantamount to atheism) or Roman Catholicism. He then expounded his 'theory':

> I can't relever the whole question that no one who has ever punched Roman Catholicism who is religious and believes in Christianity has ever not embraced it at once. *Newman* arrived at the conclusion purely *a priori*. He had a spirit of hate for Catholics and had never been inside a Catholic Church. I think it is the insolence of the Briton prevents it as a rule and type *Herbert*. Look at my sister again. She washed it at first and then punched it to argue against it – and was at once converted. Most people don't punch it at all and say, 'Oh priests and idolatry': *but* however bad priests are doesn't affect the question of, 'Is the Roman Church the Catholic and Apostolic Church of the Creed or is the Anglican?' And I think emphatically the Roman is and the Anglican is

not – and I am confirmed in my belief by the writings of Renan and any agnostic and any historian I have ever read (especially by Renan's history of the early Church). I have had a much greater spirit of hate than you not only for Catholics but for all Christians and especially Catholics. But I believe Credo in human beings. Yours M.

P.S. My uncles would much rather I was an R.C. than nothing. My uncle is [a] serious difficulty. I know everyone bows to *fait accompli*. I have not yet told you all.[13]

In December 1900 he had also written to Hubert Cornish explaining how his position had changed. A year earlier he had been quite unable to perform the 'acrobatic feat' of belief that was required even to begin to think of converting: 'But now I start from the other side. I believe in Christianity, I believe in the redemption.' Given these beliefs, should he, he asks Hubert, join the Church? Even if he should, he will not do so for at least two years: 'If you read En Route by Huysmans, his fight at the end with his reason is word for word what I have twice experienced detail for detail.'[14]

The following January (1901), he tells George Grahame again, that there is now no other course open to him – Catholicism is the only possible way forward but, as he said previously to Hubert Cornish, he is 'going to shirk the evil day for 2 years' although this was simply '*sheer cowardice* and fright of Uncle Tom'.[15] Before he went any further, though, there were other misgivings to think about, and more reading in the Catholic authors to digest. In 1906 he writes to Belloc that the only things he holds against Catholicism and its results are political and educational. He objected to the effects of Catholicism on politics as found in France and Italy and 'I hate Vatican politics and English Catholics in Rome'. On the issue of education he wrote, 'I think my sister Margaret's children infinitely better brought up than my sister Elizabeth's although both are equally nice, but my eldest sister's children are *oppressed* by their education.'[16] Family factors influenced his objections in this matter and 'fright of Uncle Tom' was a real issue for one brought up in that 'nursery tradition' of anti-Catholicism, as he was later to refer to it in *Passing By*.[17] Maurice had some very deeply-entrenched Protestant prejudices with which to contend. Family members recall, for instance, how converts were put firmly 'in the doghouse' and discoveries were made quite early in life that '*Catholic* was a dirty word, and that Catholics in general were not respectable.'[18] Conversion was something that caused at best bewilderment in the family.[19] Even today members of the family talk of how his books were, as a matter of course, 'overseen' by the priest. The Barings' Lutheran roots were very deep indeed.

The prejudice was only to be fully explored by Maurice when he came to write his novels and, most especially, *Passing By* which is set, significantly enough, in 1908, the year before Maurice's own conversion. Most of his life he had been bewildered by the 'fantastic ideas' non-Catholics had about the priesthood and its relationship with the Protestant man or woman. A typical conversation would run on these well-worn grooves:

A: 'Young so and so has become an R.C.'
B: 'What made him do that?'
A: 'Got hold of by the priests.'
B: (Satisfied) 'Of course. Got hold of by the priests.'

Quite often the person in question, like young Godfrey in *Passing By* would never have been near a priest until the decision to convert was well made. Maurice himself had never had a single 'religious conversation' with a priest until he walked into the Oratory to see Father Sebastian Bowden.

The attitude of non-Catholics continued to perplex Maurice throughout his life; in the Autumn of 1919 we find him writing to Ethel on the same subject. It was odd, was it not, he asked, that people should assume automatically that the convert had been 'got hold of by the priests' and, stranger still, was the way non-Catholics refused to 'dissociate the office and the man' when considering the role of the priesthood. The priest, wrote Maurice with confidence, 'is merely the ticket office of the journey or the *bureau d'information* . . . At one moment I came to the conclusion that human life is either causal or divine. If divine it meant a related representative.' This representative was only, for Maurice, to be found in the Catholic Church; it was the only religion that could begin to satisfy him. He rejects a 'third philosophy' or 'patent religion' (citing Christian Science, 'Spiritism', Theosophy and table-turning as examples). As for the great Oriental religions, Buddhism and the Greek philosophies, they were but 'prophecies of Christianity' whilst Anglicanism was simply a 'lopped branch' of Catholicism[20]. His time in Russia, whilst convincing him of the 'reality of the Spiritual Order'[21], had ultimately shown him that the Orthodox Church, although a tempting alternative for the disaffected Anglican, was undermined by schism and state control. Thus, 'directly I came to the conclusion *inside* that life was for me divine, and that I had inside me an immortal thing in touch with an Eternal Spirit, there was no other course open to me than to become a Catholic.' In 1919 he needed to recount this to Ethel, knowing that she would understand him when he wrote, '. . . I feel that human life which is almost intolerable as it is, would be to me quite intolerable without this belief, which is to me no narcotic but food, air, drink.'

This history of Maurice's spiritual experience, given in 1919 to Ethel, is found in a different form in his sonnet sequence *Vita Nuova*. In the first sonnet he deals with stage one of his conversion, 'I found the clue I sought not' he writes, in a lightless world where suddenly he saw 'a shining bridge to bliss'. Daring not to enter the 'topless gate' he completes stage one; he is in the "porch" of the Church but in the second sonnet of the sequence:

> One day I heard a whisper: 'Wherefore wait?
> Why linger in a separated porch?
> Why nurse the flicker of a severed torch?
> The fire is there, ablaze beyond the gate.
>
> Why tremble, foolish soul? Why hesitate?
> However faint the knock, it will be heard.'
> I knocked, and swiftly came the answering word,
> Which bade me enter to my own estate.
>
> I found myself in a familiar place:
> And there my broken soul began to mend;
> I knew the smile of every long-lost face–
>
> They whom I had forgot remembered me;
> I knelt, I knew– it was too bright to see–
> The welcome of a King who was my friend.[22]

The third sonnet rests securely in belief and tranquillity: 'My treasure and my resting place are found.'

It was a 'resting place' that Maurice returned to throughout the rest of his life. There are hints in the correspondence after his conversion that not only had Baring overcome his previous 'objections' to Catholicism, but that he aspired to be a monk. A letter to Elodie Belloc of 9 August 1911 hints that he has made this decision, a secret as yet, and is to take a retreat to confirm his decision.[23] In the 'spiritual' letter to Ethel quoted above Maurice remarks: 'You said to me one day wouldn't I like to be a monk? Yes, indeed, but I think it is like saying to a business man wouldn't you like to be a Rothschild or to a violinist wouldn't you like to play in Levi's orchestra?' He did not pursue his wish to become a monk but he never had the smallest doubt about the wisdom of his conversion and when his niece, Daphne Baring was converted in 1923 he endorsed Chesterton's remarks made in the previous year, sentiments of which he was convinced throughout his life:

> It is the scale and multiplicity of the forms of truth & help that it has to offer. And perhaps, after all, the only thing that you & I can really say with profit is exactly what you yourself suggested; that we are men who have talked to a good many men about a good many things, & seen something of the world & the philosophies of the world, & that we have not the shadow of a doubt about what was the wisest act of our lives.[24]

Maurice is on record as saying that but for his Russian experience he would never have become a Catholic.[25] Without his Russian experience in 1904–1905 he would never have had such insight into the Turkish situation of 1908–1909 into which he was plunged in May of his conversion year. From his first-hand experience in Russia in 1905, Baring was very well placed to understand the nature of the Young Turk Revolution. As the historian David Thomson points out, the situation was analogous to that in Russia where 'a generation of misrule culminated in revolution' and in both countries an already uneasy internal situation was exacerbated by failures in war. Whilst other European nations had attended to the need for broader electorates and, in general, a more satisfactory and closer relationship between state and society, Turkey and Russia had left such matters unattended to. Younger Turks, many of them from noble families, were inspired by the Russian example to intensify their demands for a policy of Westernization; the moment had come for revolt against the 'oriental despotism' of Sultan Abdul II and his profound distrust of all that was Christian, western and European. They came to realize that the key to success lay in winning over sections of the army to their cause; their main aim was to reinstate the liberal constitution of 1876 (swiftly discarded by the Sultan as soon as his own position was unthreatened) and they carried out full-scale propaganda against the 'Red Sultan'. By July 1908 the Third Army Corps, stationed at Salonica, was persuaded to join their cause and they marched on Constantinople. Sultan Abdul immediately proclaimed himself to be a constitutional monarch. Power for a time lay with the committee of Young Turks under the leadership of Enver Bey but by April 1909 Abdul was ready to stage a counter-Revolution. He entered Constantinople and overthrew the government. 'But at Salonica the Committee of Union and Progress rallied the army once more, and retook the capital after five hours of ferocious fighting. This time they made the parliament depose Abdul-Hamid in favour of his younger brother, Mohammed V, and the dreaded "Red Sultan" retired with most of his harem to a comfortable villa in Salonica.'[26] Baring arrived under the auspices of the *Morning Post* on the same day that the Sultan left the city. Living at the Little Club at Pera, a 'centre of gossip and mild gambling', he was at first very optimistic about the future of the Young Turks and the new regime. His *Letters from the Near East*, however, tell 'the story of a gradual disillusionment', his realization that progress is a near-impossibility in Muslim countries. He quotes the Near Eastern expert, Sir Charles Eliot on the issue, and comments '. . . if the Church and State must ever remain as the Prophet left them, austere, rigid and unalterable – how, one asks oneself, can Islam ever progress, and how can the new wine of Western methods be poured into the old skins of Moslim tradition?'[27] He was sceptical of the notion of 'an elastic Islam, or rather of a reformed Islam' and disbelieving of the possibility of grafting European methods on to Eastern institutions. The Young Turks were, ultimately, foreigners, puppets controlled by forces in Europe, and eventually they proved themselves as bloodthirsty and uncompromising as their predecessors. This, however, was not the view of Baring at the outset.

His first letter is optimistic; the Young Turks are the only hope for Turkey and should be encouraged as much as possible. On 6 May, 1909, he writes on 'The Political Outlook' and gives an illuminating glimpse into life in Constantinople at that time:

Last Monday morning streams of people were walking briskly from Pera to Stamboul, all in the same direction. They were making from the Galata Bridge, for the news was in the air that they had been hanging some Turkish Danny Deevers in the morning. Nobody quite knew whether they had been hanged yet or not. Some people said they had been hanged at dawn; others, that they were about to be hanged;

others, that they had just been hanged. They had, as a matter of fact, been hanged at dawn: three of them at the end of the bridge, three of them opposite St Sophia, four, I think, opposite the House of Parliament, and three somewhere else; making thirteen in all. They were soldiers, and one of them was an officer. They were hanged for having taken part in the recent mutiny and for having murdered some men.

There was a gathering crowd, 'not as a London crowd, all drab and grey, but a living kaleidoscope of startling colours – the colours of tulips and Turkey carpets and poppy-fields, red, blue, and yellow.' The victims were each covered with a white gown, and to the breast of each was fixed his sentence; 'They did not look like felons or like murderers, but rather like happy martyrs (in a sacred picture), calm, with an inscrutable content.'[28] At this stage of his experience Baring came above all to realize one essential fact: 'in Turkey the Turk must be on the top. The equality of the Christian elements with the Turkish is just as much out of the question now as it has ever been.'[29] If the Christian looked like getting the better of the Turk, the Turk drew his sword; this was the way it had always been.

Baring's third letter deals with the coronation of the new Sultan; he drove with Aubrey Herbert, the distinguished Ottoman traveller and well-known eccentric, across the old bridge into the Jewish quarter of the city, passing square and wooden houses, some bending over the narrow streets as if they would fall down, with sometimes a stone house with 'half-obliterated remains of beautiful Byzantine window arches and designs'. Eventually they reached the mosque at Eyoub; the Sultan had arrived and his carriage was waiting:

We were welcomed with great courtesy and given seats. But whenever we asked questions, every question – no matter what it was about – was taken to mean we were anxious to know when the Sultan was coming. And to every question the same answer was made gently by these kind and courteous people, as though they were dealing with children: 'Have patience, my lamb, the Sultan will soon be here.'[30]

Finally the Sultan appeared, in a large French barouche, drawn by four bay horses, and 'glittering with gilding and lined with satin':

As this large gilded barouche passed, with the Sultan in uniform inside

it, the spirit of the Second Empire seemed for one moment to hover in
the air, and for one moment I half expected the band to play:

Voici le sabre, le sabre, le sabre
Voici le sabre, le sabre de mon père,

which, as far as the words go, would have been appropriate, as the
Sultan had just been girded with the sword of his predecessors. And
this sudden ghost of the Second Empire was in curious contrast with
the people looking on with whom I was standing. For they belonged to
the Arabian Nights and to infinitely old and far-off things, like the Old
Testament. They were quite solemn when the Sultan passed and
murmured words of blessing. But there was no outward show of
enthusiasm and no cheering or even clapping. I believe there was
farther on, but not to any great extent.[31]

Maurice wondered as he watched this spectacle whether the spectre of
the Second Empire was an omen 'and whether the ceremony which
marked the inauguration, not only of a new reign but also of a new régime
– a totally different order of things, a fresh era and epoch – was destined
really to be all this, or whether under its gaiety and careless lightness, it
was in reality something terribly solemn and fatal of quite another kind,
namely, the funeral procession of the Ottoman Empire'.[32] It could of
course be hoped that the day had marked 'the marriage day of Turkey
and a new order' but Baring remained uncertain.

His letter of 19 May 1909 opens with the emphasis more on the
funereal than on the nuptial. The piece entitled 'Future Prospects' alludes
to the massacres of Adana, more brutal than any that had hitherto
occurred. The cause was, in Baring's view, the same as it always was
when any atrocities happened on Turkish soil:

The Moslim felt the Christian was getting the upper hand of him and
therefore determined to diminish the number of Christians. There is
this difference, however, between the old massacres and these. When
the Armenian massacres took place it was known that the perpetrators
of them would be *bien vus* by many persons in authority. Now those
particular persons are no more. The massacres, therefore, whatever
anyone may say to the contrary, were made for the 'wearing of the
green' against those who did not wear it.[33]

At this point the Government was in the hands of the Committee of

Union and Progress. Every Turk to whom Baring talked at this juncture insisted that the future could only be viewed with anything approaching optimism if a military dictator were appointed. Indeed, since he had been in Turkey Maurice had not met one person who believed that constitutional government as understood in the Westernized parts of Europe could possibly exist in Turkey. This did not, of course, imply that no one in Turkey believed that improvement was possible: 'What they do disbelieve is that the ideas of the French Revolution or the London County Council will ever be living realities in the Ottoman Empire.' An anecdote illustrates the point:

> After the Revolution of July, when it was announced all over Turkey that the era of freedom had begun, a certain Vali (Governor) in Asia Minor summoned the people of his district and told them that they had been granted freedom. 'What does all this mean?' asked a Moslim peasant who was present, indignantly. 'Were we slaves up till now?'[34]

An incident in Russia ran on comparable, if significantly dissimilar, lines:

> When the Emperor granted his constitutional manifesto, a certain Governor, who was utterly bewildered by this novel Ukase, summoned the local elders and told them they had been granted freedom. 'But you must remember,' he added, 'that this means you are free to do good and to behave well, but you are not free to do evil.'
>
> 'Ah!' said a peasant, 'it was just like that before, your Excellency.'
>
> The Russian was sceptical as to the efficacy of any manifesto granting freedom. The Turk simply did not know what it was all about, because he considered himself already as free as the air, and rightly so.[35]

Central to Baring's thinking at this point (despite his continued support of the Young Turks) is, once more, the idea that progress and Islam are contradictory forces at the outset so that Western methods could not be applied with any degree of success. It was mainly the insistence on forcing Western methods in inappropriate situations that caused pessimism about Turkish affairs.

However, by 21 June 1909 Baring's letter is entitled, 'Dissatisfaction with the New Régime' and reports on the touchy situation involving

Crete. Three facts stood out as all important:

> ... first, that the question impartially considered is one of enormous difficulty for the Turks; secondly, that, rightly or wrongly, the Greeks are exasperated, and their exasperation is increased, so I hear from Greek correspondents in Constantinople, with the increasing acuteness of the Cretan question; thirdly, a certain substantiation has been given to the accusation made by the Greeks against the Young Turks, of their want of Liberalism, by the more recent acts of the Young Turks. They have hanged a journalist for his opinions, and they have condemned another journalist, Murad Bey, a man, so a Turkish general told me, of exceptionally great gifts and merit, and a sincere Liberal, to penal servitude for life. Such acts savour more of despotism than of liberty.[36]

It is on this note that Baring concludes his *Letters from the Near East* at this point; he was to return once more, this time for *The Times*, to cover the Balkan War in 1912. When he left Constantinople in the middle of June 1909, he was firmly convinced of one thing; 'that the new Turkish régime was not unlike the old one, and that what a man who had lived for many years in Constantinople had told me was true. When I had mentioned the Young Turks to him, he said: "Qui sont les jeunes Turcs? Il n'y a que les Turcs."'[37] On 29 October 1912 Baring again set out for the Balkans. The situation there had remained tense since 1908–1909. Eventually the Albanians revolted against the Young Turks. War against the Ottomans required a Balkan Alliance; Serbo-Bulgarian negotiations began in 1911 to be finalized in March 1912. Meanwhile a Greek-Bulgarian agreement was reached in May 1912, after which Montenegro joined the alliance. War began in October 1912 and the Balkan allies were soon victorious; an armistice was concluded on 3 December. Baring at once discovered that there was no place on earth where 'being on the spot makes so sharp a difference to one's point of view as the Near East, and where one's ignorance and the ignorance of the great mass of one's fellow-countrymen is so keenly brought home to one.'[38] Many changes were immediately visible:

> The whole of the superficial luxuries of civilisation seem to disappear in a twinkling; and so adaptable a creature is man that you feel no surprise; you just accept everything as if things had always been so.

The trains crawl; they stop at every station; you no longer complain of the inadequacy of the luxuries of your sleeping-car; you are thankful to have a seat at all. It is no longer a question of criticising the quality of the dinner or the swiftness of the service. It is a question of whether you will get a piece of bread or a glass of water during the next twenty-four hours.[39]

At Belgrade station Baring found the place full of reservists and peasants; on the train he got into conversation with a Serbian officer, 'dressed in Khaki, with a white chrysanthemum in his cap, and a bunch of michaelmas daisies in his belt'; he had been wounded at Kumanovo (where the Serbs defeated the Ottomans) and was on his way to Uskub. It took Maurice over twelve hours to get from Belgrade to the Junction of Nish where they arrived at eight o'clock in the evening: it was dark; the station was ill-lit, and there was almost no food: 'Nish did not look like the meeting place of a lot of triumphant soldiers, but rather like the scene of an underground conspiracy in a melodrama, where a lot of tired conspirators were plotting nothing at all. One felt cut off from all news.'[40] Suddenly a sleeping-car appeared and Baring set off for Sofia. He stayed one week in Sofia until it became obvious that he was not going to be allowed to get to the Front. Told it would be easier to do so where the Serbian army was fighting, he made for Uskub, once more finding the benefits of third-class travel:

. . . under such circumstances, in war-time especially, one really gets beneath the crust of a country. Every man who travels in an International sleeping-car becomes more or less international; and it is not in hotels or embassies that you get face to face with a people, however excellent your recommendations. But travel third-class in a full railway carriage, in times of war, and you get to the heart of the country through which you are travelling. The qualities of the people are stripped naked – their good qualities and their bad qualities.[41]

Eventually they reached the station of Kumanovo and got out to look at the battlefield. It was dark and the ground was snow-covered:

Drawn up near the station were a lot of guns and ammunition carts which had been taken from the Turks. Here were some Maxim guns whose screens were perforated by balls, which shows that they could

not have been made of good material; . . . I was told that there were no
doubt cases where the Turkish material was bad; but another and
more potent cause of the disorganisation in the Turkish Army was the
manner in which the Turks handled, or rather mishandled, their
weapons. They forgot to unscrew the shells; they jammed the rifles.
This is not surprising to anyone who has ever seen a Turk handle an
umbrella. He carries it straight in front of him, pointing towards him in
the air, if it is shut, and sideways and beyond his head, if it is open.

They arrived at Uskub after eight and found 'a picturesque, straggling
place, and at that time of the year, swamped as it was in melting snow, an
incredibly dirty place'.[42] Like all Turkish towns it was poorly paved and it
was largely peopled by Albanian Mohammedans. It was the HQ of the
Serbian Army and was filled with officers and soldiers and the war
correspondents who had been forbidden to go any farther although they
could, if they wished, proceed to Kuprulu, a little farther down the line.
Uskub offered 'all the discomforts of war without any of its excitement'.
The main distraction there was having your boots cleaned, and 'as the
streets were full of large lakes of water and high mounds of slush, the
effect of the cleaning was not permanent. Matthew Arnold was once
asked to walk home after dinner on a wet night in London. "No," he said,
"I can't get my feet wet. It would spoil my style." Matthew Arnold's style
would have been annihilated at Uskub.'[43]

Baring was able to hear many accounts from eyewitnesses of the events
immediately before the occupation of Uskub by the Serbians; they were
'tragically comic in a high degree'. The people just could not believe that
it was possible for the Turks to be beaten by the Serbians. Suddenly in the
midst of their confidence came the cry 'The Giaours are upon us.' All
Turkish officers panicked and fled to the consulates trembling in
anticipation. Only the Vali (the head of the district) kept his head. Two
problems called for immediate attention: first it was necessary to prevent
further fighting in the town and second a general massacre of the
Christians must be prevented. The Vali, as it happened, acted promptly
and prevented both eventualities.

Baring learned then about the happenings after the Turkish and
Albanian soldiers had retired south from Kumanovo; they were panic-
stricken; horses belonging to batteries were put in trains and guns were
left behind; there was no doubt that the troops massacred any Christians
they came across. Baring visited the military hospital at Nish, saw many

wounded men after the battle of Perlepe, and came to this conclusion:

> At the beginning of this battle somebody on the Servian side must have blundered. A regiment was advancing, expecting to meet reinforcements on both sides. In front of them, on a hill, they saw what they took to be their own men, and halted. Immediately a hot fire rained on them from all sides. The men they had seen were not their own men but Turks. The Servians had to get away as fast as ever they could go, otherwise they would have been surrounded; as it was they incurred very severe losses indeed.[44]

With the Serbians Baring learned much about the spirit of this people; he found them full of a great patriotism, regarding war as a matter of life and death, and access to the sea as a similar question for their country. 'They have been the driving power in this war. They have had to make the greater sacrifices; and the part they have played has certainly not yet been fully realised or appreciated.' Less reserved than the Bulgarians, they were similarly single-minded. The English press had failed to do justice to the part played by this people in the campaign: 'There is no doubt that at the battle of Kumanovo and still more at the battle of Perlepe some of the severest fighting of the whole war took place.' He had heard tell of Serbian barbarities and massacres but he had found no evidence to support such things.[45] He spent just four or five days at Uskub as there seemed no chance of getting within range of the fighting and, on the way to Sofia, stopped at Nish and inspected the military hospital; 'Just outside the Servian hospital there is a small church. This church was originally a monument erected by the Turks to celebrate the taking of Nish, and its architecture was designed to discourage the Servians from ever rising against them again, for the walls consist almost entirely of the skulls of massacred Servians.'[46]

Back in Sofia he found that there was nothing of interest to do there and no chance of getting to the Bulgarian front so he settled to go to Constantinople. There was there a great feeling of gloom; but so chameleon-like was the city that within hours the mood could change. People said stories of the cholera had been much exaggerated but one thing Baring saw with his own eyes made a deep impression. Driving with two companions and a Turkish officer, they intended to reach the Tchataldja lines but they could not get beyond a certain village on the Sea of Marmora:

Not far from the village, and separated from it by a small river, is a railway station, and as we drove past the bank of the railway line we noticed several dead men lying on the bank. The station was being disinfected. We stopped by the sandy beach to have luncheon, and before we had finished a cart passed us with more dead in it. We drove back through San Stefano. We entered through a gate and drove down the suburb, where, bounded on one side by a railway embankment and on the other hand by a wall, there is a large empty space intersected by the road. Beyond this are the houses of San Stefano. It was in this space that we were met by the most gruesome and terrible sight I have ever seen; worse than any battle field or the sight of wounded men. This plot of ground was littered with dead and dying men. The ground itself was strewn with rags, rubbish, and filth of every kind, and everywhere, under the wall, on the grass, by the edge of the road, and on the road, were men in every phase and stage of cholera.

There was nobody to help them; nobody to look after them; nothing to be done for them. Many of them were dead, and lay like terrible black waxworks in contorted shapes. Others were moving and struggling, and others again were just gasping out the last flicker of life. One man was making a last effort to grasp a gourd. And in the middle of this there were other soldiers, sitting patiently waiting and eating bread under the walls of the houses. There was not a sound, not a murmur. Imagine a crowd of holiday-makers at Hampstead Heath suddenly stricken by plague, and you will have some idea of this terrible sight.[47]

Soon after witnessing this latter-day picture, of 'the Children of Israel stricken in the desert and uplifting their helpless hands to the brazen serpent', Maurice met Mr Philip, First Secretary of the US Embassy. He, too, had been to San Stefano and he and an American doctor, Major Ford, were trying to do something to help the cholera sufferers. Would Baring come and help? The next day Maurice went to San Stefano, a small, elegant suburb of summerhouses. It was deserted completely and quite silent with only a few cafés owned by Greeks where people were drinking coffee. In the Greek school, the cholera patients had at last found shelter. This was where the Americans brought Baring. It was at San Stefano that under the outside wall of the town and on the railway embankment the dead and dying were lying with no help whatsoever. Here Miss Alt and Madame Schneider came and saw the horror, took the matter into their own hands and started a relief fund with £4. They turned the school into a hospital and then were joined by Mr Frew, a Scotch minister of the Dutch Reformed Church in Constantinople. Funds came from the British and American Embassies and Major Ford and Mr Philip joined the two ladies and Mr Frew. Baring describes the school:

I have called the Greek school a hospital, but when you think of a hospital you call up the vision of all the luxury of modern science – of clean beds, of white sheets, of deft and skilful nurses, of supplies of sterilised water, antiseptics, lemonade, baths, quiet, space, and fresh and clean air. Here there were no such appliances and no such things. There were no beds; there were mattresses on the dusty and dirty floors. The rooms were crowded to overflowing. There was no means of washing or dressing the patients. It is difficult to convey to those who never saw it the impression made by the first sight of the rooms in the Greek school. . . the rooms were packed and crowded with human beings, some of them in agony and all of them in extreme distress. They lay on the floor in rows along the walls, with flies buzzing round them; and between these rows of men there was a third row along the middle of the room. They lay across the doors, so that anybody opening a door in a hurry and walking carelessly into the room trod on a sick man. They were weak from starvation. They were one and all of them parched, groaning and moaning, with a torturing and unquenchable thirst.[48]

It was as Maurice reported to Countess Benckendorff an infernal place, five little rooms filled and with no possibility of their being cleaned and a terrible smell. The Swiss woman was a saint but there were other troubles such as 'l'amour-propre des médecins (et padlockez ceci) la jalouse d'un médecin Americain contre les Anglais du Croissant [Rouge] discussions etc. etc.'[49] Eventually, with the arrival of the British Unit of the Red Crescent and that of the Egyptian Red Crescent, matters improved at San Stefano: 'What was at the beginning an ante-chamber to Hell was later, I believe, converted into a clean hospital with all the necessary appliances and attendants.'[50] His retrospective, private account of this to Bron was

. . . extraordinary. Most of the time was spent in giving patients water, in interpreting and in keeping the peace between the doctors and the

Turks by telling lies, in which the women and missionaries helped. He got one of the orderlies punished for cruelty to a patient. One punishment consisted of being beaten on his very fat bumbles with a large rake. The American and the English doctor were not on speaking terms, and on the last day the Englishman caught the American kissing the Mrs Potts woman. . . When Maurice left, the American was moving his camp bed into Mrs Potts' house. The English were scandalised.[51]

Baring has received some considerable praise for his part in this and Chesterton was moved to remark:

'. . . if I write now, I really think it is partly because it is easier to write than to talk. It is very hard for one man to tell another man how much he admires him. I can't say why; it doesn't seem to go *with the* gesture of the cigar or a walking-stick. Bring me any of the women who helped you in that magnificent thing, and I will tell *them* that they are noble, as easily as I can take off my hat in a parlour or kneel down in church. But only in pen and ink can I even hint how much I think of you.[52]

It was a time, however, that took its toll on Maurice's strength. On 12 December 1912 Bron reported to Nan that Maurice had arrived home, well but taking cholera medicine and suffering from pains in the stomach. On 15 December he had had an awful night with the pains getting worse and worse; and on Christmas Eve there was further trouble; '. . . he got up before the doctor let him to go & stay with George Curzon & returned from there & dashed straight down to Sandwich with Nancy A[stor]. The result was he returned from there & took to his bed again from which he has not risen for a week.' He was in considerable pain and on 26 December Bron told Nan that her sitting-room had become an operating theatre, the doctors having decided that Maurice had an abscess and there must be an operation:

There was a short scene about it being done here [32 Old Queen Street] – the doctors of course wanting Maurice to go to a nursing home. So your sitting room was turned into a operating room. The pictures and curtains were taken out and all the furniture except the bookcase now veiled in sheets. The twiddles were washed with carbolic. . . and the operation was done this morning. Nothing will convince Maurice that it was necessary. He's firmly convinced that it was pure doctors' nonsense. It was completely successful.[53]

Even before his involvement at San Stefano, Baring had come to realize much more fully the true nature of the Turkish situation and, above all, the cause of the reversals and misfortunes which befell this people – this was 'the devastating policy of the Young Turks and the Committee of Union and Progress' who had, as a body, set out to do the impossible with impossible expedition – namely, to *modernize* Islam. Maurice had been with those who asked in 1909 that the Young Turks be given a chance, but now he too saw how reckless they had become in the intervening years; they had tried to revolutionise 'Islam in the space of three years'.

The result was that they tore apart the Ottoman Empire by their treatment of Albania; they failed to ameliorate Christian and Turkish tensions and, when they punished, they misplaced their punishments. Thus: 'Their rule was as arbitrary as that of Abdul Hamid, only they had not one jot of his statesmanship or of his prestige. In Albania they tried to crush the Albanian nationality, to make the peoples there speak one language and to bend all one way. They failed. . . And the result is that Turkey has lost Albania.'[54]

Most disastrous was their influence on the army. They thought to get rid of fanaticism, to modernize the army and, in so doing, they felt that the soldiers must be taught to fight not for their faith but for their country. 'But the Turk is a nomad. The idea of country, *Patrie*, *Vaterland*, means nothing to him.' As a result of these misguided efforts at modernization the army was 'under-officered and badly-officered, disorganised and bewildered' at the start of war.[55] He found little reason to change his views by the time he returned to London in December 1913.

In these prewar years, from about 1909 to 1914, Maurice effectively became that exile described by Chesterton. Essentially a wanderer, a peripatetic, he remained anchored in London through his visits and his correspondence – in particular with Bron and his sister Nan (Herbert). In these years Maurice kept a room in their houses sharing a 'Triple Household' (Herbert Asquith was one who, in July 1911, was to cross-examine Nan about the details of this unconventional arrangement). Brought up by her eccentric father, Auberon Herbert, at The Old House, Burley in the New Forest, Nan, too, had something of an exile's temperament. She had spent some time in Cuba working with the Theosophists and, like Maurice, she sought out ways to travel and to help those suffering during the time of the Balkan War of 1912 (she nursed in

Montenegro). She was attracted to Maurice, drawn by his adventures, his fun and his anarchic sense of humour which they together called 'The Nonsense'. Maurice came to love her during his visits to London; he wooed her with letters when absent and, on leaving for Russia in 1909, gave her 'a most glorious string of fat ambers'[56]; perhaps he wanted more than 'The Nonsense', the constant diet of ragging and teasing; some friends, like Russell, found it all a great enigma.

Much less enigmatic were the lively evenings spent by the 'Triple Household' and their circle, tastes for Maurice amidst his adventures of what Chesterton called the 'cavalier' section of London society[57]. A typical London evening was that of 13 July 1910, a *Claque* party; the *Claque* was a circle of friends who went to the Follies and made a great deal of noise in support (to such excess that on one occasion, in August 1909, 'Maurice laughed so much he started the whole house laughing. Pelissier, beaming from the stage, threatened "to have the gentleman thrown out".'): the party of 13 July was arranged

> ... as Ld. Esher wants to meet Belloc who came, also Maurice, Bluey, [Baker], Charlie Meade [a mountaineer] and Conrad [Russell]. We migrated to North Cottage (shared by Hilaire, Maurice and Phil [Kershaw]) and all sang Russian, Basque and Provencal songs till 2 a.m. Lord Esher (who made me think of the Cat in Maeterlinck's 'Blue Bird'), smiling silently to himself. George Wyndham came in, but seemed to me very artificial and spoilt – a large soft pear rather sleepy at the core! Maurice disappeared to have supper with Pavlova, but returned later in high glee having danced many times with her.[58]

On 30 June 1911 the household held its first party at a new house (33 Grosvenor Road): 'Great nerves' Nan reports in her diary, but to pass the time they had dined at the Carlton and gone to hear *Pagliacci* 'but had made a mistake about the time and missed the opening. Home in the fastest taxi I've ever ridden in – people began to arrive at 10.30 – a deadly half-hour, and then everybody caught fire. The Russian singers sang old country songs, and the Aranye's all dressed in scarlet and fat as butter, played divinely. We saw the dawn in.' Parties and musical evenings at Grosvenor Road were interspersed with times at Picket Post such as that on 1 July 1911 when Nan went down with Countess Benck 'who adores Bron and has adopted us both'. Maurice on this occasion went back to London for a rehearsal of his play *The Green Elephant*; and on 3 July

1911, the play's first night, all the cast came to supper at Grosvenor Road. Not entirely surprisingly by 14 July 1911 the triple household had 'already decided this house is too small, so Bron, M. and I dashed off to look at a famous one near the Brompton Oratory, and three in Chelsea. No good. Countess Benck. delighted at the idea of our having a larger house.'²² Eventually, the household moved to 32 Old Queen Street, an early Georgian house in Westminster, in April 1912. There were immediately 'furious plans' for a short season in London and a rush to get the house ready; Maurice, however, had other plans. Nan reports that on 10 June 1912 he was 'in throes about his journey, and on the eve of rebellion against being sent out to New Zealand in a slow boat filled with missionaries'. When at last these plans were settled, Maurice was to go to New Zealand on 21 June and Nan, by now firm friends with the Bencks., was to go to Sosnofka. The King's birthday was 14 June, so Bron had a holiday 'and we all buzzed off to Kew where Maurice made incredible nonsense by pretending to pick the flowers and accosting the keepers, until Bron (as B[oard] of A[griculture]) became really angry'. A dinner party on 18 June consisted of the Laverys (the painter and his wife), Evan Charteris, Nathalie [Benckendorff/Ridley], Dorothy Browne, Diana Manners, Belloc, Bron, Maurice and Nan: 'A huge success, although the electric light went out seven times. Afterwards masses of other people came in, and the party did not end till 2 a.m., when it broke up in fearful hullabaloo over a picture which Maurice had previously given to B and now gave to Natalie.' The following night, 19 June, they dined with the Laverys and looked at Lavery's pictures of Tangiers 'and ragged till nearly 2 a.m., Maurice making a stunt picture in chalks. Hazel Lavery ended by giving us her sketch of Pavlova, which we like much better than Lavery's academy picture.' The next day, Maurice left for New Zealand 'very blue, but not so blue as we are' as Nan recorded in her diary.⁵⁹

Correspondence for the newspapers, his *Letters from the Near East* as they were called for publication, was not Baring's only literary activity at this time. In July of 1909, the year of his return from his first appointment in Turkey, Mills and Boon had brought out *Orpheus in Mayfair*, a collection of short stories and sketches; and the *Morning Post* began to publish his series of *Dead Letters*. Dedicated to Bron, these are 'collected from the Dead Letter Office of the World' and contain highlights such as Walter Raleigh's complaint about the exorbitant cost of cloaks; Guinevere's letter to Arthur about the guest list for the Camelot jousts:

'Oh! I quite forgot. There's Lancelot. Shall we ask him to stay? He's been so often, so if you would rather not have him we can quite well leave him out this time. I don't want him to think he's indispensable to you.'[60]; and, one of the best of all, 'Lady Macbeth's Trouble', a 'Most Private' letter to Lady Macduff inviting her to come to Forres for a few days with her son Jeamie and confiding that unfortunately Macbeth is 'not at all in good case' after the terrible tragedy at Inverness. He had grieved so much over King Duncan, his 'favourite cousin':

> I shall never forget the evening when the King arrived after the battle against those horrid Norwegians. I was very nervous as it was, after having gone through all the anxiety of knowing that Macbeth was in danger. Then on the top of that, just after I heard that he was alive and well, the messenger arrived telling me that the King was on his way to Inverness. Of course I had got nothing ready, and Elspeth our housekeeper put on a face as much as to say that we could not possibly manage in the time. However, I said she *must* manage. I knew our cousin wouldn't expect too much, and I spent the whole day making those drop scones he used to be so fond of.
>
> I was already worried then because Macbeth, who is superstitious, said that he had met three witches on the way (he said something about it in his letter) and they had apparently been uncivil to him. I thought they were gipsies and that he had not crossed their palm with silver, but when he arrived he was still brooding over this, and was quite *odd* in his way of speaking about it.[61]

Then there is the memorable letter from Nero's nursemaid reporting that it is impossible to leave her charge with the new nurserymaid, Virginia:

> She left him all alone in the night nursery while I was getting ready to bath him and the poor darling set fire to his cot with one of the birthday candles, and luckily I came back just in the nick of time. I heard the pet calling, 'Nanna, 'ook at fire' (Fancy his being able to say all that!)

Or, Goneril to her sister Regan in the letter 'King Lear's Daughter' which opens thus:

> I am sending you this letter by Oswald. We have been having the most trying time lately with Papa, and it ended to-day in one of those scenes

which are so painful to people like you and me, who *hate* scenes.

And ends with the postscript: 'P.P.S. – It is wretched weather. The poor little ponies on the heath will have to be brought in.'[62]

Enshrined in the *Dead Letters*, too, is 'Peter the Great', a letter from the English architect, Detmar Lutyens from St Petersburg:

> . . . a man of genius can make bricks without straw. The Czar has proved it. He has built St Petersburg on a marsh. He has built a fleet and organized an army. He has made palaces, schools, academies, factories, and dockyards, and he has inspired others with his fever for work. Like all great workers, he never gives one an impression of hurry. . .
>
> He seems to delight in finding out a project which appears to be impossible, and in achieving it forthwith. No scheme is too large for him to devise, and no detail of it too small for him to attend to. He has the gift of discovering any useful scrap of knowledge either in men or books.[63]

In *The Russian People* Baring gives a further view of Peter the Great:

> Emerson says that Napoleon enlarged the meaning of the word business. Peter the Great enlarged our conception of the word energy. He had developed to its very fullest extent the quality of frantic energy, which I have said is sometimes characteristic of the Russian. Only there is this difference which we have already noted, that the Russian is generally more capable of a short spurt of frantic energy than of a prolonged, sustained effort. Peter the Great's energy was not only superhuman, but constant. Energy was his normal state.[64]

The next period of Maurice's life was to be dominated above all by one man of whom it would also be true to say that 'Energy was his normal state' – Colonel Hugh Trenchard.

[IV]

Royal Flying Corps
1914–1918

– 11 –

Unlikely Soldier

IN November 1914 Colonel Hugh Trenchard, formerly in charge of the
Royal Flying Corps Military Wing at Farnborough, arrived in France
to take command of the First Wing. (By now there were two
operational wings of the RFC.) He was met at Boulogne by Maurice.
Maurice, who was on the staff of General Sir David Henderson, the
General Officer Commanding the Royal Flying Corps in France, had been
detailed to take Trenchard to RFC Headquarters at St Omer. It was not
an auspicious occasion. Trenchard had arranged a car but no petrol;
obtaining petrol took time and they did not start the journey until after
dark. After a while it became rapidly obvious that they were driving in the
wrong direction, towards Calais not to St Omer, indeed almost straight
into the German lines.[1] All too clearly this was a blundering idiot who
couldn't even read a map properly, better fitted to the cultured life of
Paris, Vienna or Rome than to the exacting practical duties required of an
employee of an Air Chief. Trenchard was well aware of Maurice's
reputation. He knew of his ability as a writer and linguist, of his
aristocratic background and his social flair, but what possible place could
there be for him in the Flying Corps? As Trenchard's biographer has
commented, he had a point; he was not simply being philistine but was
genuinely anxious whether Baring had the necessary competence for the
job. Once again, too, Maurice's reputation for elaborate practical jokes
had rebounded on him. In the following August, when Trenchard was
given command of the RFC and 'inherited' Maurice from General
Henderson, he wanted a 'second memory' not a 'court jester'.[2]
Unfortunately on that previous November day, there had already been
signs of the jester – in the drive to St Omer, in the tales of Maurice's ham-
fisted efforts to do up his own puttees and of his frequent port-balancing
act (in moments of ennui Baring was quite likely to enliven the dinner

165

table by placing a full glass of port on his balding head). There was just too much of the aristocratic Quixote about Maurice Baring for the tougher, more rigorous 'Boom' style. Trenchard was to become the most important person to Maurice throughout the war years and Maurice the finest Staff Officer 'Boom' could have wished for.

Only seven months before that meeting in Boulogne, Maurice had returned to Russia little thinking that it would be his last visit before 'tremendous events and the changing of the world'. Alone in the Benckendorffs' house at Sosnofka during an idyllic early summer, he worked hard on his *Outline of Russian Literature*, breaking off only to take a swim in the river or to listen to the nightingales. But one day he was seized with a presentiment: 'Pack and be gone' declared his *Sortes Shakespearianae* when he opened it at random; and when the same thing happened a second time he felt unable to stay in Russia.[3] He arrived in Berlin on 30 June to find the newspapers full of the Archduke's assassination. On leaving Russia he might, he comments, have realized that this was the start of a new life for him but until he reached Berlin he had felt merely a 'small cloud' in the sky.

It was a cloud that was to intensify with astonishing speed, for the murders at Sarajevo gave the Austrian leaders an excuse to attack Serbia. On 23 July an ultimatum was issued to the Serbian Government which conceded almost all the points demanded. Nevertheless, the Austro-Hungarian empire declared war on Serbia on 28 July, having already made sure of German support. On 30 July Russian mobilization began on behalf of the Serbs; the Germans followed suit and declared war on Russia on 1 August. The French started their mobilization on 31 July and Germany declared war on France on 3 August. Most awkwardly of all for Britain, on 2 August Germany sent an ultimatum to Belgium demanding that German troops should be given freedom to march through their country. The invasion of neutral Belgium began on 4 August.

During this rapid sequence of events many people underplayed the news; Maurice was faced with contradictory impressions: meeting Russian acquaintances at the Hotel Bristol in Berlin, he found their reaction to be very serious indeed; back in London in early July the prevailing mood seemed thoughtless, gay and frivolous. On hearing of the Austrian ultimatum, with the headline 'To Hell with Serbia' emblazoned on newspaper placards, Maurice understood from a friend at the Foreign Office that Austria did not mean to pursue matters but at the Russian Embassy the impression was very different. Like many of his compatriots Maurice felt that war would be contained within the Balkans. Russia might become involved but a Slav War was the only certainty. Bron, Maurice and Nan had the idea of taking a 'galloping ambulance' to Serbia, taking advantage of Maurice's experience in the cholera camp in Constantinople in 1912 and Nan's nursing experience in Montenegro. This idea did not develop and Maurice became determined that he must make another journey to Russia. Hearing that the Empress Marie was to return to St Petersburg after a visit to her sister, Queen Alexandra, he decided he would join her private train. But on the evening of 31 July, the day the French mobilization began, he dined with Count Benckendorff. If Britain did not enter the war, advised the Russian Ambassador, Maurice would arrive in Russia at a time of great disappointment and there might well be unpleasantness. Even on 31 July, however, only four days before Sir Edward Grey's famous speech in the House of Commons, neither the French nor the Russian Ambassador thought there was any chance of Britain entering the European struggle. In spite of his many contacts Maurice too thought it unlikely, a mistake he was to repeat some twenty-five years later thinking of the Second World War from his sick bed at Rottingdean. In his novel *Cat's Cradle*, published ten years later, he was to re-create this mood of scepticism as one of his characters remarks light-heartedly at a dance: 'It's like the ball the night before the Battle of Waterloo, isn't it?'[4]

Later, in 1916, he was to admire his friend H.G. Wells's novel, *Mr Britling Sees it Through* for its evocation of the pre-war mood. Wells's Mr Britling presents an American visitor with England 'as a great and amicable spectacle of carelessness and relaxation . . .' despite the fact that the country was 'drifting towards a real disaster'. It was, emphasized Wells, all too characteristic of the English state of mind in the summer of 1914 that 'Mr Britling should be mightily concerned about the conflict in Ireland and almost deliberately negligent of the possibility of a war with Germany.'[5] The Irish situation had come to a head in March when fifty-eight officers stationed in Ireland to undertake the coercion of Ulster had resigned. At the outbreak of war this question was still quite unresolved; and Asquith himself was to write in July to Lady Ottoline Morrell, 'This will take attention away from Ulster, which is a good thing.'[6]

Of course the outbreak of war was to do much more than simply redirect British attention away from the Irish problem, from which it was in fact diverted until the Easter Rising of 1916. On 3 August Grey argued the case for entering the war to support Belgian neutrality, receiving strong support from all his colleagues except the Labour leader, Ramsay MacDonald. (MacDonald, in fact, resigned his leadership as soon as his party conceded the need to be involved.) On the night of 4 August, Britain entered the war.

Maurice 'sleepless and nervous' had discussed with Bron and Nan every possibility of England's joining in; then Asquith had made his speech, read, Maurice felt, 'in a quite low, clear voice, but with emphasis laid on just the right tones, so that no one could ever forget till their dying day the pause and the word *midnight* cutting through the air, stirring the house into an uproar of applause.'[7] Maurice had experienced war at first hand during the Manchurian campaign and had written at that time of how he had recalled '. . . all the heroes of the past, from the Trojan War onwards'.[8] This romanticism was attuned to the spirit of 1914 and he would not greatly have disagreed with Julian Grenfell's wistful comments written from South Africa in August:

> It must be wonderful to be in England now . . . a wonderful speech of Grey's . . . And don't you think it has been a wonderful and almost incredible rally to the Empire; with Redmond and the Hindus and Will Crooks and the Boers and the South Fiji Islanders all aching to come and throw stones at the Germans. It re-inforces one's failing belief in the Old Flag and the Mother Country . . .'[9]

Nor clearly did he dispute the terms of Asquith's address to the Commons on 5 August:

> No nation has ever entered a struggle – and this is one of the greatest in history – with a clearer conscience and a stronger conviction that it is fighting not for aggression and for the advancement of its own interests, but for principles whose maintenance is vital to the civilised world.[10]

Maurice never had any doubts about the rightness of the war with Germany. For all his intense enthusiasm for the country and its culture, his love especially for its music and poetry which he had discovered at Hildesheim, he felt that war was now an inevitability and decided without hesitation to take an active part.

There were two alternatives: either he could make use of his linguistic and interpreting skills in Russia, the country of which by now he had such wide knowledge and experience, or he could join the Expeditionary Force. Nan notes in her diary entry for 10 August, 'The terrific pressure of preparing Wrest [as a war hospital for naval ratings] has almost knocked everything else out of one's head, except consciousness of Maurice's struggles to get out to France as interpreter with the Expeditionary Force . . .' With this in mind Maurice had visited his old friend, David Henderson, GOC of the RFC in the Field, but Henderson was not immediately encouraging: 'Do you want', he asked, 'to go to war to serve your country or do you want to go to war for the fun of going to war?' Maurice hesitated and then replied, 'for the fun'. This was disingenuous:

> As a matter of fact this was not the whole truth. I thought I could be of some use as an interpreter and in fact I added that I thought the two things were not incompatible, with which he agreed, but he said that if I wanted strictly to serve my country and nothing else I would probably be put in an office. It was for that very reason and anticipating that answer that I had said what I did say, because I was convinced that I could be of very little use in an office and of some positive use at the front in France.[11]

Henderson was still discouraging and over the next few days Maurice's hopes diminished fast. An office post began to look dispiritingly probable when he heard that he had only been put on the waiting list to go to France. Russia was the only hope and he went to see Sir John Hanbury-Williams, who was leaving for Russia, and offered his services provided that an opportunity to work with Henderson did not arise. On 8 August the situation suddenly changed. A note from Henderson told him that he was to accompany him to France and that he should report to the War Office the next morning. There he learned that he was to be a Lieutenant in the Intelligence Corps attached to Headquarters Royal Flying Corps.

On 9 August friends came to say goodbye at the home of the 'Triple Household', 32 Old Queen Street. There had been difficulties with Maurice's uniform and no time to buy the correct clothes. Luckily he had ordered some khaki in advance and this was then equipped with the appropriate badges of rank. But his puttees remained an insuperable problem. Try as he would he could not get them done up: six people tried in vain to help but it was not until David Henderson came round in the evening of 9 August that the problem was solved (and this was only a temporary solution since, having got them done up, Maurice would not

take them off again; it was unthinkable to go through all that pain again).
Laughing at his unwillingness, Henderson told him firmly that he would
have to take them off and put them on again a great many times before the
war was over. Conrad Russell and Bron came round too. Conrad was in
the Yeomanry and mobilized but not yet going to France; Bron, too, who
had been in the Army for seven years had not yet received his orders. Nan,
his sister, comments in her diary:

> . . . One of the greatest of all the impressive things has been the quiet
> way men vanish to France – one is talking with a man one day, by the
> next he has disappeared . . . Evan [Charteris] came in consumed with
> desire to get out as interpreter – he will leave soon I suppose. Countess
> Benck came in so harassed and worn that one understood even less
> than usual of her English . . . finally Maurice left with his Wolseley [i.e.
> General], struggling hard to keep his puttees up. They've all gone. It's
> ghastly for Bron – but he is working 15 hours a day, which helps him.[12]

In August 1914 Maurice did not even know there was a Flying Corps let
alone what its function was to be. There was a great deal of interest in
aviation but flying was still very much in its infancy. The first cross-
Channel flight had been undertaken as recently as 1909 and, before the
war, although a civilian would certainly have known of Blériot and the
Wright Brothers, he might well have had little knowledge of the Corps.
The British administration too was conservative about developments in
flying; in 1912 the Wright Brothers' offer to sell their invention was
refused as was Dutchman Anthony Fokker's bid to sell his aircraft design
to the British. Until very shortly before the outbreak of war, government
opinion held that if the aeroplane were to be of any use at all, it would be
as an extension of the cavalry. The official historian of the war in the air,
Walter Raleigh, comments: 'The Germans, who as a people fall easy
victims to agreeable sentiment, indulged extravagant hopes from war in
the air . . . the English, who are less excitable, were comparatively slow as
a nation to appreciate the importance of the new invention.'[13] But the war
gave an unprecedented impetus to the development of flying. In 1914
there were only four squadrons in the Royal Flying Corps and 2,073
officers and men in the service. By Armistice Day 1918 there were eighty-
five squadrons and five special flights operating in France and 291,175
officers and men. In August 1914 the RFC took 64 aeroplanes to France,
with another 116 left in the U.K. (of which only about 20 were fit for

operational flying). In November 1918 there were over 22,000 aircraft.

These increases were matched by other developments. At first the sole purpose of the RFC was reconnaissance; the pilots were to be the 'eyes of the army'. But this was to change. More sophisticated techniques were developed; wireless installation was introduced; photography from the air was refined as was contact patrol (reports by low-flying aircraft of the enemy movements); most important of all, was the development of battle in the air (and this was, also, of particular significance in terms of Maurice's attitude to the heroism of the war pilots). Although one-to-one combat in the air was comparatively rare until the second year of fighting it developed rapidly thereafter as methods of air fighting became more advanced. In the early months of the war, officers would take a revolver, a carbine or a rifle into the air with them and into an aircraft that was not specifically a fighter, a two-seater BE2C, for instance, the machine in which Maurice took his first flight in February 1915. In the spring of 1915, the Germans began to use their Fokker aircraft as fighters and by the summer it was clear to the RFC that specialist fighters were a necessity. As a result of increased activity by the Fokkers, the British pusher biplanes, the FE2B and the DH2, and the French Nieuport Scout, were introduced and, in 1917, the famous SE5A, a machine that contemporary pilots believed to be one of the greatest fighter aircraft of the time. In 1917, too, the new Bristol Fighter came into operation and, despite a disastrous beginning, became invaluable to the British. Not only were there advances made in the aircraft themselves; there were also developments in the weapons carried; early experiments in firing from aircraft were followed by the introduction of Lewis and Vickers guns. Methods of bombing were also much refined particularly after the German raids on London in the summer of 1917.

Something of the quality of the early RFC is seen in the autobiography of Sholto Douglas, a fighter-pilot at the time. Here he reports on his method of photography: '[I] cut a rectangular hole in the bottom of [my] cockpit in a BE2A, and [my] practice when the area to be photographed nearly filled the aperture, was to push [my] camera through the hole and take [my] snapshot.' On meeting his first enemy aircraft in the air, Douglas describes how he and the German pilot simply noticed and then avoided each other with gentlemanly restraint. The fellow-feeling between British and German fighter-pilots was strong; when the great German pilot Boelcke was killed a British parachute dropped a laurel wreath over the enemy lines with the inscription: 'To the memory of

171

Captain Boelcke, our brave and chivalrous foe. From the British Royal Flying Corps.'[14]

During August and September 1914 Maurice helped set up aerodromes in Northern France and then moved with Henderson to Headquarters at St Omer. Henderson was clearly very pleased with Baring's work, reporting to his wife that Maurice was a 'treasure'. She wrote, Henderson 'loves him & says he is an angel to all the men in the Flying Corps & they all adore him. . . . David asked him . . . if he wasn't bored & wouldn't he like to go to some more exciting regiment or staff job & he was very touched when Maurice said he would like to stay with him.'[15] Henderson had been promoted to the command of the First Army Corps in November 1914, but had returned to the command of the RFC in late December, taking Maurice with him in both moves. When Henderson returned to England and Trenchard came to take up his permanent post with the Flying Corps in France, both he and Maurice were dispirited. On Henderson's departure in August 1915 Maurice 'felt adrift, like a stranded bondsman face to face with a new Pharaoh, and a bondsman who felt he had no qualifications'.[16] Trenchard, the 'new Pharaoh', had, at first, definitely intended sacking Baring as soon as was decently possible; but he soon became impressed by his 'unselfishness and the loyalty he showed to Sir David Henderson and others'.[17] He agreed to give Maurice one month's trial.

By November 1915 Trenchard's view had changed completely and his many reservations had been dispelled. Baring's memory was invaluable; his skill as an interpreter was undoubted; and he had the conviction and concentration to give himself whole-heartedly to the task in hand. With little or no interest in engineering as such (a lack of interest he shared with Trenchard) and with absolutely no technical ability, he believed whole-heartedly in the cause for which he was working and he liked the General. His only reservation was, in fact, throughout the war, to be that as he confided to Chesterton, he felt 'very inglorious' being on a Staff.[18]

In September 1915 Maurice wrote to Lady Desborough (his old friend and confidante Ettie whom he had known since childhood), that he had been 'dog lousy' ever since 'Boom' took over command. He had been fully occupied doing the work of Military Secretary for him and going about with him all day with a notebook and doing all the necessary talking – Trenchard could speak no French: 'It is dog interesting – He is v. energetic, v. quick and v. drastic; but not a Heygate. He is v. shrewd and has . . . the lucidity and instincts of a clever dog.' Trenchard had been pleased with him and had said 'dewdrops' to the adjutant about a letter Maurice had written for him. It had been exactly what he had wanted. Maurice wrote: 'Lots of people can write more or less what you want said but so many people put it in a way in which you don't want to put it and in which you would never put it yourself. And after I had done the interpreting at a Conference between him and the French Flying Officers, he said "I shall use you more and more" . . . I hope it will last and I shan't lose him suddenly.'[19] Of course it was not without its strains; Trenchard never repeated anything he said and complicated details of induction pipes and *monosoupapes* must have been taxing indeed. What was more awkward was the way Boom could be quite distressingly tactless and overbearing with a squadron. But by now a certain intimacy had grown up between the two men and Maurice knew how to deal with his superior. If a reprimand was needed but difficult to deliver Maurice would use one of his 'Field Punishments'. There were two favourites: on driving off after an inspection, he would lean abruptly forward in his seat and look urgently up into the sky as if sighting enemy aircraft. Eventually Trenchard would be forced to ask what the matter was only to be told that his Staff Officer was enjoying watching the birds. Trenchard would then know that he had not behaved quite correctly. If this failed there was always Field Punishment Number Two. Back at St Omer he would find that his pipe had mysteriously vanished and would know then that he had committed a serious infringement. 'The Child' as Maurice was later to name him, could be tamed with a little careful strategy.

But there was a threat to this situation. Maurice did not lose Trenchard as he had feared but in January 1916 Mr Balfour suggested that he should go to Russia to help organize propaganda. Balfour was 'immensely kind' but was firmly convinced that Baring in France was 'a square peg in a round hole' and, with his knowledge of Russian, would be of a great deal more use there than in France. Once more Maurice called on David Henderson, now at the War Office, who told him that he need not go to Russia if he did not so wish. Lord Robert Cecil, however, the Minister of Blockade, was less amenable: 'Do you expect anybody . . . to believe that you are of more use in the Flying Corps than you could be in Russia?'[20] Odd though it might seem Maurice felt that this was indeed the case; there was an enormous amount of work to be done in France with French aviation staff and aircraft manufacturers; Trenchard couldn't speak French so an interpreter was essential; and this interpreter should be familiar with the details of what was being discussed. Cecil remained firm but in a final interview with Henderson on 22 January, Maurice was told that he would not be 'ordered' to Russia. On 23 January he returned with relief to France and the Flying Corps.

More than he realized at the time, his interpreting skill was badly needed to solve knotty communication problems between French and English leaders to aid collaboration; and things could go very wrong:

> Later on I listened to conversations at conferences at Versailles and elsewhere on the subject of aviation, when a fluent interpreter who understood English perfectly would nevertheless translate a phrase about aviation in such a way that it meant the exact opposite of what was being said, simply from ignorance of the subjects that were being discussed. Luckily there was always someone else present who pointed these slips out to the General, and the misunderstandings were rectified, but it showed one how easy it was for a conversation of this kind to go wrong when the interpreter knew French and English but not aviation.[21]

Maurice ensured that mistakes like this were not made; but even more important was his interpreting and recasting of Trenchard's prophetic views on the war and the role of the Flying Corps. Baring was particularly in tune with this task; were not the feats of the Flying Corps a romantic episode in the history of British fighting? Although British air aces were not given the fulsome star treatment the Germans offered their fighter pilots, British pilots could be classed with those past heroes Maurice had recalled when in Manchuria. For a man of his temperament, it is likely that he could have found a place for his heroic view of war only with the Flying Corps; in the hardship and squalor of the trenches it would have been wildly out of place. The best place to put his literary skills to use was clearly in presenting Trenchard's inspired but hopelessly disorganized views, 'a feat comparable to bottling a mountain torrent while yet preserving the tingling fury of its natural state'.[22]

The 'mountain torrent' expressed itself in comments that remain relevant to modern air tactics and, as reported by Baring, carry his unmistakable imprint and clarity. September 1916 saw further operations on the Somme. To date British supremacy in the air was unchallenged and Trenchard was quite justified in saying that if the war had ended then the Flying Corps would 'go down to history in a blaze of glory'.[23] But he was apprehensive on two counts. Surely the Germans would not stand their defeat for long? Would they not improve their aircraft and adopt a more aggressive policy? Should this be the case there would undoubtedly be a British outcry for more defensive measures. On this issue Trenchard was immovable: a defensive air policy could only spell disaster. His worries crystallized after the fighting on the Somme on 15 September. Maurice cast his ideas in a memorandum, afterwards printed and included in an official pamphlet, *Offence and Defence*. The gist of this document is that the aeroplane is an offensive not a defensive weapon. Owing to the 'unlimited space in the air' it is quite impossible to prevent hostile aircraft from crossing the enemy lines should they have the initiative and determination to do so. Although valuable as a weapon of attack, the aeroplane must not be considered as a viable defence against other aeroplanes. Previous experiences at Verdun and on the Somme had proved these points and, stated Maurice, British aviation had rightly continued its offensive policy. What, however, should be done if the Germans changed their tactics and ceased to use their aircraft as defensive weapons? Should this happen the demand for protective measures would increase because of the 'moral effect' produced on the troops by the presence of hostile aircraft. Trenchard had strong ideas on the only 'sound policy': this was 'to exploit this moral effect of the aeroplane on the enemy, but not let him exploit it on ourselves. Now this can only be done by attacking and by continuing to attack.' Experience had shown that the presence of enemy aircraft, even when Germany was doing only *half* the work done by the British Flying Corps, tended to generate an immediate call for defensive measures. Such a call must not be met: 'any machine at the front has five times the value of that the same machine would have behind the lines.'[24] Defence by sea against submarine attacks was difficult enough; in the air, the much greater area involved made it nearly impossible. In the event of changed enemy tactics, the British would have to step up the air offensive and increase the area of air operations but, warned Trenchard, nothing should be taken as certain and German policy could well become much more aggressive. This, like so many of Trenchard's prophecies, was proved correct and by August 1917 it was necessary to review developments in the air since the battles on the Somme. It had become clear that British aircraft could not compete with the new German fighters and by early 1917 German supremacy in the air had become an established fact. The Germans had realized that an offensive air policy was crucial, reorganized their Flying Corps, changed its leaders and accelerated aircraft manufacture.

Trenchard's memorandum that August pointed out that there were other factors with which both sides had to contend. The area of fighting now extended upwards and, with greater numbers of aircraft in operation, battles of whole formations had taken the place of single combat. More problematic still, flying not only extended upwards but also downwards and soon the Germans, following the British lead, attacked enemy forces on the ground. In future, defence against low-flying aircraft would have to be carried out by strategic shooting from the ground. Trenchard thought this of great importance since in his view low-flying aircraft were likely to become an integral part of air tactics. Here again he felt that offensive strategies were the only sensible course of action. There must too be closer co-operation between infantry and air services and specifically the infantry must be educated about the uses of the 'newer weapon'. Whatever new developments might arise Trenchard saw one fixed principal strength of the aeroplane in its 'power to attack the enemy, to force him to fight, and to defeat him'.[25]

Trenchard continued to make use of his Staff Officer throughout the war, making Flying Corps matters clearly known to the authorities in England and Maurice remained with him when he was appointed Chief of Air Staff in England in 1917. Their wartime partnership turned into a long-standing friendship even after Maurice, with regret, refused Trenchard's requests that he should write a history of the RAF for him. In 1919 he was best man at the General's wedding, a best man with a wine glass balanced on his by-now very balding head listening to Trenchard's farewell words as the train took the bridal couple away on their honeymoon: 'All right, Baring, you may go. This is a journey I shan't want you on.'[26]

Busy drafting Trenchard's memoranda, taking notes, interpreting for him and solving all kinds of problems from the domestic (getting hold of Trenchard's favourite 'Oxford' marmalade) to the strategic, Maurice it would seem would have had little time for that other side of his life which had been so dreaded by Trenchard on their first meeting. What, in wartime France happened to Maurice's artistic bent, his talent for friendship and his carefully-staged jokes? Astonishingly, given the amount of time devoted to Trenchard and the Flying Corps, it was very much alive. Almost every day he wrote to Lady Juliet Duff, daughter of the Earl of Lonsdale and Lady de Grey, and married to Robin Duff who was killed in action in October 1914. Juliet was an old friend, sometimes ridiculed by her contemporaries for her gaucheness and tendency to miss the point. Lady Cynthia Asquith remarks acidly in her war diaries that she always thought her a 'very ugly beauty';[27] and even Maurice who was very fond of her, had moments of irritation with her lack of understanding. Later in the war he tells Belloc that Juliet has sent him a book that has 'every qualification for a book that I can't read now or ever'. (Among its other deficiencies it was a contemporary novel by a woman and, at this time, Maurice preferred to read the classics or the novels of Henry James to which Eddie Marsh had introduced him some years earlier, or else, for pure relaxation, a really good detective story, the only genre with which he felt contemporary women writers could cope with any real skill).[28] Juliet was, however, thought to be a 'good sort' and a very sympathetic listener; Belloc was attracted to her probably for this reason after the death of Elodie. His biographer suggests this as a possible interpretation of his flagrant infatuation.[29]

Maurice's letters must in large part have passed by the dull wits of Lady Juliet full as they are of classical allusions, elaborate literary references and multilingual jokes. Why should this cultured, highly literate man have chosen such a correspondent? A clue comes in his loathing of intellectuals and (despite exceptions, such as Vernon Lee) his especial hatred of clever women: 'The intelligentsia are the same all the world over. I feel for them an elemental hatred.'[30] His joking specification, admittedly a little worrying today, of what 'Bints should be' casts further light on this strange choice of correspondent:

GOOD; KIND; DOMESTIC; EXPERTS IN COOKING (NOT IN WINE); (IF POSSIBLE BEAUTIFUL); INCAPABLE OF NAGGING; Able to sew; ALWAYS READY TO LISTEN; Discreet; DEVOTED; INFINITELY SYMPATHETIC; Always ready to go to the zoo if necessary.[31]

Whatever her deficiencies Juliet filled this bill to perfection. None the less a certain querulous tone creeps into Maurice's letters: 'The G. has been marvellous and wonderfully prescient, if you know what that means; if not, look it out in the dictionary.'[32] 'Do not mix up Marie Corelli and Hall Caine. Hillary [Belloc] will explain the vast difference between them.' Directions to apply to Belloc or Marsh for explanations or translations are quite frequent in these letters and it *was* tiresome to have to spell out his linguistic jokes:

That Italian letter was really very clever. Every phrase in it was the beginning of a very well known song such as 'Batti Batti'. There was no word in it that didn't belong to the beginning of a song and sometimes but not always it made a certain sense just enough and not too much. That was the point.[33]

If Italian arias passed Juliet by Maurice's translations of Horace fared even worse. 'I have sent Juliet', he wrote to Eddie in April 1917, '*dozens* of translated odes of Horace in letters; but she doesn't know they are Horace. She merely thinks it is my form of rhetoric.'[34]

Tiresome as Juliet may well have been as the recipient of Maurice's more subtle *jeux d'esprit*, the correspondence clearly filled a great need for him and was a lifeline with the world of Edwardian London. A great deal of thought could be put into apparently trivial needs. A perfect cigarette box would be much appreciated but its nationality was very important. It must not on any account be 'Scottish Finnish Japanese German Swiss or Belgian. And Not Egyptian.' He would like a seal for his birthday with an inscription 'like the Mona Lisa's smile'; and a small wedding present for a Frenchman which should not cost more than five pounds and not less than four pounds ten shillings. Then there were the problems with the minutiae of his life: he needed further supplies of the special cigarettes he used to buy from Marcovitch in Regent Street, the same as those 'they supply to Bron' but with a different kind of mouthpiece; what could he do about a favourite flannel shirt that had shrunk? Was it a permanent casualty? Juliet, his typewriter 'named after Romeo' needed a new ribbon.

In France Maurice wanted details of Juliet's life at home: 'write me a page of gossip. Are you wearing the tonneau skirt or the spinning nosedive skirt?' Clothes were always very important to him and he admitted that he would 'cool' considerably were Juliet to become dowdy, if there were to be even a hint of Sloane Street about her dress; and his friends remember how very important it was throughout his life to look smart for his visits. Juliet mustn't think her letters dull; the 'smallest detail' was of interest to him, whether of her clothes, her garden, the food she had had for dinner or the parties she had been to. So she passed on such details and Maurice responded well: 'Your letter about the dinner made me scream with laughter. Dinner in Lent with Hillary is always a trouble.' In turn he wrote her a flood of letters wittily addressed to *Chère Pointe d'Asperge*; *Donna Immobile ou immeuble*; *Mrs Bouverie Pusey*; or *My dear Malverina* (Molly, after the water); and signed himself variously as *Macbeth (beware of Macduff)*; *Brougham and Vaux*; *Simple Cymon*; *Macgillicuddy Reeks*; *Your Evanescent Vacuum-Control*; *Ben Gun*, and many other aliases.

As the war progressed he still found time to devise pieces of 'fun' for Juliet. In 1917 there were many American soldiers in London on their way to the Front; would it not be 'tremendous fun' if Juliet were to send an invitation to the American Club in Chesterfield Gardens and ask two or three officers to come and stay with her for a few days? She would 'find them quite charming and they would love it and be quite natural about it.' History does not tell whether Juliet took up this suggestion; one suspects that she might have thought her friend could have been joking this time. Anecdotes continue throughout the war years in the letters to Juliet; inevitably there was trouble with Mess cooks and fights in the billets; the soldiers complained, among other things, about the French bread because it had holes in it unlike the American bread which became impossible to obtain. There were also some unlikely events such as this one in July 1918:

> Yesterday one of the chinese labourers engage[d] on making aerod-romes was delivered of a child. This caused great surprise. It is unprecedented in the annals of labour and war work.
> But the chinese always were an original people.[35]

Juliet was also clearly to be trusted with some of Maurice's personal feelings as well as with his anecdotes. Here the combination of poetic response and a sense of horror is characteristic:

> Yesterday it was beautiful in the air.
> The sea mysteriously fringed the coloured world and the lights and shadows made a wonderful chequerboard.
> Today it was hideous. The sky was grey and full of rolling clouds the earth was as colourless as a photograph.
> The fields are scarred and chewed up by the shell fire and the devastation on the ground beyond the Somme is past belief. Every single tree has been methodically cut down; every rose tree and every Virginia creeper.[36]

A few days later on 29 June 1917 he admitted to his intense weariness of the war and of the 'constant wonder as to whether those who have flown away will come back'.

Maurice's humour found an outlet not only in his correspondence with Juliet but also in some of his official duties. During the cold autumn of 1917 he brought the artist William Orpen (who had previously painted Trenchard) to visit 56 Squadron. Orpen reports that he went along with Maurice and found the Major very excited because they had just completed a little circular saw to cut firewood for the squadron that winter:

> The Major had a great idea that, as the A.D.C. to 'Boom' was lunching, after lunch there would be an 'official' opening of the circular saw. It was agreed that all officers and men were to attend (no flying was possible that day) and that Maurice should make a speech, after which he was to cut the end of a cigar with the saw, then a box was made with a glass front in which the cigar was to be placed after the A.D.C. had smoked a little of it, and the box was to be hung in the mess of the squadron. It was all a great success. Maurice made a splendid speech. We all cheered, and then the cigar was cut (to bits nearly). Maurice smoked a little, and it was put safely in its box. Then Maurice was given the first log to cut. This was done, but Maurice was now worked up, so he took his cap off and cut this in halves. He was then proceeding to take off his tunic for the same purpose but was carried away from the scene of execution by a cheering crowd. It was a great day.[37]

Trenchard had mistrusted Baring's artistic talent; it found a safe outlet in the letters to Juliet and in his literary 'war baby', the anthology English Landscape. Throughout 1915 Maurice's friends were applied to for advice; Eddie was asked to advise what should be included and in November 1915 Belloc was requested for his opinion on the ten best poems dealing with English landscape, 'English not Scotch or Irish or Welsh ... When I say landscape I mean in the sense that Gray's Elegy and In Memoriam deal with English landscape.'[38] Originally Maurice had intended that the volume should be published anonymously and that the proceeds should go to the Russian prisoners of war but his publishers were not amenable so he had to say that the compiler's profits would be so disposed, 'but as you may well imagine, there wont be any compiler's profits. The Publishers will take good care of that.' Publishers, he remarked in a letter to Belloc, made him sick.[39] Eventually, with many difficulties about getting hold of the relevant books at the Front and the impossibility of arranging for proof corrections, the volume was published on 22 July 1916.

English Landscape cannot have added much to the comforts of the Russian prisoners if indeed it added anything at all. It was not particularly well-received. The *New Statesman*'s reviewer, John Squire, complained that Baring had not included a few lyrics from *A Shropshire Lad*, a few lines from Pope, Shenstone or Denhan, or something from John Dyer. Squire remarked, too, that the book would surely provoke nostalgia in those fighting at the Front.[40] Normally Maurice never replied to reviews believing this was inevitably a mistake; but *English Landscape* was different from his previous publications – he particularly wanted it to sell because of the one penny that would go to the Russian prisoners (eleven pence to the publishers) in Germany. This time, therefore, he replied to the reviewer; it was he said precisely because he did not want to instil nostalgia that he had not included extracts from *A Shropshire Lad*, a 'desperate book', and he had no wish to 'torture' his readers merely to remind them of the landscape of England.[41]

In 1916 Maurice's preoccupations could not long remain with this *gepack*. As the year wore on he had to turn his attention back to London where impatience was growing with the ineffectual Asquith government. Public opinion was aimed with particular ferocity at the Prime Minister himself, who to many British people seemed quite unable to summon up the necessary energy to deal with the emergency. Asquith's habit of referring all important matters to a full cabinet provoked wide-scale irritation and decisions took far too long to make. Numbered among the Prime Minister's most influential critics were Lloyd George, Sir Edward Carson, Max Aitken, owner of the *Daily Express*, and Lord Northcliffe, owner of *The Times* and *Daily Mail*. By November 1916 these critics had rallied the support of the Conservative leader, Bonar Law, and lobbied for the establishment of a War Council led by Lloyd George. If he remained Prime Minister, Asquith was in effect to be debarred from leading the war effort. Lloyd George finally instituted a new coalition government, a government that was to have important effects on the way the war was waged in France and on the role of the Flying Corps.

Maurice's wartime relations with the media were often fraught; his heroic view of the events from 1914 onwards and his profound loyalty to Trenchard and the Flying Corps made this inevitable. As early as May 1915 he had written to Chesterton that the Harmsworth Press's campaign against Kitchener was 'disgustingly mean and cowardly', that 'treasonable' was 'too exalted a term' to be used of their articles.[42] In January 1916 he was anxious that the Harmsworth papers were launching an attack against the air service (as indeed was the case since the Zeppelin raids on London had called forth a rush of heavy criticism about Britain's inadequate defence in the air). Maurice wrote to Eddie Marsh (Marsh was Winston Churchill's Private Secretary until Winston went to the Front and had very influential contacts). On 26 January Maurice's argument to Eddie was that no change in the administration of the Flying Corps would make the slightest difference to the speed with which machines were being produced; all that could be done was being done by all the available people. The shortages were due to the fact that at the outbreak of war certain aircraft parts were made in Germany and Switzerland. If 'blame' were in any way an appropriate term, it lay either with the Treasury or with the German Emperor for making war in the first place. The Flying Service had not been ill-organized at the start of the war; surely the fact that British aviators had taken the initiative was sufficient evidence of this point? Public opinion tended to listen to the pilots' complaints and this was a mistake since they, like 'the prima donnas discussing an orchestra' knew only a fraction of what was happening and were unaware of the larger policy that determined their instructions.[43]

On 23 March Maurice again took up the cudgels, this time in reply to the Oxford military historian, Spencer Wilkinson, who had published an article in *The Times* on 'Bungling Ignorance' in the Flying Corps. To the points already made to Eddie, Maurice added his remarks about Trenchard, 'one of the biggest men I have ever come across . . . were anything to diminish his influence, I should feel as I have already said, that the Germans had won a victory.' Combined with his support of the General was Maurice's equally strong loyalty to David Henderson who he felt had also been shockingly treated by the press. It was a 'disease' to which even his friends were susceptible; at the bottom of Wells's 'war hysteria' for example lay a bad attack of 'Harmsworthia'.[44] At the beginning of the war Maurice had made a deliberate 'sacrifice' in taking up a position in which he could not write on public concerns; in spite of this he managed, through his newspaper contributions and his many friends and contacts to make his views felt and to influence the way in which the Flying Corps was perceived in England.

The 'scaffolding falls about one daily' Maurice wrote to Ethel on 20 September 1916, at a time when he felt 'mortally tired' and living in a world without seasons.[45] His war diary is all too often punctuated with news of the deaths of his many friends and their children. On 4 June 1917, he attended an Old Etonian dinner at St Omer with three hundred guests. After dinner, 'everything in the room was broken; all the plates, all the glass, all the tables, the chandeliers, the windows, the doors, the people. A bomb raid was nothing to it.' It sounded like one of those youthful dinners in King Edward Street, Oxford but it was tragically different: 'There was not one representative of the Julian and Billy Grenfell generation. They have all been killed. The rest were either much older than me or much younger than the war.'[46]

Of the deaths in 1915, Julian Grenfell's was one of the most poignant for Maurice; he had known this son of Ettie's since he was a little boy 'with golden curls and little green knickerbockers'; and when Julian's brother Billy was also killed Maurice felt that that generation of 'radiant beings' had gone for always.[47] But in spite of these and many other losses Maurice's attitude to the war was not profoundly changed. His anonymous poem in *The Times* of 5 June carried a note of sincere celebration: 'Because of you we will be glad and gay,/Remembering you, we will be brave and strong;/And hail the advent of each dangerous day,/And meet the last adventure with a song.' In 1916 Ettie published her *Pages from a Family Journal*, chronicling the lives of her children, including Julian and Billy. Maurice responded that the book was much more than simply a record of the boys' lives, it was 'an emblem, a banner, and microcosm . . . of all we are fighting for. It is a reflection of the soul and spirit and the CORE of England . . . like a Constable landscape, or a speech in Shakespeare.' He would, he told Ettie, read and re-read it as 'a testament of the War and for the War'.[48]

His Russian connections were also severely affected. In June 1915, Maurice felt what he was so often to feel in this war 'that the death of a particular person meant the close of a whole chapter of one's life which was different from other chapters and could never be repeated'; this one person was Pierre Benckendorff, son of the Ambassador. His death marked the end of Maurice's direct connection with Russia and looked forward to the events of 1917 which were finally to conclude his visits to that country.

Particularly heart-rending, too, was the death of Raymond Asquith. He could think of 'nothing but Raymond'. Yet somehow during the war Maurice could endure the loss of so many of his friends; it was not a waste and he could never for one moment conceive how it could be seen as such. Raymond's service at the Front was 'The most triumphant thing that could have happened to him', and 'part of the sacrifice that has to be'.[49] Less than two months later Bron was killed. Despite his loss of a leg in the South African War, Bron had joined the Flying Corps and served as a pilot. He was killed on 3 November 1916. His death gave Maurice the inspiration for one of his greatest poems, *In Memoriam A.H.* His friends and literary mentors were unprecedentedly admiring: 'Good verse' pronounced Belloc which was high praise from him; whilst Gosse commented on this 'noble and passionate Elegy, which I have just read to myself and then read aloud to my thrilled ladies with an emotion to which I can give no expression'.[50]

He had never before had to come to terms with a loss of such magnitude; the condensation of all that he had lost and all that he had felt about the war finds its way into this poem, a far cry from the muted Georgianism of some of his earlier verse:

No one shall take your place.
No other face
Can fill that empty frame.
There is no answer when we call your name.
We cannot hear your shout upon the stair.
We turn to speak and find a vacant chair.

In this spare, modern tone he deals with the experiences of waiting for Bron when he was first reported missing, how he 'cheated his despair' imagining that his friend was safe, wounded but safe; and how after days of waiting the fatal news came. Bron died in a 'war with Gods', a war in the air, of a kind that neither Hector nor Achilles knew. This invocation of heroes of the past is characteristic; they could here be invoked with justification. With a moving economy, the poet states his position as to 'waste'; there is no 'burning might-have-been', 'No bitter aftertaste'; Bron had gone to his death as 'to a bride'. Underlying this feeling is the firmly-held idea that his friend's memory will survive 'on the entablatures of truth', that his name will sound throughout the halls of fame; and there is, of course, the profound conviction that Bron's life is not over, that he will have found his place with the 'Knights of the Round Table' in the next world. The poem is a restatement of Maurice's faith, of his attitude to war, and a means of coming to terms with the deaths of his friends.

In Memoriam A.H. does not understate the loss for those who still live; as the dead will know 'They think of you, and when you think of them/

You know they will wipe away their tears, and cast aside their fears'; but to 'cast aside' the sense of loss must have been very painful indeed; and all the more so because other factors of Maurice's pre-war life were coming to a close. In August 1916, he heard of the death of Mr Cornish, Vice-Provost of Eton; he felt then as if 'part of the scaffolding' of his life had disintegrated; and on 16 October 1916 Aunt M'aimée died. Asking Gosse to write something about this 'beloved aunt', he said, 'I feel that with her death a curtain falls on an epoch'[51] – the epoch of his childhood and youth and the happy Membland days that he was later to record in *The Puppet Show of Memory* (1922).

'Major Baring' as he had become in July 1917 was awarded the OBE and mentioned in the *London Gazette* for gallantry and distinguished service. General Foch summed up the extraordinary career of this unlikely soldier: 'there never was a staff officer in any country, in any nation, like Major Maurice Baring.'[52] He returned to England with Trenchard, now Chief of Staff in England in 1917 and later went back to France again with him when Trenchard took command of the Independent Air Force, and served with him until the Armistice. But, after the Armistice and 'mortally tired' he felt he could no longer work with him; and he turned, in 1918, to a full-time literary career and the task of coming to terms with what he had lost, with evocations of his childhood, with the world of his parents and with his conversion. As a professional full-time writer, his life for the next period was his novels.

[V]

Retrospect On The Enchanted Land

Cat's Cradles:
Baring the Novelist 1918–1929

THE decision to become a full-time writer was not without its problems for Maurice. Living in post-war England was a great deal more expensive than living at European embassies before the war. John was as usual willing to help; he had always insisted that his brother was quite right to pursue his literary ambitions but he must not do so without proper remuneration. By 1920 John was especially willing to help his brother, now back from the war and intent on carving out a place for himself amongst the literary figures of the day. Maurice had been ill and John offered to book and pay for a passage on a ship to help him recuperate; and on 10 May sent him a cheque for an extra £100 and the decision to increase his allowance. Sister Elizabeth, too, was sensitive to her brother's needs and willing to bail him out of difficulties with a well-timed cheque. Although he would accept this kind of family support he would not capitalize on the family name. In 1924 he had told Chesterton that he did not feel able to accept directorships of any kind lest this give a false impression;[1] he was not that kind of Baring and, as his dealings with the ever-generous John show, he was always on the verge of financial disaster, and a very poor relation of the bankers. John would pay his bills for a time but Maurice had to try to rely on the 'outcome of [his] pen'.[2]

This meant an all-out effort directed towards his writing. In December 1918 he had written to Trenchard, 'I should like to be with you wherever you go, whether it be Abyssinia or Farnborough or West Africa or East Ham; or the Colonial Office or the War Office or the Cecil, the Savoy or the Russian coast.'[3] By March 1920 this no longer applied, Maurice had started with some success to pick up the threads of his literary life, abandoned during the war years, and he had been subjected to difficult bouts of ill health. Trenchard asked him to return to work for him but Maurice felt:

. . .too old and too tired – I think you want a younger man and not a bald-headed $\frac{1}{2}$ blind crock with $\frac{1}{2}$ his inside cut out and an inflamed bladder and an inflated prostate gland and in perpetual danger of having colitis. Long drives in motor cars is [*sic*] the worst possible thing for me – and I pay for it afterwards in the nights – I am mortally tired too; tired by and of the war.

He simply could not imagine doing half a job for the General, a man who was not the type to accept a partial commitment whatever the circumstances; 'you might just as well if you were a strap say you would help the dynamo from time to time!'

Quite apart from his ill health and moral fatigue Maurice wanted to devote all his available time to his new career: 'I make no bones about it, I want to make money; not a lot but some – and I can – but in order to do so I want all my time, as my work is in 2 channels. Channel A journalism, simply done for money; Channel B – books I write for my own pleasure whether they pay or not but I have to do A to make B possible.' It wasn't easy to refuse Trenchard; the problem had been on Maurice's mind for some weeks in March 1920 ever since the General had sent a 'female battery' in the form of sister Susan to try to persuade him; and he was genuinely worried that his friend would take his refusal amiss: 'Don't be cross with me – you are the biggest thing I've had in my life and don't want to spoil [it].'[4]

In March 1924 Trenchard was to make another effort to enlist the help of his former Staff Officer, this time with the writing of a history of the RAF. By this time, however, Maurice was on surer ground: 'now after thirty years I have at last opened the doors of the book world so that I can get books accepted without hawking them all over London, and they pay well enough for people to want to publish them, so that if I never wrote anything more I should still think that I might at any moment, and that if I did I should get a hearing.' It was possible that he might be wrong in making this 'grand refusal' of his life but he would not be deterred.[5]

The novels to which Baring now devoted himself were not, however, his sole activity; full time career it may have been but the books were written 'through the interstices of other occupations, distractions, relations' as one reviewer remarked of C.'s love affairs.[6] These years, all very full of a succession of visits, travels, friendships, follow a certain pattern. Every summer Maurice would go to Scotland to stay with his friend Lady Lovat (Laura) and her family at Beaufort. This was a most congenial place for Maurice – it was full of children whom he loved; it was a beautiful piece of countryside and a 'divine household' where his faith was more than respected (his non-Catholic family and friends were inclined to feel that he was on a traitorous path of trying to convert all with whom he came into contact – a deep-rooted if unjustified view). Lady Maclean, one of Laura's daughters, remembers the fun they all had when Maurice was making his yearly summer visits, the incidents when he 'would play the fool in a delicious way' and Laura would get rather cross as her children became thoroughly out of control. There were huge luncheon parties; Lord Lovat was very hospitable and Beaufort was usually filled with guests, but although there were at least twenty servants it was always informal. There was rather a grand cook who made rolls for lunch. Maurice said 'The Romans never used to eat the inside. They used to take it out and clean their hands on it and throw it away.'[7] So the young Fraser children would willingly take up the hint, throwing theirs as far as they could.

A frequent guest was Ronald Knox, the Roman Catholic priest, writer and a most appreciative critic of Baring's novels, who joined with the utmost seriousness in the many games. He would take these on a very intellectual level and could not bear it if anyone did not treat even the simplest game with the proper degree of concentration. Sometimes this became intolerable and, if Ronald were taking an extra long time to plot his next Halma move, Maurice would take a box of matches, light them all and throw them into the middle of the game.

There was an irresistible opportunity for jokery with Laura's driving. In 1924, with considerable difficulty, she had obtained a driving licence which she unwisely left for two minutes on her writing table. When she returned she found the space left for 'Endorsements and Collisions if any' had been filled:

August 1st — Collision with train
August 2nd — Collision with motor cycle
August 3rd — Collision with donkey cart
August 4th — Collision with perambulator
August 5th — Collision with goods train
August 6th — Licence withdrawn

With some effort, and after paying a heavy fine, Laura managed to procure a second licence. Maurice, however, was not to be deterred and the new licence was similarly 'endorsed':

August 27th — Collision with bicycle
August 28th — Collision with hand tricycle
August 29th — Collision with motor scooter
August 30th — Collision with charabanc
August 31st — Collision with go-cart
September 1st — Licence withdrawn[8]

Despite his unquenchable appetite for jokes like this (we might wonder whether the recipients of such tricks did not ever become wildly irritated by Maurice's unfading but very contrived sense of humour) and the very busy social life there Maurice still found time to write. He and Ronnie Knox were each given a quiet room in which to study and write and the children were given very strict instructions that neither man was to be disturbed while he was working.

Little work can have been done on those expeditions on Naval Exercises which Maurice joined at the invitation of his friend Sir William Fisher (later husband of Cecilia Cornish.) Very rare for a civilian, these voyages were the source of huge enjoyment to Maurice. In 1908 he was invited on board HMS *Indomitable*, then on her way to Sardinia for special gunnery practice. Maurice, 'the most popular guest any wardroom could have' had originally intended to leave the ship at Gibraltar but he was persuaded to stay on board until Aranci Bay. Suddenly he became restive: there was business to be done in London about his house in North Street and he must get back; another officer was returning home to take up a new appointment, he and Maurice would travel together. They set off by steamer but the weather defeated them:

> . . . Baring was brought back to the ship for the night and was then overruled and persuaded to stay on as fate was evidently against his going. In the morning his luggage was fetched, the steamer sailed, his passage was cancelled, and after we had finished our gunnery, we brought him back to England. He did, however, make one dramatic gesture, very like him. After dinner we were on the quarter-deck when Baring, suddenly saying he must catch the steamer, dived overboard. Of course he only swam round the stern to the other gangway. But after the irons were sent for Baring was safely secured and fed with whisky until he promised to make no further attempts to leave.[9]

Top left: Count Benckendorff by John Singer Sargent. *Top right*: Countess Sophie Benckendorff

MB in St Petersburg

The home of the Benckendorffs at Sosnofka

Picnic, Sosnofka, 1894

Left: 'My sleeping quarters on the summit of Tsien Chan'. *Right*: 'The Mandarins of Mukden'

Left: 'Buriat Cossacks at home'. *Right*: 'Lama Priests'

Constantinople, 1912

MB at San Stefano

Dame Ethel Smyth

Lady Diana Cooper, 1924

Ethel Grenfell (Lady Desborough)

Lady Juliet Duff from a portrait by Sir
John Lavery (detail)

Lady Lovat by E. Barnard, 1909

MB with Dempsey during his
last illness

In a letter William Fisher commented during this cruise: 'We gave Baring a great dinner last night . . . It's extraordinary the hold he has got on all hands from the Cook's Mate to the Commander! We are dreadfully sorry he is going tonight. He has been the life of the mess.'[10]

So much 'the life of the mess' must Maurice have been that the invitations to go on Exercises were continued throughout the 1920s and 1930s: 'I am in a battle ship as you see, on my way from Malta to Majorca', he wrote to Gosse in 1925, as if it were the most natural place in the world for him to be. *En route* he had spent a night in Paris and dined with André Maurois whom he had found 'delightful' and with whom he was shortly to enter into a spirited literary friendship. Then during three days in Rome he had had a private audience with the Pope. He reported this to Gosse. In the first throne room there had been three 'very talkative Italian ladies' waiting. One of them dark and voluptuous was a little too *décolletée* and one of the plum-coloured servants went up to her and told her in an audible whisper that he thought her dress needed a little adjustment, 'but never mind,' he said, 'I will myself lend you a pin,' which he did and the lady was made respectable. Then Maurice was ushered into the Presence:

I thought him a little like Mr Bain père [Maurice's bookseller] . . . He began to speak in French and then the talk slipped into Italian . . . as soon as he began to talk Italian I felt everything was easy. At first I was shy beyond all words as if the words wouldn't come and as if when they did come they were miles away . . . then he talked of all sorts of things, Rome, Russia, Malta, the Navy, the Poles, the Japanese . . . till he made the gesture.[11]

To a closer intimate, Diana Cooper, Maurice confided that, while waiting to be ushered into the throne room his 'teeth were chattering'.[12]

These two months on HMS *Bahram* were the 'wildest fun' and, as he told William, he had 'never enjoyed anything more' in his life.[13] On 4 January 1927, he was again preparing for another treat, this time on HMS *Nelson* but without William. There he found a very agreeable Admiral 'who at once gave me some gin and made me comfortable' before leaving him to settle down to playing vingt-et-un with two captains 'one courageous and the other furious'.[14] On 12 January 1929, he reported to Ethel that he was again off on HMS *Nelson* to Gibraltar; and in March

1931 he told his friend William Rothenstein, the painter and Principal of the Royal Academy, that he was 'Between Malta and Gibraltar, somewhere near Algiers'. On this voyage there was a party very like those riotous King Edward Street parties in Oxford, a reminder that this kind of 'fun' had not been totally submerged by the War. Maurice thought it 'divine' (he never wholly grew out of his enthusiasm for schoolboy slapstick) and especially relished

> ... seeing the waiters dance musical chairs to a chorus ... Last night I had dinner in the gun room and got away by a miracle to go to the Governors [of Malta] at 9.30 in white tie and medals. Although the table was already in *pieces* used as a battering ram and all the crockery flying about the room like in the Duchess's kitchen in *Alice in W.*[15]

With his love of sudden dramatic gestures and wholesale breakage Maurice himself must have seemed something like a character from *Alice* transported into the wardroom.

Back in London there were more serious matters to attend to. In the 1920s Maurice had also to take up his Russian connections, in many cases severed by the war and by the 1917 Revolution. He still often saw Sophie Benckendorff, lunching with her in London and visiting her at Lime Kiln Farm, near Claydon in Suffolk until her death in 1928. But there were more pressing needs of his Russian friends. In September he received a letter from his former acquaintance, Prince Dimitri Mirsky, from Athens. It was with the 'keenest joy' that, having lost touch with Maurice, Mirsky had fortuitously seen his name in the *London Mercury* (for which publication Maurice had worked as a reviewer since April 1920). Now the time had come to tell of his own doings. Mirsky had been in the army since 1914 and had left only three months previously after escaping from a concentration camp 'where the Polish dogs had treacherously interned a portion of our army and where, I am sorry to say, the British representatives would not move a finger to help us'. He had also been in America 'and other funny places'. These years had treated Mirsky harshly; his brother had been killed and 'all my friends'; it was a time of bitter disillusion:

> Russia came first with Rasputin, Kerensky, the bolsheviks and all, and Europe followed close behind with the infamous treaty of Versailles, that damned humbug Wilson, that despicable coward Lloyd George

and those traitors the French. If it were not for the two reviews I just mentioned [The *London Mercury and La Nouvelle Revue Française*] and all that they stand for, I should not have the inkling of a doubt that England's and France's case was worse even than Russia's.[16]

With views like these we might wonder why Maurice so keenly wanted to maintain his connection with this angry, disaffected Russian and, had he known that Mirsky would later convert to communism, to be last heard of in a Siberian prison camp, he might not have gone so whole-heartedly to the Prince's aid. But go to his aid Maurice did; by December 1920 the *London Mercury* had published his first article written in October of that year, the month after he had re-established contact with Baring. As the recent scholar Nina Lavroukine remarks, Mirsky's introduction to this publication was his 'passport to England'.[17]

A passport to English literary life Mirsky certainly now had but he had no money; in July 1921 Maurice told Sophie Benckendorff that he had sent his friend £10 but to do so he had had to sell the rest of his collection of Henry James. From Beaufort in August 1921 Maurice wrote to Juliet that he would like her to be kind to this Russian friend who had arrived in London with a mere £5 in the world: 'He is a very nice man and very intelligent and trying to get literary work in London.' But 'remember that he is penniless and don't suggest anything that will entail expense, such as a trip on an aeroplane or a good feed at the Ritz.'[18] Clearly there was still a need to explain things to Juliet whose brief marriage to Major Keith Trevor seemed to be doing little to brush up her understanding. Luckily for us, however, Maurice did not carry out his threat in his lines on the occasion:

I've written plenty enough
To Juliet Duff;
I'll write nothing whatever
To Juliet Trevor.[19]

Having got Mirsky installed in London, Maurice helped him build a reputation and he went on helping him even after Mirsky's appointment to a Lectureship in Russian Literature at King's College, London. Articles in Mirsky's name continue to appear in the *London Mercury* until 1931; and he worked with Maurice on the *Oxford Book of Russian Verse* published and well-received with Mirsky's annotations in 1924. From 1927 the two men would seem to have parted company; Lavroukine suggests that this was mainly due to Mirsky's 'recantation of his former literary values'. In any event by this time, the appeal of communism was beginning to strengthen his resolve to return to Russia. His book *The Intelligentsia of Great Britain* leaves Baring alone unscathed (and unmentioned) but figures whom Mirsky had previously admired get the rougher edge of the party-line – Chesterton, once described by Mirsky as a man of truly 'democratic passions' had now become a 'mere journalist' whose paradoxes are simply a 'mechanical trick' whilst the *London Mercury* to which he owed so much is brusquely dismissed as a 'petty middle-class publication'.[20] Petty and middle-class the *Mercury* might well have seemed for the Russian prince but for Maurice it provided the necessary means to pay for his other, more important activity – writing his novels.

Since he was nineteen Maurice had known Ethel Smyth, that 'formidable old egoist and eccentric'[21] and she was improbably to remain one of his closest and most intimate friends until her death in 1944. The women Maurice knew well at this time divide sharply into the Beauties (that succession of aesthetically lovely women with whom Maurice populated his life and, later, his house at Rottingdean, which included Lady Lovat, Lady Desborough, Countess Benckendorff and, of course, Lady Diana Cooper) and on the other hand the redoubtable intellectual Sapphists led by Dame Ethel herself and accompanied by Vernon Lee and Edith Somerville. Maurice's loathing of clever women does not seem to have extended to them possibly because, at least in the case of Ethel and Vernon, he met them when he was very young indeed. When working on his biography Ethel commented further that she was not the kind of person to attract him romantically, 'He wanted sheen. His men friends were of any class. His women always of the one . . . Of the two requisite ingredients in his passions, I don't know which was stronger, "smart-ness" or (to be fair to him), intelligence . . .'[22]

He was obviously very fond indeed of Ethel and it was to her that he felt able in the autumn of 1919 to confide one of his deepest preoccupations of the post-war years and one that was to profoundly influence his novels, his conversion to Roman Catholicism in 1909. The 'divine household' at Beaufort was a most appropriate place for him to work on his fictions and it was, fittingly, there that he learned of and was overjoyed by his great friend Chesterton's conversion in 1922. His own conversion was well in the past and yet there were still bewildering facts to be confronted.

From some of the residual perplexity and the response he had received towards it, Maurice, in part, wrote his first novel, *Passing By* (1921); it is in the form of letters from Guy Cunninghame, a young diplomat, and the diary of Godfrey Mellor, a rather dull, reserved Protestant who reads only *The Times* and (repeatedly) *Jane Eyre*. Set in 1908, the year before Maurice's conversion, it introduces Riley, an Oxford friend of Godfrey's who gradually comes to the Church. In so doing he expresses almost verbatim Maurice's views on the subject as included in his letters to Ethel.[23] Against the process of Riley's conversion is set the conflict of Mrs Housman, a Catholic woman unhappily married but in love with George Ayton. Even after her husband's death, however, she does not marry Ayton but obeys the 'categorical imperative' of her vocation and enters a convent.

Maurice was not entirely at ease with the themes of this first novel. 'Pink Tights' was the family expression for a convert; it registered a mild disapproval deriving from that very English 'nursery tradition of anti-Catholicism' as Mrs Housman expresses it in *Passing By*.[24] The 'Pink Tights' issue was undeniably very much present in this novel and Maurice worried that this might jeopardize the book's popularity. He was, however, quite prepared to defend his position, believing that if the issue were vital in personal relationships it was quite legitimate to write about it. French writers, such as Bourget and Claudel wrote, he remarked, of little else and their books weren't dismissed as tracts but were thought to deal with a crucial clash of interests. 'Just think,' he wrote, 'first my sister [Elizabeth] put on pink tights, then a great literary friend [Reggie Balfour] and then I myself . . .'[25] This was a real factor in life as he knew it and he wanted and needed to write of it. Still, doubts remained; a first novel was, after all, very important to his plans. He must try and get it right. So he asked discerning friends, Madame Bulteau and Sophie Benckendorff, whether they thought *Passing By* was too polemical or tract-like. Both were reassuringly firm; they could see no reason for such a criticism.

Although hardly a whirlwind success and there were some quibbles about the 'Pink Tights' concerns, *Passing By* aroused considerable interest. In September 1921 Belloc wrote that he had just read and enjoyed it and believed that it would last 'though aimed at a narrow target'. It was 'a remarkable triumph and will seem bigger still when I read it again'. He also reported that everywhere he had found people discussing the book – among others, the Herberts and their guests at Pixton, all those at Mells and many more. Edwin and Venetia Montagu [Stanley] had spent a whole Sunday too reading it aloud to one another.[26]

The sense of life going on around Baring's books is very typical of his life at this time (as indeed it had been with his very early literary efforts such as *Entr'actes*). Above all, in the 1920s his books were one way in which Maurice managed to rekindle friendships that had faded during the war years, and he received an enormous amount of mail in response to them. *Flying Corps Headquarters 1914–1918*, published in 1920 and hailed as 'one of the few war books that will survive', in particular, brought back old friends and called forth enthusiasm from members of the Flying Corps. An Air Ministry friend commented, with justice, 'I think everybody in the Air Force will get it and it will become a classic.' 'Boom' was thought to have smiled at many parts of the book and Edmund Gosse wrote by return that it had kept him from his bed: 'I read all the pieces of verse first, like a child that scoops the cream out of the marang [sic]. "I killed a beetle in the night" ranks with England's noblest triolets':[27]

May 26th, 1916
I killed a beetle in the night
   That soared in spirals round my bed.
Do you agree that I did right?
I killed a beetle in the night.
It would persist with all its might
   In soaring round and round my head.
I killed a beetle in the night
   That soared in spirals round my bed.[28]

Shortly after his first novel, Maurice's autobiography, *Puppet Show* (1922) appeared. This retrospect on the enchanted land of Membland and his childhood and youth was praised by both critics and friends. On its publication Blanche Warre Cornish wrote that it had 'absorbed the past week, ever since Hubert found his, your splendid gift, on his table at the office and came to lunch to tell me about it . . . Arthur Benson wrote to me that there was not enough of yourself in it.' But Benson had also commented with approval that Maurice was now clearly 'making his mark'. Vernon Lee felt that the book made her understand something of Maurice's eternal quality of childishness, something of the character of the man who wrote magical books for children and sophisticated literary jokes like *Lost Diaries* and *Dead Letters*; that he had been such an exceptionally happy small boy explained much even if he had (regrettably from her point of view) been part of a 'very silver-spooned class'.[29] Maurice would have been particularly pleased with Gosse's praise. Gosse saw Maurice as 'A Citizen of Europe' and wrote in *The Sunday Times* that his prodigious linguistic ability 'has not only taken him where he went, but has positively made him what he is, for the remarkable thing about his intellectual apparatus is that he is a complete cosmopolitan. As no language presents any difficulty to him, he is able to pursue his own line of imaginative thought wherever he finds it.'[30]

Irish friends liked the book also: Edith Somerville much enjoyed it when Ethel brought it with her on one of her visits to Drisheen, Edith's home on the West Coast of Ireland, and *Puppet Show* brought with it, too, news of schoolfriends with whom Maurice had lost touch during the War. His ex-housemaster at Eton was especially gratified. Here was 'an excellent alternative to a poisonous book' that he had recently had the misfortune to read – namely Shane Leslie's scathing attack on Eton, *The Oppidan*. Mr Tatham (from Northcourt House, and mentor and friend from Maurice's cramming days in the 1890s) responded in the appropriate triolet form favoured in his dealings with Baring: In the elegant tome/Of your Autobiography/You mention my home,/In the elegant tome.[31]

Another ex-scholar from Tatham's, Augustus Ralli, was pleased to find his name enshrined in Baring's Memoirs and Donald Tovey, the musician, was prompted to write, 'Your memory is too sensitive an artist to have recorded what I can't imagine myself forgetting: viz., that in those King Edward Street days you presented me with a ticket to Bayreuth.'[32] From Boston, where he was attempting to raise money from lecturing, Belloc reported that *Puppet Show* was 'vastly popular' in the United States; 'many talk to me who do not know I know you and have all bought it'. Belloc also advised that Maurice should write *any book at all* 'about Europe and it will sell here well, for you are now much liked'.[33] Although, at forty-eight, he was quite young to publish an autobiography Maurice found that *Puppet Show* not only increased his American reputation; it also helped him to pick up the threads of his pre-war life and distance the experience of war and the cruel loss of so many of his friends.

The year 1924 was an important one for Maurice; not only did it mark the publication of his first widely successful and substantial novel, *C.*, it was also his fiftieth birthday. As was by now his habit this was celebrated at the Royal Albion Hotel in Brighton, owned by his friend and fellow wrestling and boxing enthusiast, Harry Preston. Chesterton writes in his *Autobiography* of the 'godlike joy of life that induced a gentleman to celebrate his fiftieth birthday in a Brighton hotel at midnight by dancing a Russian dance with inconceivable contortions and then plunging into the sea in evening dress'.[34]

Sadly, Diana Cooper was away in New York playing in *The Miracle* but Duff attended the party and reported to her on 27 April. There had been a dinner for fifty-two people including Belloc, Chesterton, E.V. Lucas, the writer and publisher, and 'lots of sailors and airmen'. Maurice made a rhyming speech and Chesterton, Preston and Duff made speeches in prose. As Chesterton remarked, Maurice, with his usual penchant for jumping into the sea at odd moments, wanted to bathe after dinner. There was a howling gale and almost all the guests tried to dissuade him. Duff, however, thought that on his fiftieth birthday Maurice had every right to swim if he so wished: 'He finally got into the water and an energetic sailor stripped stark naked and plunged in after him. He didn't stay in long. I [Duff] brought him back and gave him a hot bath.'[35]

At this time Maurice relied very much on Diana and was always dispirited if she did not write regularly to him, feeling that he was simply sending his many letters into a void if she didn't respond. Back from America and living in a house in Bognor which she had recently inherited, Diana was one audience to whom Maurice read *C.* aloud. As with performances of Duff's literary efforts, Diana was deeply embarrassed and 'quite incapable of fair criticism'. Must her friend cause her so much awkwardness with these public readings? Could she not be allowed to read the books on her own? She is happier recalling those summer seasons when Maurice never 'got older or laughed less or resisted the candles at any London ball. Almost nightly . . . we ate our quail and drank our champagne together, while his trembling hand wrote verses on the back of menu-cards'.[36]

Maurice's devotion to Diana did not lessen; although retrospectively she admits that his attention was sometimes a great strain. After Maurice's death she confided to Conrad Russell that there was a time, just before he got really ill, when her balls and parties each season were

. . . really ruined for me by Maurice. I'm ashamed now – but it was a certain two hours' supper that he would arrange by telegram and from which there was no reprieve. He'd stand at the foot of the stairs at the appointed hour and wait till he could see me to claim. I got to dread the monotony and mastery – only bearable if one is *in love*. I think no one was ever in love with Maurice, and curiously enough, I never felt absolutely comfortable with him. I think it was his own nervosity that infected me. Admiration and pride in him attached my heart to him more than delight in his company.[37]

It was not only on the backs of menu cards that Maurice inscribed his affection. *The Times* personal columns would be filled with messages to 'Mrs C.' She recalls this one from 1924:

> *Mrs C.*
> I told her she was beautiful, tis true;
> But I said nothing when I wrote to you.

The following day Diana inserted this:

> Nothing shall come of nothing; speak again!

And on the third day, Maurice answered:

> Yet out of nothing God made time and space,
> The stars, the sun, the summer and your face.[38]

Diana may well have been worried by her friend's insistence on reading C. aloud but many others, relations and critics, were enthusiastic about this novel of Baring's fiftieth year. Vernon Lee and Desmond MacCarthy both praised it and on 1 June 1924, John wrote to his brother that he had read C. in the car on the way to the country, before, at, and after dinner, and had finished it only at 2 a.m. Reviewers praised the 'really flawless quality of its emotion' and 'its air and tone of faultless taste'. It was compared with the work of Forster (rather oddly in view of the fact that *A Passage to India* is the novel published by Forster in the same year as C.) and Wodehouse; and Maurois said that he had found comparable pleasure only in the work of Proust and Tolstoy. J.B. Priestley remarked justly that C. had something in common with Maurois's *Ariel* (he reviewed them together in the *New Statesman*) and that it should, perhaps, be read as a 'novel approximating to memoir'.[39]

C. is partly memoir, a record of Baring's childhood and youth up to the turn of the century; it is also one of the most characteristic of his novels. Written during the period of the great modernist experiments in fiction, Baring's novels have little in common with the best-known literary events of the day. By the time C. was written and published, the Bloomsbury group was well-established in London: from 1906 onwards Strachey, the Woolfs, Bells, Garnett, Forster, Fry and others, had begun their regular meetings; and by the mid-twenties Virginia Woolf's work was well-known to the public (*Jacob's Room* appeared in 1922 and *Mrs Dalloway* was to be published in 1925). She was one of those who professed to be quite unable to read Maurice's novels; in her diary she includes her comments on C. under the uncompromising heading 'Second Rate Art': '... Within its limits, it is not second-rate, or there is nothing markedly so, at first go off. The limits are the proof of its non-existence. He can only do one thing: himself to wit; charming, clean, modest, sensitive Englishman . . .'[40] In C. Maurice takes a look at some 'sham literary people'. These are the literati of the 1890s but there are echoes of Bloomsbury in the description and Maurice's irritation about professional literary people is given some rein. The parties were definitely the worst of the matter; they were a sad contrast, he remarked to Vernon Lee, to those of his youth, those at his father's house in Charles Street, or at Mrs Wyndham's: 'When I compare [them] to parties I have seen given by the modern intelligentsia in Bloomsbury or Chelsea – where . . . well, the tone is different and sometimes (to the unmarried!) *à faire rougir les singes*.'[41]

Still in middle life disliking intellectuals, out of tune with Modernism, and frankly embarrassed by the breaking of sexual taboos, Maurice was not surprisingly bewildered by James Joyce's *Ulysses* (1922). He confessed to Sophie Benckendorff that he found the work very indecent as well as very boring, advising her that it was not a book to leave lying around on the table for the public gaze.[42] The more modern intelligentsia were also inclined to dislike Baring's characters, his cast of aristocrats, landowners, socialites (including many 'beauties'), diplomats and successful musicians, living in an international world of continental travel, country house-parties, embassies and balls. Vernon Lee commented, 'Of course . . . I *dislike* your people, personally. I dislike their mixture of footling uselessness and devouring passion . . . They have *time* for it, as they never do anything but go to parties.' On this one Maurice was firm: 'It is surprising,' he replied 'how much time is taken up by parties in the lives of busy men. Henry James puts on record 244 dinner parties in one year! Robert Browning, between 1870 and 1880, would have beaten that, I think.'[43]

Many parties and social distractions were certainly part of Maurice's own life at this time and, with C. successfully through the doors of the London publishing establishment, he could take time off to enjoy them. There were many entertainments with Diana, small dinner parties in Maurice's tiny bachelor flat at Gray's Inn Square with catering done by the London Embassy, many 'good gossiping, scandal-talking, literature–discussing lunch[es]' as Arnold Bennett was later to describe a meeting including Diana's family and Maurice.[44] There were society weddings, such as that of Mona Grenfell on 2 July with its large reception at Hampden House in Green Street, and there were race meetings to attend, in particular, this year the Derby where Lord Derby's own *Sansovino* won, and there was a celebratory dinner afterwards in which Maurice was included. (Baring's prodigious memory for things in which he was interested included the names of every Derby winner since the inception of the race in 1786.)

Maurice did not neglect his interests in the Air Force: on 24 June he attended the Annual RAF Club Reunion and the RAF Annual Pageant on 28 June. After his usual summer visit to Beaufort he returned to London to see three short humorous plays of his own acted at Seaford House. These included such characteristic *jeux d'esprit* as a short piece presenting the rival dinner-parties of Calpurnia and Lucullus. With his now assured place in the literary world Maurice was among those paying tribute to the poet Ronsard at Bedford College in the company of Lord Curzon, Walter de la Mare, John Galsworthy, Thomas Hardy and Yeats. On 18 October he enjoyed a private boxing entertainment put on by Captain Buckmaster (although unathletic in the extreme Maurice greatly admired physical skills and beauty in others) and the next night he went to hear Galli-Curci at the Albert Hall.

The year 1925 opened with the good news that Baring had been made an Honorary Wing Commander (in spite of this new title he remained 'The Major' throughout his life to many of his friends and acquaintances and later to his much-loved Nurse Neill). There was another Air Force Reunion dinner in June and an Air Force display at Hendon in July. In September he attached himself to No.4 (Army Co-operation) Squadron on exercises in Hampshire and Berkshire. Eton, too, was still much part of Maurice's life at this time, as it was of his novels since C. and in July he attended a dinner for the former pupils of his ex-housemaster, Walter Durnford. He also agreed to donate a large number of books from his personal library to the College.

Gray's Inn Square was the setting of two more dinner parties in July; one a small gathering with Lady Derby, Laura Lovat, Belloc, Dorothy Grosvenor and Evan Charteris; and a more ambitious affair attended by Diana, Venetia Montagu, Mrs Dudley Ward, Valentine Castlerosse and Lord Beaverbrook. Parties at Gray's Inn Square were not always very easy affairs; Maurice worried about whether or not his carefully-chosen guests would mix. On occasion they did not and were 'like ice and vinegar, never a happy juxtaposition'. Gosse was a particularly awkward proposition now that he was in his mid-seventies, tending to arrive with extreme punctuality and to get exceedingly irritated if he was not fed at once. At one luncheon at Gray's Inn Square Maurice had been through his usual catalogue of worries; the food had all been ordered from Luigi's Restaurant (hot eggs, grilled chicken, brie, burgundy, port and brandy, the last habitually referred to as 'brumble' of which much was drunk that day) but it had not arrived when Maurice returned home from High Mass at one o'clock. He had thought that there was not enough to eat and drink in any case and had already rushed out to Buck's Club for some vodka and some sandwiches. The food from Luigi's finally arrived and with it the elderly Gosse who 'hopped up the stairs like a nilex'.[45] Luckily on this occasion Gosse and Valentine Castlerosse did mix; but this didn't satisfy the fractious Gosse who complained, looking repeatedly at his watch, that he could not bear to be kept waiting; and then, on being offered some luncheon, immediately interrupted one of Evan Charteris's stories which promised to be very funny indeed. Such awkwardnesses needed a quite considerable quantity of 'brumble' before they could be smoothed out.

Back from Air Force Exercises Maurice visited Venetia's home at Breccles (Edwin Montagu had died in November 1924) for the second October Meeting at Newmarket and returned to London in time to receive some gratifyingly good reviews of his next novel – *Cat's Cradle*.

Cat's Cradle is a central book in Baring's life and it is a novel with an intriguing history. In September 1923 Sophie Benckendorff had read an obituary in *The Times* for a Mrs Dering of Baddesley Clinton. It told a curiously romantic tale of two married couples living together at this historic Warwickshire house – the story of the strange ménage of Heneage Dering, Lady Chatterton, Rebecca Orpen and Marmion

Ferrers.* Was not this, thought Sophie, an excellent subject for one of Maurice's novels? She cut out the obituary, passed it on to him and it became the inspiration for the second part of the book.

Alton Leigh (the estate in *Cat's Cradle*) was not, however, Maurice insisted, Baddesley Clinton. His settings, like his characters, must not be open to easy identification. He was always very definite about this, repeatedly refusing to tie down such memorable characters as the fascinating, cruel siren Leila Bucknell in C. (who she was was never established, and never could be; she has elements of Pamela Plowden, Lady Lytton, all his favourite 'beauties' and many others). Alton Leigh was 'composite; the front is like the house I saw but the rest . . . is Stanway, Winchcombe, Lord Wemyss'. This was written in 1925 to Daphne Baring, Maurice's niece, the novel's illustrator. Maurice was extremely careful about these pictures and their details and, as Daphne was at work on them, would bombard her with minute illustrations as to places, characters and, above all, details of dress. *Punch*, he insisted, was the best guide for men's clothes whilst the couturier, Hayward & cie., was a possible source of information about women's fashions; the dating of the costumes must be very carefully observed; Daphne working in her studio received copies of *Punch* for 1873, 1889 and 1914; and in June 1925

*The obituary of Mrs Dering of Baddesley Clinton in Warwickshire, an 'exquisite example of domestic architecture of the fifteenth century . . . perhaps more celebrated as an ancient shrine of the Roman Catholic faith, since the Reformation' continues thus:

> The maiden name of Mrs Dering was Rebecca Dulcibella Orpen. She was the only daughter of Abraham Edward Orpen, of Dublin, and niece of Sir William Chatterton, Bt of Castle Manor, C. Cork. Chatterton married Georgiana, the only child of the Rev. Lascelles Iremonger, of Winchester, her mother being a daughter of Admiral Lord Gambier. Chatterton died in 1855, and the widow married four years later, Edward Heneage Dering . . . in 1865 – Dering, his wife, and Miss Orpen, her ward, were received into the Roman Catholic Church. Georgiana, Lady Chatterton, as she continued to call herself after her marriage . . . at the time of her second marriage [she] was 53, and Dering was twenty-two years her junior. *Indeed there is good authority for the statement that it was for the hand of the young Miss Orpen, the ward, that Dering had really asked of Georgiana Lady Chatterton, and when the latter, in the mistaken belief that it was she who was being wooed, extended her own, Dering was too well-bred to explain.* Soon after her reception into the Roman Catholic Church, Miss Orpen married Marmion Edward Ferrers, of Baddesley Clinton . . . Ferrers and Dering had been old friends . . . On the invitation of Ferrers, Dering and Georgiana Lady Chatterton went to live at Baddesley Clinton, and there the two married couples lived together for the remainder of their lives. (*The Times*, 13 September, 1923)

In *Cat's Cradle* there is an important scene based on the lines in italics.

Maurice emphasized that it was 'important that the 1914 dresses and coiffures should be correct in every detail'; Daphne must go out and 'glean' from Mme Hayward and it was all in order that Blanche, the heroine, 'WEAR a MEDICI COLLAR in 1894!' in June too Daphne received the directive that men 'at suburban parties wore *top hats*: at a garden party probably grey hats with a black band'. Although Maurice allowed that the illustrator might wish to modify the author's suggestions as to coiffure, if she did so, she *must* take an idea from *Punch*.[46]

One of the most difficult problems for the young artist was the heroine's appearance. She is the greatest of Baring's fictive beauties and is singled out as being especially difficult for the painter to capture. Unlike her ward and rival, Rose Mary, she is not a 'footlight beauty'. In March 1925 Maurice sent another photograph to Daphne – it was of Desclée, the actress 'of whom Blanche had a *look* but Blanche was *much* prettier'.[47] Not only was Blanche very pretty, she appeared subtly distinguished and slightly foreign (here she has traces of Maurice's beautiful sister-in-law, Lady Ulrica and her sisters, the Duncombes, beauties one and all, as well as, perhaps, of the great French beauty, Mme de Greffuhle). It was not always easy to come up to Maurice's very exacting standards about these illustrations; his attitude to female beauty and appearance was highly romantic – his aesthetic as important in his fiction as in his life; the heroine must look exactly right.

The trouble taken with this novel, this story of tragic 'cat's cradles' of impossible marriages and intolerable disappointments repaid Maurice well. The book came out in the first week of October; within two or three days Belloc had read it from cover to cover and pronounced it a 'remarkable book'. 'Its unity of purpose not less than its unity of technique sets it beside *Madame Bovary*' said *Punch*. Fellow-writer Edith Somerville commented, 'A pageant of an epoch, such as no writer has ever come near, astonishingly vivid . . .' and André Maurois wrote: 'C'est un grand roman aussi bon que les très bons, dignes des grands Russes, dignes des grands Anglais.'[48]

There was some awkwardness with Vernon Lee. In the novel, Prince Roccapalumba, the impossible first husband of the heroine, is the victim of a 'mysterious nervous disease'; unable to walk, he never moves from his bed and dislikes any one talking to him (although he is a most 'energetic monologist'). Maurice had met Vernon's brother, Eugene Lee-Hamilton, and reported the meeting to Gosse in the 1890s; Eugene 'had been on his back a helpless invalid for over twenty years, and had suddenly in a marvellous manner, recovered, and his first act had been to climb Mount Vesuvius'.[49] The fictional Prince Roccapalumba had made a similarly mysterious and sudden recovery. Vernon was worried and hurt when she did not receive the usual complimentary copy of Maurice's latest novel and could only assume that this was because of the character of Guido. She wrote and confronted Maurice with this who replied that he was simply waiting for the second impression (without the many printer's errors of the first) before sending Vernon her copy: 'It was nothing to do with Guido . . . Guido wasn't your brother . . . also I meant Guido's malady to remain a complete mystery – as indeed your brother's did and does to me.'[50]

Cat's Cradle is, like all Baring's best books, a tragic story in which history endlessly repeats itself; the ending, one of the most chilling moments, indicates the tone. The young Rose Mary is at last, after many years' unhappiness, married contentedly to the man she has loved all along. This could have been a happy ending but the final scene shows her husband, Bernard, newly married but deep in conversation with another woman – Leila Bucknell, the siren making her first devastating fictional appearance since C. Rose Mary asks her new husband if he knows Leila well:

'No; I have always just missed knowing her somehow, but she was telling me to-night how fond she used to be of Blanche.'

There was a note of reverence in his voice which was more noticeable when he said the word *she* than in the word *Blanche*.[51]

Maurice had come back from the War 'finished' as he had told Trenchard; in a letter to George Grahame he had written, 'you don't realise what has happened to me in the last 3 years. It is simply this: the main spring is broken. Another thing you don't realise is that my life is now minus Madame Sottise. It is torn out by the roots and has been for three years ever since the war. But [it] leaves the kind of feeling of having had a tooth out with laughing gas.'[52] Again and again the novels repeat this feeling, leaving the reader with a profound if undefined sense of a very melancholy man, and of a cast of characters who refuse to grasp the happiness stretched out to them. Who was this 'Madame Sottise'? Ettie was the original claimant to the title but Maurice's connection with her (and his brother John's affair with her) lasted throughout their lives and he often visited her at Taplow, entertained her in London and so on.

Possibly the term is a code word for anyone for whom he had a *culte* [enthusiasm]. In any case it is this feeling that is constantly worked and reworked in the novels; in *Daphne Adeane* (1926) the young Leo Dettrick, a writer, had 'formulated and established the principle that with the death of Daphne Adeane his life – that is to say his sentimental life – had come to an end.'[53] Maurice had clearly, and with many *ridges* made a similar decision. It is not a decision that comes from the records of his lived life but from the novels; they are ultimately very sad books which make us feel that *Comfortless Memory*, the title of his novella published in 1928 could well be the descriptive subtitle of all his major fiction. They are unhappy love stories which show above all that 'Love is too strong to be overcome by anything except flight' as he remarked to Belloc, quoting Cervantes, in the Dedication to *Cat's Cradle*. In *Darby and Joan* (1936) one character is asked whether he thinks he will marry one day. Maurice would have agreed with his reply: 'I don't think so. I haven't been lucky so far, and perhaps it's just as well.'[54] He did not marry and had returned from the War not only 'finished' but also a confirmed bachelor; his novels are a fitting expression of a life lived in retrospect.

Nevertheless his life gives little evidence of this fictional disposition; this is possibly also due to the kind of records he kept; Maurice's tracks are very well-covered. A less private man might have kept a diary, might indeed have taken up his Eton housemaster's advice that he do so. It was advice he did not take; it was just too much of a risk to his privacy. Instead he compiled detailed scrapbooks with photographs, reviews, programmes, occasional letters, sermons: an assortment of things, important and, at times, annoyingly trivial. These albums tell a much more public story than a personal diary.

Following the début of *Cat's Cradle* Maurice was back in London. In October he went to Welbeck Abbey with Raymond de Trafford, Lady Cranborne and Venetia Montagu. On 23 November, there was a concert given by the London Symphony Orchestra with Casals playing; and on 30 November he joined Desmond MacCarthy for a performance of a play by Arnold Ridley. Christmas this year was spent with the Charteris family at their house at Stanway.

Early in 1926 he went to a Private View of the late John S. Sargent's paintings at Burlington House: 'such a curious exhibition so many epochs so many people one knew . . . Lady Wemyss looking at her dead self . . . it was rather like the last day.'[55] Race meetings to attend included the *2000*

Guineas in April as well as the usual June visit to the Derby. In the Spring, Maurice discovered an enthusiasm for the acting of the Italian Ruggero Ruggieri. He went to the first night of *Hamlet* with his sister Susan Reid and with Nan saw the same actor in Sacha Guitry's *L'Attore*. These performances prompted him to write to *The Times* on 24 April 1926 imploring readers not to miss Ruggieri's acting and not to ignore him in the wilful manner they had failed to notice the young Duse: 'The moral for the young is: "If you care for fine acting go to the Globe Theatre *now*. In 30 years' time there may be no room in the theatre and Signor Ruggieri will be older."'

In May came the General Strike and Maurice's temporary attachment to General Trenchard as ADC from, 3 to 13 May. When this was over he left London for Vienna to see the première of his play *June and After* at the Burg theatre. Up until this time his drama had enjoyed only private success and very little critical acclaim. *June and After* was his first genuine theatrical success as he commented with considerable pleasure to Sophie Benckendorff; he loved Vienna and was delighted with the way his play had been produced.[56] One attraction for first night audiences was Maurice himself: the *Neue Freie Presse* commented, after a good notice, that the theatre's management should really try to persuade Baring to prolong his stay so that he could appear at the end of each performance; his charming awkwardness as he hurried away at the end rather than acknowledge applause would draw ever larger audiences.

In London in the summer of 1926 Maurice made several visits to the opera, including one with Max Beerbohm to Covent Garden. His regular summer visit to Scotland this year was marked by the Fraser children, together with the young Trim Asquith (son of the late Raymond and Katharine) putting on two of his plays – *The Fatal Rubber* and *Brutus and Cassius*. Then came the publication of *Daphne Adeane*, a novel of 'seriousness almost unrelieved' as the *New Statesman* put it.[57] It is the saddest of all his love stories, a romance dedicated to a dead woman, and an investigation of the impossibility of being true to memory. The deaths of many of his friends during the war had given Maurice cause to think that memory *did* matter; this is a keynote in his correspondence after 1918. His best books are brilliant fictional studies of how memory can and cannot be controlled.

Temperamentally a traveller even now Maurice could not remain for very long in one place; and in January 1927 he returned to his German home of the post-Eton period, Hildesheim. Diana was once more appearing in *The Miracle*, this time at Dortmund. Those friends who had been unable to see her in Reinhardt's piece in America went to Germany to see it there. Maurice reviewed it; he was not, perhaps, as generous about Diana's performance as he might have been. One friend remarked to her, 'Sarah Bernhardt was an ugly old bitch but the terrible gift of beauty is yours. Maurice doesn't mention that.'[58] Back at home there was a performance of *Der Rosenkavalier* at Covent Garden with Lotte Lehmann singing the part of the Marschallin. Maurice and his brother John went together to Bayreuth for the fiftieth anniversary where from 13 to 17 August they heard the complete 'Ring'. Maurice made two visits to Beaufort this year in September and December and it was a fertile time too for literary work. *Tinker's Leave*, a novel based on his experiences in Russia was published and well-reviewed in August. *What I Saw in Russia* followed in October and his short book *French Literature* appeared in November.

But changes were again to come. In the early part of 1928 Maurice again went on Naval Exercises this time on HMS *Nelson* (Prince George was on board as lieutenant), on the destroyer *Westminster* and then on the battleship *Resolution*. This treat was much clouded when they reached Malta to find that his nephew, son of Margaret, Cecil Spencer, an officer serving on the *Queen Elizabeth* had had a serious riding accident. His pony had shied against a wall during a thunderstorm. The accident proved fatal and Cecil was buried at sea after a funeral on board ship. Baring's commemorative poem 'Cecil Spencer' describes this:

> The sun was shining in an azure sky,
> When Queen Elizabeth went proudly by,
> Through the grand harbour bound for Hagiar Khim,
> And bugles sounding the salute
> (Whole ships were at attention stiff and mute)
> Rang like the trumpets of the Seraphim.
> Destroyers, submarines raced through the blue,
> And overhead the roaring seaplanes flew;
> Resolution, Valiant, Warspite were under way;
> (Their firing was that day).[59]

In London again parties and races were overshadowed by the deaths of two very close friends: Edmund Gosse on 16 May and Sophie Benckendorff in June (she, in particular, left an 'irremediable gap'). Her funeral at Claydon was followed by a Requiem Mass and Memorial Service at the Russian Orthodox Church in Buckingham Palace Road in London, attended by the Benckendorff and Ridley families (the Ridleys had married into the Benckendorff family) and also by Serge Obolensky, Laura Lovat, Katharine Asquith, her daughter Perdita, Ettie Desborough, Juliet Duff and Lady Lucas. As if to underline the changes that were scarring his life, Maurice's scrapbook notes, without comment, that Membland was in the process of demolition.

On 19 April John Revelstoke died of a heart attack in Paris; he was only sixty-five. It was the end of an unobtrusively illustrious career. In 1890 he had been admitted as partner of Baring Brothers; eight months later came the 'Crisis', a situation that was rescued to an appreciable extent through his efforts. Philip Ziegler comments:

Those traditions [of the bank], established towards the end of the eighteenth century, had been carried through for almost one hundred and fifty years with astonishing consistency . . . Intelligence was desirable, clubbability no defect, but integrity was indispensable. Lord Revelstoke had done as much as anyone to ensure that this scale of values had survived. He had good reason to be proud of his accomplishment.[60]

In 1897 John had succeeded to the title; in 1907 he became a member of the Privy Council and in 1908 a member of the Council of the Prince of Wales. In 1911 he was made Receiver-General of the Duchy of Cornwall and was awarded the GCVO in that year. In 1926 he became Lord-Lieutenant of Middlesex. The *Morning Post* gave a fitting obituary with a résumé of the Baring history up to that time: 'Four Barings have seats in the House of Lords, and they all trace their descent to a Franz Baring who was minister of the Lutheran Church in Bremen in the Seventeenth Century.' Maurice clearly felt able to endorse the opinion that the family had made considerable strides since Franz Baring's day:

Franz Baring's son, John, settled in England in 1717, and became a merchant and cloth manufacturer at Larkbeer, near Exeter. John Baring's son, Francis, who was created a baronet, founded the London firm of Baring's. Sir Francis's son was created the first Lord Ashburton and his grandson became in 1885, the first Lord Revelstoke; another grandson, Sir Evelyn Baring, was raised to the peerage as Lord Cromer in 1892, becoming an earl 9 years later, while a third, Francis Thornhill Baring, was created Baron Northbrook in 1866, his son being advanced in the dignities of Viscount and Earl in 1876.[61]

John was much mourned not only by his family but also, more publicly as 'the greatest personality in banking and finance in this country' and as a man of a 'rare business genius'. The King sent a telegram to Elizabeth Kenmare:

> The Queen and I are terribly shocked to learn the news of Dear John's death. He was one of my oldest friends, and I shall never forget his devotion to me.
>
> I cannot yet realise that I shall never see him again. We send you all our heartfelt sympathy in the loss of such a wonderful brother. How dreadfully we shall all miss him.

Although Membland was partly demolished, John was buried near his former childhood home at the church at Noss Mayo. Many members of the family and numerous friends attended the funeral; but it was Ettie, accompanied by her daughter Imogen, who was the Chief Mourner, 'more shattered than I have ever known her' as Maurice remarked in a letter to Diana. He 'never thought I could be so sad again'.[62] For Maurice, John's death was not only the start of a more affluent life; it was also the end of an era and a style of life which could be enacted and written like the courtship story of John and Ettie, that discreet romance that continued until 19 April 1929.

Half-Way House and a Novelist with
'A Large Cloudy Reputation'

JOHN's death certainly eased Maurice's financial worries and he was quite soon able to buy Half-Way house in Rottingdean, his main home for the next few years (he also rented a small house in Chelsea, 18 Cheyne Row from his brother Cecil for a nominal sum). Diana Cooper remarks, 'Maurice, who had never before had juggling money, felt himself a Croesus . . .'. Both these houses were arranged in the taste of Maurice's youth; there was William Morris paper of olive branches, with water-colours of France and Italy accompanying photographs of Sarah Bernhardt, famous beauties and an international cast from Russia, Denmark and France. In particular, Diana recalled one of Sosnofka: 'I remember it because Maurice told me that when he was asked to stay by his hostess she said there were two trains, one arriving at 4 a.m. and one at 4 p.m., and asked him if he would do his utmost to arrive by the 4 a.m. one, as the servants enjoyed this so much.' In the main room there were refectory tables with stacks of books '. . . holding snapshots, theatrical programmes, menus scrawled with verses and sketches, letters, Royal Navy jokes and touching mementoes from the several weeks a year that Maurice spent aboard His Majesty's ships' – Interspersed with these stacks of books were blue and white oriental bowls of potpourri, and, in the garden (rather suburban and overlooked according to Diana) there were pinks and pansies. Privately, she thought this 'modern villa' was 'awful'.[1]

Above the main room was Maurice's private chapel with specially commissioned Stations of the Cross executed by his niece Daphne. The French critic Gérard Boutelleau commented in his reminiscences of Maurice that the house had 'Un raffinement d'un autre âge, et ce luxe discret que les Anglais appellent confort . . .'. Maurice's own room, however, was as cold as a cell and furnished only with a wooden table and camp bed.[2]

A near neighbour was Enid Bagnold [Lady Jones]. Desmond MacCarthy had insisted that Maurice would not like her; she just did not have the kind of appeal that he responded to. This, thought Enid, was a definite 'facer' but she had to own that she knew what he meant. She 'had no relation to that kind of Henry James charm' that singled out women like Laura Lovat.[3] Their first meeting was excruciating; alone for dinner, Maurice 'was so alarmingly shy himself that he made me as tongue-tied. If I said anything "clever" he instantly asked his butler to bring some bread. I couldn't repeat it: I couldn't go again. I didn't'.[4] Later Laura Lovat persuaded her, insisting that Maurice really did want to see her and after that she went almost every night for years. It was something of a relief to Maurice. He was already beginning to feel strained with the illness that was to haunt his last years and, at least, Enid had not known him in his 'larky days'. She comments 'like Emmanuel after his stroke, Maurice liked seeing me because I hadn't known him in his well days'.[5]

Enid did not, however, always 'mix' easily with Maurice's other friends and acquaintances; and there was a certain tension with Juliet Duff, for instance. One tea-time in winter Enid received a telephone call from the Theatre Royal in Brighton to come and read a Prologue at the opening of a play *Heil Cinderella*, an amateur production brought by Cecil Beaton and Olga Lynn to Brighton in aid of war charity. Juliet was supposed to read it but she had fallen ill. Enid put herself into tall, slim Juliet's dress, 'safety-pinned across the back as in the days of mourning for Napoleon'. It was a great excitement to find herself behind the lights and she spent all night learning the Prologue. Juliet, however, got up the next night and gave her performance. Enid felt she could kill her. 'Make a play of it,' said Maurice; so she wrote *Lottie Dundass* with its ruthless and utterly selfish heroine who will do anything in order to act – including strangling her rival who threatens her chance to perform.[6]

As well as new friendships with people like Enid, Maurice continued to see Ethel and through her he finally met Virginia Woolf in 1932. 'Yes,' she remarks in a letter to Ethel of February 1932 'I liked Maurice B.'[7] Virginia wondered whether Maurice had ever been in love with Ethel (unlikely); and, after a visit to Sissinghurst, she went to tea at Half-Way House: '2 dirty footmen to hand anchovy sandwiches, which I loathe and so had to put in my bag. When asked for a match by Baring I handed him a sandwich.'[8]

Virginia and Ethel disagreed about Baring's writings. In December 1933, Woolf comments that this is in part a matter of generations: 'I was thinking how you admire *Robert Peckham* and I hate it, no, not hate; but merely feel that a spider has walked across a garden pond . . .'[9] Smyth tried to convince her of Maurice's literary standing, but, replied Virginia, although he was perhaps better than she thought, she could not fail to be distressed with his 'superficiality'; 'compare him with Turgenev now that's a masterpiece maker, now and then, in M's own line too; but MB seems to go out like candle shine before it.'[10]

In July 1934 Woolf writes, in reply to another of Ethel's efforts to get her to read Maurice's fiction, that she supposes she must get hold of his *Lonely Lady of Dulwich*, 'but oh dear me, I don't want to. I never can submit myself to his silvery bald fingers (as a writer, I mean) with any gusto. He's too white waistcoated, urbane, and in the old Etonian style for my rough palate . . . But I'll try once more in deference to you.' A little later, Virginia was even less convinced. Ethel just couldn't get away with her high praise of *Lonely Lady* and, as for her comparison with Mérimée, that was merely absurd; Ethel had clearly been influenced by her affection for Maurice: 'What a flurry love sets up – what a dust – what in short, to speak plainly, a vacuum.'

Carmen! Oh Dear! Oh Dulwich! Oh my God! Why Carmen which I read 2 weeks ago by chance, is like an oak tree; this is a piece of chewed string. Every word in Carmen has the thickness of a giant's thigh: this is thin as a blade of green that a butterfly makes wobble. *There* the shade is ink black; here thin as weak tea. *There* the sun is blue; here a watered wisp. Its a conjuring trick of a hack. 'Behold – my hat! Look well – now there's a rabbit.' That's all it is – a book without roots; veracity, shade or sun. A parasol of a book – an empty white waistcoat.'

A few days later, Woolf was unrepentant about her opinion of this 'brash' (babies' diarrhoea): 'As for Dulwich, read the denouement – I mean the chapter about the journalist publishing her life – and ask yourself if anything of such palpable meretricious falsity could be used in that place save in a tenth rate book.' And Woolf couldn't seem to drop it; 'No, I can't understand, seriously, your feeling about Dulwich. If you'd likened it to something say by Edmund Gosse or Andrew Lang, I would have been delighted to praise it – for of course it has merits – on those terms. But to drag in Stendhal and Carmen! Dear me, how we differ.'[11]

To some extent Ethel's views were conditioned by her great affection for Maurice and by the fact that she had been a close friend of Aunt M'aimée from 1893 until the latter's death in 1916. Her consequent enthusiasm for almost all of his work emerges in the biography *Maurice Baring* which she published in 1938. Writing it cannot have been the easiest of tasks and, although Ethel had long thought a biography of her friend a good idea, it was not until the late thirties that this came to be. His weakening condition made it necessary to be especially sensitive. In March 1937 she wrote to Eddie Marsh, 'He's now almost entirely bedridden, can't even read as it fatigues him too much and can converse but little for the same reason. In fact his life is a martyrdom . . . The only thing he likes is being read to.' To some extent the work on Ethel's book revived him but he became quite difficult about the use of letters and photographs. Ethel had quite enough cause to complain to Eddie for he would understand – 'You know how granite he can be.'[12] Most tricky of all, given that she must have known a fair amount about it, was the taboo on any comment whatsoever about his personal life. When Virginia had quizzed Ethel about Maurice, Ethel had been firm that they had never been lovers: their relations were 'always a family affair minus incest'. Ethel had every respect for Maurice's breadth of culture, his appreciation of music in particular and for his literary work but she couldn't fathom his relations with women. 'Maurice's loves were always amazing to me . . . I feel certain he can never have had one happy affair.'[13] There is not one unqualifiedly happy affair in Baring's fiction and I am reasonably certain this is also true of his life. In writing his life story Ethel could not answer the questions that must have been asked by many of his friends and acquaintances. For example, both Conrad and Diana wondered whether any woman had ever been in love with him. They thought it unlikely; there were rumours that he had, when in Copenhagen, been engaged to a French girl but that it had been broken off; to Conrad, Maurice's relations with Laura Lovat were something of a puzzle; Katharine Asquith had hinted that Maurice 'was a burden, an incubus at times. Difficult for her to leave him as he minded her going away so much.' There was Sophie Benckendorff. Conrad supposed they were lovers, 'hard to believe, but in my old age I grow to believe that all things are possible'. Then, there was Nan Herbert; that was also extremely puzzling; 'He must have asked her to marry him', thought Conrad.[14] Throughout the production of Ethel's biography Maurice was somewhat troublesome and insisted that Eddie read the proofs to make absolutely sure they were free of solecisms. If her friend Maurice had been well, Ethel would quite simply have told him 'to go to blazes' as she confided in Eddie; instead she anxiously awaited his response; it came in the form of a long telegram full of congratulations signed, 'Your grateful, devoted and overwhelmed Maurice'.[15] Elsewhere and to other friends he was less delighted, loathing the exposure the book gave him.

Woolf's views of Baring's growing *oeuvre* were, fortunately, not typical of this period. In the late twenties, first of all *The Coat Without Seam* had been welcomed: Chesterton was especially enthusiastic and discerning, and 'much uplifted' by it. He realized, however, that the reception of such books could be full of misunderstanding:

It is, as you say, extraordinary how the outer world can see everything about it except the point. It is curiously so with much of the very good Catholic work now being done in literature, especially in France. The Protestant English, who prided themselves on their commonsense, seem now to be dodging about and snatching at anything except the obvious [.] I am only a vulgar controversial journalist, and never pretended to be a novelist; my writing cannot in any case be so subtle or delicate as yours. But even I find that if I make the point of a story stick out like a spike, they carefully go and impale themselves on something else. But there are plenty of people who will appreciate anything as good as *The Coat Without Seam*.[16]

This novel is a narrative interwoven with the story of the Coat which soldiers took from the body of Christ and which is passed from age to age. It is also the life of Christopher Trevenen, a brilliant but doomed man, one fated to miss every opportunity (one acquaintance remarks he is 'always hiding, always getting into the background');[17] his life consists of a series of fractured friendships, unhappy liaisons and unfortunate career moves. Most painfully, it is a life of evaporating possibilities.

Different legends of the Holy Coat feature in the novel which is patterned around them, but each time Christopher meets with one some great sadness follows. He hopes here to marry Alex, daughter of an Austrian countess. Together they read an old manuscript of the story of that St Christopher who had been martyred in Hungary:

'It is strange,' he said, 'that this story should have cropped up in my life again. The first time it was just before something sad. I hope it doesn't mean that something sad is going to happen to me now.'

'I think it will be the contrary,' said Alex, 'I think that something wonderful is going to happen to us.'[18]

Shortly after this their relationship is broken off.

Later, Christopher falls in love with Esther, daughter of a man well known in the world of music; she was believed to have a great future as a pianist. In the library of a country house where they are visiting, she and Christopher find another version of the legend; next day, Bruce Lawless (one of a recurring fictive family in Baring's work) arrives, only to fall violently in love with Esther. Christopher, sensitive in the extreme, thinks there has been a plot against him. The engagement is broken. Esther's planned marriage to Lawless devastates him; it 'brought his last fort of illusion, dream and hope to the ground'.[19]

His last and greatest love for Antoinette d'Albert is similarly doomed; she loves him also but dares not tell him so (Christopher meanwhile is racked with an unfounded jealousy for Count Altamura). Antoinette marries the Count through a sense of duty for past events and it is only at their last meeting that Christopher discovers that she has loved him all along.

During the war Christopher dies; he and Lawless ironically lie beside each other in their dying moments. The novel ends with this scene; Lawless dies and the Curé hears Christopher's confession (he is not a Catholic):

I found the Coat without Seam, after all, M. le Curé. The real one, you told me about at Vernay, when you gave me the mirliton, but I needn't have searched, because it was there all the time. It was my life that was a Coat without Seam. But I tore it into shreds and now you have mended it. There is no seam in it now.

'Oui, oui, mon enfant,' said the Curé, thinking that Christopher was delirious.

Later, when the ambulance came back, and the doctor and the orderly came to look after Christopher, they saw it was not necessary to send him back to the base, for he was dead, but they took back the two Germans.[20]

Robert Peckham, a different kind of spiritually-based narrative,

218

constructed from the epitaph sent to Maurice by Reggie Balfour in 1899 as a 'tragedy of conflicting allegiances' set at the time of the dissolution of the monasteries, was well-received, too, as 'a sad little story, resting upon definite religious presuppositions, but one woven with subtle threads of poetry on a warp of history'.[21] Even more warmly welcomed was *In My End is My Beginning*, a version of the life of Mary Stuart told from the point of view of each in turn of her 'Four Maries'. Ever since he was eight years old Maurice had been under the spell of Mary and *In My End* is evidence of that spell. G.M. Thomson wrote, 'I am jealous that this book, so nobly felt, so finely phrased, with its subject the most famous of Scotswomen, was not written by a Scot.'[22] John Buchan in the *Spectator* commented that it was both a 'brilliant pastiche' and also a book with 'much sober and subtle history':

> . . . he is not a fascinated sceptic like Andrew Lang, or a wholesome condemner like Froude, or a single-hearted apologist; nor does he follow Swinburne in seeing in her one who was fated, like Clytaemnestra, to sin on the heroic scale. In Mr Baring's eyes she is more intricate and more human, and I for one think that he has come very near the truth.[23]

It was not only Buchan who appreciated this truthfulness of Baring's. In their different ways both Belloc and Chesterton were impressed by his 'amazing accuracy of mind which proceeds from his great virtue of truth' as Belloc expressed it.[24] Edmund Gosse had found this 'accuracy' and 'realism' in Baring's greatest poem, 'In Memorian A.H.';[25] whilst Chesterton had early discerned Baring's strength in realism in *Flying Corps* and on C. had remarked: 'God moves in a mysterious way; and considering that most people would expect Catholic literature to be rather romantic, it will be very amusing if the new Catholic literature turns out to be strictly realistic; and beats the realists at their own game.'[26] Earlier still, Chesterton had suggested that Baring had that kind of mind that would appreciate that 'medieval men were men and medieval minds were minds';[27] that he indeed did so and could make creative use of this knowledge and of his belief in realism (so crucial to his criticism of Russian letters) is borne out by *In the End* and *Robert Peckham*.

Friday's Business (1932), another version of realism and a book based on Maurice's experiences in the Near East and on his time at Eton, was also well-received. The *Morning Post* responded typically:

> Never does the action flag, never for a moment, does the author intrude
> his literary personality (one almost has the sensation that the book is
> entirely written in words of one syllable), and yet the picture is
> individual to the last degree . . . Mr Baring is rarely better than when he
> writes from his great affection about his old school . . .[28]

Far from being thought pallid and meretricious, as Virginia Woolf
believed, *Lonely Lady*, a deeply tragic novella and a book very
characteristic of Baring's literary personality, was discerningly praised.
Desmond MacCarthy's important review sums up Maurice's literary
standing in the mid-thirties. He was 'aloof from the trend of modern
fiction':

> . . . although he has an admiring circle of readers, it is noticeable that he
> is more discussed in France than here. He is a novelist who, in his
> handling of the general picture of social life or the emotions, takes for
> granted a certain social quickness of perception which seems more
> common on the Continent . . . He eschews analysis completely, and the
> temptation is to read him far too fast. Many of his effects are produced
> by abstaining from statements, not from refining upon them. Still, in
> yet another respect he does resemble Henry James. He will attribute
> extraordinary penetration to normal, not to say commonplace and
> conventional people. Indeed, one of his favourite situations, and it
> recurs in this story, is one in which a self-centred possessive sort of
> Philistine (he is normally a husband), the last person to whom one
> would attribute subtlety of perception, proves himself at an important
> juncture to possess not only an extraordinary power of guessing but
> adroit delicacy of feeling. Now there is a great deal of truth in this
> estimate of human nature.[29]

MacCarthy's comments on Baring's French reputation are only just; in
1932 he was considered the Mauriac of contemporary English literature,
his work preoccupied with the most serious religious issues, with a strong
Christian meaning and spirit. *Daphne Adeane*, in particular, is found
admirable. Thanks to the help of André Maurois, 'People are applying
for translation rights . . . from every conceivable place in the world'
Maurice wrote gratefully on 22 February 1929.[30] Quite widely reviewed

in France, Baring's work was particularly pointfully, to use his own family's word, seen by Maurois, a man who came to understand many of the contradictions of 'Mon Ami Maurice Baring' as his sympathetic article in Les Nouvelles Littéraires was entitled in February 1938. As well as taking the religious aspect of the novels as a given, Maurois was able to appreciate the characteristic combinations of the spiritual and the infantile, the deep seriousness with the penchant for practical jokes.[31] The reviews in French periodicals also much approved the sense of ordinary life conveyed by Baring's books, their extraordinary and deceptive simplicity. MacCarthy understood this when, at one time, in talking about the reasons for Baring's greater popularity in France than in England, he 'likened Maurice to a junket which the English swallow at a gulp, not realising it could possess subtler qualities'.[32] Mauriac felt that Englishmen did not on the whole rate Baring as a novelist at his proper worth commenting, 'What I most admire about them is the sense he gives you of the penetration of grace – without making you aware of it.'[33] Mauriac's remarks were typical of the high regard in which Baring was held in France. In 1945 Robert Speaight wrote, 'Almost everyone who reads novels at all is in love with "la Princesse Blanche" [Cat's Cradle]; and the speed with which the novels were translated into French seems to bear out his popularity on the other side of the Channel'.* Arnold Bennett sees the point of Maurice in a letter to André Gide when he comments that he knows no one in London 'except possibly Maurice Baring, who at once thinks continentally about literature and who has an expert creative acquaintance with literature as a craft'. Baring, he added, 'is a wonderful man, not only reads but speaks 18 or 20 languages . . . but not strongly creative'.[34]

By contrast with his French audience, Speaight believed that Baring was little read in America. By 1932 there is some evidence to the contrary. Belloc had already pointed to the popularity of Puppet Show across the Atlantic and there is, notably, a long article in The Bookman of August 1932 reviewing and praising much of Baring's work and concluding: 'what modern writer is more productive or more versatile? . . . Few people know that he is perhaps the only English author who visited this country, gave no lectures, and wrote a book of unreserved admiration for our land.'[35]

*Daphne Adeane was translated into French in 1930, Cat's Cradle [La Princesse Blanche] in 1931, Robert Peckham and The Coat Without Seam in 1932, C. and Comfortless Memory in 1934, Lonely Lady in 1936 and Tinker's Leave [La Clé des champs] in 1937. Passing By and Puppet Show appeared in French in the 1940s.

Of course, it was not only fiction that occupied Baring during these years. *Lost Lectures* appeared in 1932 and J.C. Squire attests to his reputation in that year. Baring had been almost as versatile as Belloc, although he had not written on economics or on religious politics:

> Had he written only his books, three or four, about Russia he would be regarded as a 'Russian expert', he might even be commonly known as the sagacious observer who predicted in 1907 that there would be a Bolshevik Revolution in 1917 . . .
>
> Had he written only 'Dead Letters', 'Diminutive Dramas', and 'Lost Diaries', he would have a narrow but intense reputation of the Max Beerbohm sort, as a man familiar with many climes and languages imbued with the sense of 'Plus ça change' who had shed light on the history of politics and literature through the medium of parody. But he has written books, short stories, essays, and reminiscences; and though he has obtained a large cloudy reputation, people do not know where they are.

The same critic commented that, whether Baring wrote slowly or fast, 'The man is always there, and in a state of perpetual, natural youth; feeling never swamping humour, and humour never withering feeling; in the background an enormous, if unsystematised culture, and an interest in all things except mathematics – which, one gathers were disastrous to him in early life.'[36]

In 1933 *Sarah Bernhardt* was published. He was, as Shane Leslie commented, 'the one and only Englishman who could have written this book'. David English makes a similar point: 'If ever the appetite for good writing returns to the public this short biography will be praised and talked about as it deserves to be. Nobody but Mr Baring could have written it.'[37] The *Times Literary Supplement* of 12 October 1933 wrote: 'His purpose is to record his own impressions under the influence of Sarah Bernhardt on the stage. He does it so well that we almost seem to see and hear her still. And he does more than that, he sees her as one of the sources of inspiration of modern art.'

Desmond MacCarthy wrote an approving article on the subject which 'satisfied [Maurice's] greedy avid avaricious grasping exigent insatiable nature'; MacCarthy, in particular, praised Baring's descriptions of Bernhardt's parts as 'examples of the way in which the sensitive critic may perpetrate the very thrill and quality of the actor's art'. Above all, Baring as a critic had convinced the public that there was absolutely no need to apologize 'for her having had to act Racine' as he wrote to Belloc on her death in 1923.[38]

As well as making new friends near Rottingdean, Maurice continued to be in close touch (by letter if not in person) with Belloc and Chesterton, friendships which did not diminish. Letters of 1931 and 1932 show that they were brought together literally for sittings for James Gunn's well-known 'Conversation Piece', a great success at the Academy Summer Exhibition in April, and which today can be seen in the National Portrait Gallery. *Punch* captioned a cartoon of the portrait as 'Mr Chesterton takes a note of another Sussex tavern, discovered by Mr Belloc, where they sell very good ale'.[39]

Illness kept Chesterton mostly at Top Meadow but Baring continued his cruises under the auspices of William Fisher; in March and April 1935 he took the last of these. He had always been very much involved with the ships on which he voyaged and had been especially sad when one of them had to be scrapped. His commemorative poem on HMS *Tiger* makes this clear:

Now Tiger has crept back into her lair;
She will not go a-fighting any more;
And there are few that know and less that care.
But there are some whose hearts are very sore.

They'll skin her of her coat and break her neck,
And spoil her brasswork and her spotless deck,
Her purring padding engines (Tigers proper!)
And every shining piece of steel and copper.
For all that pomp and power of black and gold,
Drenched in story,
Scarred with glory.
Must now be broken up and sold,
And broken up and sold and thrown away,
And Tiger shall not live to fight another day.
For Tiger once the Flagship of Lord Beatty
Must now be scrapped forthwith, so says the Treaty
And once upon the scrap-heap, not all the king's men
Will ever put Tiger together again:
Not all the king's horses; not all the king's men.[40]

Tiger had been condemned but Maurice also rose to occasional verse, in collaboration with Chesterton, in an attempt to avert the threat posed to the trees opposite the Church of the Holy Redeemer in Cheyne Row. Their favourite ballade form came into its own in these verses:

> They're breaking down the bridge at Waterloo;
> They've daubed the house of Henry James at Rye;
> They've caught a man and put him in the zoo;
> They've let the Japanese into Shanghai;
> They may destroy St Peter's on the sly;
> They all agree that dogma has to go;
> From pole to pole the shattered temples lie;
> They're cutting down the trees in Cheyne Row.[41]

In losing Gilbert Chesterton, who died in 1936, Maurice not only lost one of his closest friends but also a literary collaborator and sympathetic critic. Maurice was too ill even to attend Mass when his friend died in June. It was an almost unbearable loss as he wrote to Gilbert's wife, Frances: 'I feel as if a tower of strength had crumbled and one's crutch in life had gone. That I saw but little of him lately is neither here nor there. I knew he was *there* and knew what he would think of things . . .'[42]

Despite the successes and critical acclaim for his novels on the Continent, by the late 1930s, Baring's energy for fiction begins to diminish. His last novel, *Darby and Joan*, did not inspire the enthusiasm of many of his earlier novels. Masterly as realism, it is based on fact, on events which took place between 1546 and 1629 (Baring transposes these to 1855 and 1930) and 'one of those cases in which truth outdoes fiction in odd misadventures and coincidences'; and yet the novel as a whole 'takes on a greyness from its heroine's character' and does not, perhaps, entirely satisfy.[43]

Thereafter Maurice left fiction to devote himself to his last full-scale work, *Have You Anything to Declare?*, a different kind of book altogether, an example of his favourite genre, a *gepack* and a more appropriate coda to his literary life. In a dream he was asked, as he tells us in the Preface, by the Customs Official of the 'Chemins de fer de l'enfer' to declare his literary baggage; he opened his trunks and unpacked. The book is the result, 'a record, a confession, and a challenge, both unique and universal, a setting of jewels with consummate skill'.[44] It is also a testament to the wealth of Maurice's learning, a fitting close to his active life as a man of letters.

[VI]

The Last Years
1936–1945

– 14 –

A Broken Toy?

My body is a broken toy
Which nobody can mend.
Unfit for either play or ploy,
My body is a broken toy,
But all things end.
The siege of Troy
Came one day to an end.
My body is a broken toy
Which nobody can mend.

. . .

My soul is an immortal toy
Which nobody can mar.

. . .

Though rusted from the world's alloy
It glitters like a star.[1]

By 1936 illness was becoming all too obvious; on 16 June, Maurice is 'too paralysed with neuritis and "agitances" to hold pen or pencil' and is not allowed to travel except for his once weekly doctor's visit.[2] The diagnosis was Parkinson's Disease and it was by now clearly well-established, with all its inconveniences of awkward movement as well as difficulties with speech and controlling the hands and limbs. By 1937 Maurice had been to any number of doctors in search of any 'cure'; he relates these experiences to Ronald Storrs:

My doctors have become like Chinese Puzzle boxes, but it is their doing not mine. Plesch, whose name you spell wrong, when he had finished with me put me on to a man called Martin, who, in his turn called in the aid of Gonin. Between the three they cured me of Neuritis, and agreed that they had done all that orthodox medicine could do towards alleviating 'Paralysis Agitans', and that there was nothing more to do but chance the unorthodox.[3]

The unorthodox included Alexander, recommended via Ethel by Bernard Shaw who considered him an undoubted genius. By the 1930s a number of doctors in Britain had started to take an interest in Alexander's work although it never received the recognition of the profession as a whole despite the fact that Alexander numbered among his pupils many illustrious persons including Aldous Huxley, Sir Stafford Cripps, the Earl of Lytton and William Temple, Archbishop of Canterbury.[4] Shaw has written that Alexander:

> ... a musician-reciter ... found himself disabled by a complaint known as clergyman's sore throat. Having the true scientific spirit and industry, he set himself to discover what it was that he was really doing to disable himself in this fashion by his efforts to produce the opposite result. In the end he found this out, and a great deal more as well. He established not only the beginnings of a far reaching science of the apparently involuntary movements we call reflexes, but a technique of correction and self-control which forms a substantial addition to our very slender resources in personal education.[5]

Maurice remarked: 'I think his theories are sound, and I agree with Bernard Shaw in thinking him a genius.' To H.G. Wells, he wrote that Alexander seemed to be doing him some good although he was far from certain. But by September he had deteriorated further; Eddie could come to Half-Way House for lunch if he liked but he should realize that Maurice had all his meals alone as he could only sit still for five minutes (mealtimes were awkward affairs because of difficulty with swallowing; this could cause an embarrassing dribbling).[6] He writes to Ettie wondering if she would come for the night or for the evening: 'Luncheon is very unsatisfactory as I don't have my meals downstairs. I eat upstairs on a tray, and alone, very quickly, and if I don't have a rest from 2 to 4 I get no quiet in the day and generally a bad night.'[7] Then to Eddie:

> My general health is perfect, but I cannot walk a yard; I cannot sit in a chair for more than ten minutes, and when I lie down I have fits of shaking all day long, and these wake me four or five times in the night.

It is like having an angry wasp inside one's chest. I cannot hold a book in my hands and I can only bear being read to at times.[8]

There were books he would have loved to have read, including Rothenstein's autobiography but this, like many others, was 'too big for my desk or my hands and I cannot even attempt it'.[9] And, as he wrote to Rupert Hart-Davis, 'I am always glad of books. The trouble with me is size and shape. I cannot manage tall or fat books. I can't hold any book in my hands and I can only manage books that open flat on my reading desk. What is best for me are unbound books, page proofs.' (Ethel had, with this in mind, thoughtfully had her biography specially bound for him in three easily held volumes.) Maurice at this stage could most pleasurably 'read Trollope and a certain kind of detective story, that is to say, crime and detective stories that are not too difficult or too puzzling. I can read any crime story that has no problem in it and any detective story that is not in the nature of a Torquemada crossword puzzle.'[10] Unfortunately, Ethel had told many friends, including some in Germany, that Maurice was much better. This had greatly increased his correspondence and it tired him very much indeed to dictate.

In 1937 Leonard Woolf had developed a Parkinsonian tremor in his hands; Maurice wrote to Virginia to compare their experiences with Alexander. Teaching no 'fantastic theories' Alexander had, Maurice thought, stumbled up against some basic truths, despite the fact that he was a very bad teacher, always liable to go off at a tangent and far from good at explaining. His discoveries were essentially common sense:

> . . . namely that if you control the head you control the body, that if you throw your head back you lose your balance, that if you put your head forward and up you achieve the poise of a Greek statue or a Zulu; that if you use the strongest muscles to do the heaviest work you will find everything easier; that if you sit down and get up and walk doing this you will be more comfortable than if you slouch and crouch. I think then he has further discovered that most people when they think they are applying these rules are really doing the opposite, and to counteract this he has invented a technique of inhibitions which I think is quite successful when properly executed.

It wasn't that this technique was any sort of universal panacea but it did teach one to sit and walk properly and to control the nerves and with

Maurice, a very keen and assiduous pupil who attended his classes every day for several weeks, Alexander had some qualified success:

> He has been successful with me in getting rid of the superficial tremors from a spasmodic internal throbbing in the chest. This comes on worse when I lie down and especially at night. It began to be much worse after my first four lessons from Alexander and has practically been getting worse all the time.

The final question was, however,

> ... whether he is training a race horse with a broken wind. He says the horse would be worse without the windpipe he is putting in, but the question I ask myself is whether he is putting in a windpipe or just teaching the horse to jump better and whether the jumping is not wearing the horse out.[11]

By January 1938 Maurice was anxious not to suggest that he did not respect Alexander; he owed it to himself 'not to give other people the impression that I was ungrateful for what he had done to me or that I thought his work negligible'.[12] Indeed he had much to thank Alexander for: 'I did not mention the fact, talking of his treatment of me, that before I had lessons from him I could not get out of a chair, I could not walk across a room, and it took two people to haul me out of a taxi. That I can do these things and that I can hold a pencil or pen I owe to him.'[13] Later in the same month he reports to Enid that he has been to Brighton in an ambulance for an X-ray, but has had a series of bad nights and was shaking 'like a steam-piston'.[14] The results came and were passed on to Enid on 1 February; in the backbone there was 'lateral curvature and rotation'. Maurice wrote:

> I don't know what rotation means. It means the whole thing is crooked. Lower down there is calcification of a cartilage, spondylitis; further down, arthritis, and further down again sacralisation. In fact, it bears out exactly what Dr Martin said and exactly what Alexander meant, although Alexander called it impaction. But then, he always calls things by wrong names. In fact, he does not know the ordinary scientific medical names at all, nor, as we know, does he pretend to.

It was looking likely that all question of any cure should be ruled out.[15]

In November 1938 Enid suggested a treatment using Bulgarian Belladonna. Folklore had long held that certain plants could cause the mouth to dehydrate and, in the late nineteenth century, Charcot and others exploited this to control the drooling of saliva. They also discovered that improvement might also occur for stiffness and trembling: '"The Bulgarian belladonna treatment" introduced by a plant collector Ivan Raeff gained an unwarranted reputation although it contained no more than an elixir of belladonna supplemented by white wine, charcoal, bread dough, sawdust and nutmeg . . .'[16] Maurice was doubtful having already tried 'the most extraordinary treatment, being inoculated with ordinary garden flowers, such as sweet geranium and lavender'.[17] He had heard of the Belladonna course from Plesch and made some enquiries of the Italian specialist in tropical diseases, Aldo Castellani:

> Knowing what effect these kind of drugs have on me, namely, that they make me worse, I decided I would certainly not try it till I knew at least of one case where it had been successful. The great thing now is not to be made worse by any treatment. Before I went to Alexander I should have pinned him down and instead of being content with the vague hope that he could do me some good, I should have said, 'Have you ever cured *anybody* of this'? And I think the answer would have been in the negative.[18]

There was, and indeed is, no cure for Parkinson's Disease, and the cause remains unknown, although effective symptomatic treatments have been developed, particularly in recent years.

Although there were many people, and visits, from Cecilia Fisher, Diana and Maurice's sister Susan, as well as the almost daily one from Enid, and he was still able to appreciate literary matters like Beerbohm's wonderful parody of his writing which appeared in *John o'London's Weekly*, it gradually became too much for Maurice. When war broke out, he was bed-ridden in Rottingdean, 'enduring with saintly fortitude a long and merciless overthrow'. The weekly visits to Half-Way House were very painful for Diana. She would dress her best to please him, and to satisfy his 'high standards of a grander epoch' and get together a quantity of jokes and plans for a future in which he never lost hope, 'but for all his laughter and good spirits I felt my offerings insufficient and beggarly, and myself a shadow of what I wanted to be'.[19] Later, after his death, Diana was to reproach herself for not being adequate in her relations with Maurice at this time, and earlier; a letter from Conrad Russell remarks that she should not feel badly; she 'couldn't pretend to be in love with him'.[20] On 6 July Diana went to Rottingdean: '. . . poor Maurice. He is half the size he used to be. A bright blue budgerigar sits on his shoulder always chattering into his ear, pecking his cheek and making little messes. He claims that Dempsey (that's his name) talks. I doubt it. I wasn't allowed to drive along the front where the camouflaged six-inch guns are.'[21] Later in July she 'found Maurice in high spirits today owing, he said, to being in acute pain. His blue budgerigar was pecking hairs out of his ears and talking to him incessantly. The visit passed in a flash. We both felt so gay, sipping sherry and nibbling chocolates and arguing about the Pope.'[22] On 14 August 1940 her impressions were much more sombre:

I went to see poor shrivelling, palsied Maurice today. I took my tin hat along. I do not think he will bear the front line much longer. Compulsory inactivity under bombing is not to be borne. He had best take his last patience to Laura Lovat in Scotland, where there will be fewer alarms. The high white cliffs are bristling with guns.[23]

Laura had been with him in 1939

. . . on those hot days in September and we wheeled him over the lawn to cut off the heads of over-flowered roses that they might flower once again. It was warm, a St Martin's Summer, and he spoke of planting the border for the following year, but the next summer came, and though the garden was fuller of roses than ever before, his windows had been shaken by gunfire, and the noise of air-raid warnings had become unendurable.[24]

Thus it was that he moved, at just a moment's notice, to Scotland. He believed it was for just a few months, until the armies had progressed further from the coast: 'but this was not to be, and he remained there, a loved and honoured guest, from August 1940 until his death in 1945. His existence had changed; for from this date onward he remained in constant pain within four walls, in a lonely part of the Highlands.'[25]

Although it was wartime and travel difficult, nevertheless friends came to see him at Eilean Aigas, the island, and a 'place of rare and unexpected beauty' in the river Beauly. In the winter of 1942–43, Enid and Diana journeyed up to see him; it was to say goodbye. Diana wore her porter's clothes, navy blue trousers and a peaked cap, and each had a small knapsack, as there was no food at all on wartime trains. Enid writes:

> For some reason we sat in a sort of long saloon; perhaps a restaurant car that had no restaurant. She [Diana] told me the fabulous stories of touring America in *The Miracle*. Some of the tales (to do with millionaires and glass floors) were hair-raising. Twenty soldiers and sailors and their wives were riveted. Who was this perfectly beautiful woman-porter who was saying these things? I could see 'tart' in one eye, 'actress' in another; but most of the eyes were baffled.

Enid thought it would be an ordeal to say goodbye to the dying man but it wasn't like that at all: 'Once past the shymaking outer fence – with Maurice all was natural.'[26] Diana writes:

> Though he did not die until December 1945, we knew we should neither of us ever see him again. What an awful finality in saying 'I shall never see him again' of someone so near to one's heart and still alive and alert. Maurice was playful all his life and to the end – playful as snow, weightless as it dances down, white on a dark background of cloud. Newman said there were angels in disguise; some get canonised, some, like Maurice, don't. The budgerigar Dempsey still sat on his shoulder, chirping sweet nothings, the indefatigable nurse still dedicated her soothing gestures and words, her life itself, to his service. He was in a centre of the Faith he proclaimed, yet leaving him was so dreadfully sad that one wished he would soon win his last battle.[27]

The last battle was not yet quite over; it was only a few friends who were able to come to Eilean Aigas and Maurice obviously missed his friends a great deal, a disadvantage of his being in Scotland. At intervals, Belloc and Lady Lovat corresponded about the possibility of moving him back to Rottingdean but it was impossible: 'I think it wise to keep him away from the guns as long as possible. The strain is cumulative and the accumulation goes on unconsciously . . .' So wrote Belloc on 28 January 1941.[28] Sad news, too, constantly assailed Maurice; in February 1942 Half Way House was bombed, and, as the paralysis became worse, it was increasingly difficult to do more than dictate the shortest of letters and some verse. But Maurice's life was not over and 'he threw himself with zest and no expression of outward sorrow into this next existence.' Very important at this time was the help of his Australian nurse, Jean Neill, 'whose gaiety and understanding almost rivalled his own'.[29] She knew all that could be done to alleviate his suffering and she helped him with her optimism and her humour:

> 'You are not even a "mallard imaginaire", dear Major' she used to tell him – which was the answer the late Godfrey Webb gave on being asked what he had shot when out duck flighting. She gave him confidence and security in a martyrdom which we all realised could only be terminated by death.[30]

The fact was never mentioned though Maurice clearly wanted it to be an established fact and for there to be no more talk of possible cures. It was forbidden in the Eilean Aigas household to ask about his health and, should anyone inquire if he had slept well, he would reply 'That is a secret.'

In some ways these last years were among the richest of his life because of the family life and group of children of which he was the centre. Every new baby was placed in his arms and every birthday celebrated in his bedroom with only nannies and children, those same children to whom previously he had promised a prize for the one who could make the biggest mess. Every evening each child was lifted on to his bed and 'given a sweet hidden in his frail hand, which had to be blown on, or sometimes kissed, until the sweet was released.'[31] They would then sit beside him sucking their sweets and telling him about their day. Jean Neill writes:

> His years in Scotland were happy ones. The winter was spent in the Castle, summer in the dower house on Eilean Aigas, where his room looked out on a sea of rhododendrons, molus azaleas, to an avenue of elms, beeches, limes etc. The babbling of the Beauly could always be heard. Many old friends came to visit – one, Lord Trenchard, I think, said 'To be with Maurice in this setting is like being in a cathedral'. Winter months in the castle were a delight – he had the daily joy of visits by the young Fraser children, whose day was not complete without seeing Uncle Maurice, to hear his stories and having a sweet appearing with a gentle puff from his delicate and trembling hand.[32]

Dempsey was always a good companion but trouble came when his seed was no longer available, so when Jean Neill's family asked what she would like to be sent from Australia her answer was simply 'bird seed'. It arrived in time to prevent Dempsey losing weight.

The days passed with much listening to the wireless, not just to war bulletins but also to music and plays. When the wireless was not interesting, Laura would read to him (by candlelight for there was no electricity) – Dickens, Meredith, Scott, Stevenson, Jane Austen, the Brontës, Trollope, Conrad and all the English classics. Of the war news, naval disasters were the most affecting for Maurice; his many happy times at sea with William Fisher and his long association with the Navy made 'the death of a ship an almost unbearable agony'; but he was involved in all aspects of the war. When the news of the liberation of Paris reached Beaufort, a French military chaplain on sick leave there recited the Te Deum standing at the salute at Maurice's bedside.

From this time on his anxiety over the war relaxed and his curiosity about outside events diminished. He had, in any case, as Laura says, sung his Nunc Dimittis and

With the end of the summer he seemed to grow more remote from the events of this world, except those which affected his immediate surroundings; for these his sympathy and care never varied, and if possible increased. But the problems of the world's agony he felt could now be left only to its Creator.[33]

He died on 14 December.

The burial and service were on 18 December at Askadale. Lady Fisher writes:

When we reached Askadale there were the usual group of stalkers and keepers under the great oak as on a Sunday – Shimi in his black mourning jacket and Lovat Kilt, looking so like his own son, the Little Master, so young but tremendously tall – the birches, the midsummer nights dram moss and the river flowing so quietly as it does near by there, and the ineffable line of the hills beyond . . .

Maurice's coffin was covered with the Union Jack which would have so pleased the Navy. It had gone everywhere for the last five years with Father McGuire, given to him as Chaplain of the Forces to the Canadians during the War . . .

Laura was wonderful and took me up into her room and told me everything of the last few days of his life. How Maurice made her say the Rosary in French and German, feeling the beauty in each language and then Salvadore, the Italian prisoner came into his room to say it in Italian . . .

It seemed so beautiful that he had no strangers to deal with in those last weeks of suffering . . .

Then the miracle of Father McGuire coming two days before the last – when Maurice had asked for him early in the morning, and again later on – and then at noon he appeared straight from Germany – although not expected till Christmas itself – he stayed with him till in the End is my Beginning, came to our St Maurice.[34]

There was also a Requiem Mass at Farm Street in London. Molly MacCarthy wrote:

'it was most beautiful – dignified –. . . quiet – and we were much moved. It was all that Maurice himself would have liked. The 6 lighted candles were round about the black velvet pall covering the bier – and reminded me of Shakespeare, and days in England before the Reformation, when England was as full of dignified and poetical ceremonies as Maurice would have wished.[35]

All aspects of Maurice, this 'great European' as Laura Lovat called him, were remembered in letters and obituaries; he would, it was said by a writer from Russian House, be remembered by Russians as an enlightened friend who 'gave many of his abilities not only to studying Russian with an understanding heart but to acquaint[ing] public opinion in this country with the real state of affairs in old Russia in a manner worthy of the best traditions of British fairness and justice'.[36]

Above all, he was seen as a most special personal friend; Eddie Marsh wrote to Susan that he was 'full of memories of my old friendship with Maurice – one of the most important of my life – his charm, his brilliance, his kindness are among the joyful things of life, and his long suffering at the end one of its sorrows, although his shining courage made that too a thing to marvel at.'[37]

Trenchard (who also wrote an obituary in *The Times*) felt that Maurice was 'truly the best character I ever knew', a man whose spirit will live 'especially in the Air Force – I feel that there will be thousands waiting to welcome him on the other side . . .'[38] Conrad Russell commented to Diana, with some justice, 'But no man ever got such praise as Maurice got from Trenchard. I was very glad. It's strange to think that Maurice's real claim to greatness may be as a staff officer – not as a man of letters.'[39] Frank Mildmay, one of Maurice's cousins from Devon, recalled his abiding impression of Maurice as 'a very beautiful little boy . . . racing about the "Waterwitch" at Cowes, thoroughly enjoying himself – a delight to watch! How devoted to him was your dear mother.'[40]

It was not surprising that at Farm Street there was 'little sorrow' now that 'the martyrdom of Maurice Baring was over and those who mourned were mourning their own last hope of seeing once again, in this life, their incomparable friend'.[41]

Glossary

This Glossary only contains terms quoted in the text above. For a fuller commentary on 'The Expressions' see Edward Marsh, *A Number of People* (London, 1939)

Bird: happy
Block: to put someone/something on the block: to bring up a subject; to discuss
Culte (pronounced as in French): someone very nice and lovable; to have a culte: to have a crush on someone
Curlingtoes: an attack of extreme shyness
Dentist: a heart-to-heart talk
Dewdrop: a compliment
Dog: very, extremely
An Ethel: an undue display of rage
Fou-rire (as in French): uncontrollable laughter
Mrs Hunter: vulgarity, lewd conversation
Heygate: second-rate
Ibsen: ordinary, straightforward, what everybody has always said or thought
Leveson-Gower: a sudden, mad plan
Loser: a cad, someone third-rate
Molasse: something very nice, a treat
Padlock: a secret, keep secret
Punch: to have a go at something, to do something with enthusiasm
Pink Tights: to become a Roman Catholic, to be a Roman Catholic
Relever (French): to talk about, to talk over, to gossip [MB also uses rel. in the letters]
Robespierre: shabby
Ridge: depression
Sobheart: a comforter, a confidante, a sympathetic person
Tea: as in 'great tea', a very good thing
Type (as in French and so pronounced): used as a prefix to almost anything, as in 'Type Rio', 'Type novel'
Umble: used as suffix. MB sometimes known as 'Mumble', for example
Washed: got rid of
Wolseley: a General

Notes

Chapter 1

1 MB, *Round the World in Any Number of Days* (London, 1919), pp.3–4
2 MB, Letter to Countess Benckendorff, 22 June 1922
3 MB, *The Puppet Show of Memory* (London, 1922), p.56
4 Vernon Lee, Letter to MB, 17 November 1922
5 *Puppet Show*, p.63
6 MB, *Cat's Cradle* (London, 1924), pp.72–8
7 *Puppet Show*, p.3
8 Ibid., p.21
9 Philip Ziegler, *The Sixth Great Power: Barings 1762–1912* (London, 1988), p.187
10 Ibid., p.29

Chapter 2

1 *Puppet Show*, p.91
2 Ibid., p.14
3 Ibid., p.63
4 *Round the World*, p.79
5 MB, *Lost Lectures* (London, 1932), p.13
6 *Puppet Show*, p.77
7 *Lost Lectures*, p.14
8 *Puppet Show*, p.74
9 Ibid., p.81
10 Ibid., p.78
11 Ibid., p.37
12 Ibid., p.82
13 Ibid., p.83
14 Ibid., p.84
15 Ibid., p.86
16 *Lost Lectures*, p.20
17 Ibid., p.18
18 MB, C., (London, 1924), p.67
19 Ibid., p.53
20 *Lost Lectures*, p.21
21 Ibid., pp.23, 25

22 MB, Letter to Vernon Lee, 14 October 1903 (as quoted in Smyth, *Maurice Baring* p.200)
23 *Puppet Show*, p.88
24 MB, Letter to G.K. Chesterton, 29 September 1916
25 *Puppet Show*, p.91
26 *Lost Lectures*, p.26
27 Ibid., p.27
28 *Puppet Show*, pp.105–106
29 *Lost Lectures*, p.39
30 *Puppet Show*, p.111
31 Ibid., p.112
32 C., p.87
33 Ibid., p.111
34 *Puppet Show*, p.113
35 Sir John Clapham, *The Bank of England* (London, 1944), p.8
36 Ibid., p.330
37 Philip Ziegler, *The Sixth Great Power* (London, 1988), pp.260–61
38 Ibid., p.260
39 *Puppet Show*, p.114
40 Ibid., p.104
41 Ibid., p.117
42 C., pp.103–104

Chapter 3

1 *Puppet Show*, p.118
2 Ibid., p.132
3 Ibid., p.120
4 MB, Letter to Arnold Ward, 20 March 1892
5 *Puppet Show*, p.135
6 Ibid., p.138
7 *The Memoirs of Ethel Smyth*, abridged and introduced by Ronald Crichton (Harmondsworth, Middlesex, 1987), p.181
8 *Lost Lectures*, p.85
9 *Puppet Show*, p.141
10 Ibid., p.143
11 *Lost Lectures*, pp.44–5
12 *Puppet Show*, pp.145–6
13 Ibid., p.146
14 Ethel Smyth, *Maurice Baring* (London, 1938), p.5
15 *The Letters of Conrad Russell*, edited by Georgiana Blakiston (London, 1988), pp.253–4

16 Evan Charteris, *The Life and Letters of Sir Edmund Gosse* (London, 1931), pp.239–40
17 MB, Letter to Edward Marsh, 27 August 1897
18 MB, Letter to Edward Marsh, 23 January 1899
19 MB, Letter to Edward Marsh, [?] 1897
20 *Puppet Show*, p.147
21 The quotations following on pp.45–55 are from the Lost Lecture, on 'The Nineties' included in *Lost Lectures*, pp.91–113
22 MB, 'M. Anatole France', *The Yellow Book*, V (April 1895), p.265
23 *Puppet Show*, p.157
24 Ibid.
25 *Puppet Show*, p.161
26 Ibid., p.166
27 Ibid., p.167
28 MB, Letter to Edmund Gosse, (1896?)
29 *Puppet Show*, pp.167–8
30 Ibid., p.168
31 Ibid., p.169
32 Ibid.
33 MB, Letter to Hubert Cornish, 27 May 1897
34 MB, Letter to Hubert Cornish, 31 May 1897
35 *Puppet Show*, p.172
36 Ibid., p.173
37 Ibid., p.175
38 MB, Letter to Hubert Cornish, 31 May 1897
39 *Puppet Show*, p.176
40 Ibid., pp.176–7
41 Ibid., p.179
42 Ibid., p.180
43 Ibid.

Chapter 4

1 *Lost Lectures*, pp.120–21
2 *Puppet Show*, p.181
3 *Lost Lectures*, p.122
4 *Puppet Show*, pp.181–2
5 Ibid., p.182
6 *Lost Lectures*, p.123
7 David Thomson, *Europe Since Napoleon* (Harmondsworth, Middlesex, 1966), p.373
8 *Lost Lectures*, p.127
9 Smyth, p.13

10 *Lost Lectures*, p.125
11 Ibid., p.126
12 Ibid., p.127
13 Smyth, p.11
14 MB, Letter to Blanche Warre-Cornish, November 1899
15 MB, Letter to the same, 6 February 1900
16 MB, Letter to the same, 17 January 1900
17 MB, Letter to the same, 4 February 1900
18 MB, Letter to the same, 14 October 1900
19 MB, Letter to Edmund Gosse, 29 December 1899
20 MB, Letter to Blanche Warre-Cornish, 27 May 1899
21 *Puppet Show*, p.193
22 Ibid., p.194
23 MB, Letter to Blanche Warre-Cornish, 22 February 1900
24 MB, Letter to Edward Marsh, 23 March 1900
25 MB, Letter to the same, 11 January 1900
26 MB, Letter to Edmund Gosse, (1899?)
27 MB, Letters to the same, 17 March 1900, 21 January 1900
28 MB, Letter to Edward Marsh, 19 March 1900
29 MB, Letter to Blanche Warre-Cornish, 23 March 1900
30 MB, Letter to Vernon Lee, 14–15–16–17 October 1903
31 Paul Horgan, *Maurice Baring Restored* (London, 1970), p.12
32 C., pp.177, 179, 180
33 *Puppet Show*, pp.239, 242
34 Ibid., p.242
35 Ibid., p.243
36 MB, *Punch and Judy and Other Essays* (London, 1924), p.25
37 MB, *Sarah Bernhardt* (London, 1933), p.109
38 *Puppet Show*, pp.216–17
39 *Sarah Bernhardt*, p.83
40 Smyth, pp.18–19
41 MB, Letter in *Saturday Review* 17 June 1899
42 *Puppet Show*, p.195
43 MB, Letter to Blanche Warre-Cornish, 7 February 1900
44 MB, Letter to Hubert Cornish, 9 February 1900
45 *Passing By*, p.32
46 *Puppet Show*, p.198
47 Ibid., p.199
48 Ibid.
49 Ibid.
50 Ibid.
51 MB, Letter to George Grahame, *c.* January 1901

52 Daphne Pollen, *I remember, I remember* (privately printed, 1983), p.37
53 *Puppet Show*, p.207
54 Mary Ponsonby: *A Memoir, Some Letters and a Journal*, edited by Magdalen Ponsonby (London, 1927), pp.205–207

Chapter 5

1 *Puppet Show*, p.209
2 MB, Letter to Hubert Cornish, 10 August 1900
3 *Lost Lectures*, pp.135–6
4 Ibid., p.136
5 *Puppet Show*, p.209
6 Nathalie Brooke, 'Baring and the Benckendorffs', *Chesterton Review*, XIX (February 1988), 103–106
7 *Puppet Show*, p.209
8 Ibid., pp.212–13
9 Ibid., p.213
10 MB, Letter to George Grahame, 1 November 1901
11 MB, Letter to Edward Marsh, n.d.
12 *Puppet Show*, p.215
13 Ibid., pp.215–16
14 Smyth, p.17
15 *Puppet Show*, p.139
16 MB, Letter to Henry Brewster, 21 December 1903
17 Smyth, p.217
18 Ibid., pp.202–203
19 Ibid., p.203
20 MB, *What I Saw in Russia* (London, 1927), pp.215f.
21 *Puppet Show*, p.220
22 MB, *Tinker's Leave* (London, 1927), pp.70–71
23 Ibid., p.73
24 MB, Letter to Edward Marsh, 16 December 1901
25 MB, *Collected Poems* (London, 1901), p.60
26 *Puppet Show*, pp.246–7
27 Ibid., p.250
28 Ibid., p.253
29 MB, Letter to Hilaire Belloc, 8 November 1902
30 Ethel Smyth, *What Happened Next* (London, 1940), pp.196–97
31 *Puppet Show*, p.254
32 *Lost Lectures*, pp.86–7, 90
33 MB, Letter to Vernon Lee, 31 January 1906
34 *Puppet Show*, p.260

35 Ibid.
36 Ibid., p.261
37 MB, *His Majesty's Embassy and Other Plays* (London, 1923), I and II
38 MB, Letter to Vernon Lee, 31 January 1906
39 *Puppet Show*, p.261

Chapter 6

 1 *Puppet Show*, p.261
 2 MB, *The Russian People* (London, 1911), p.284
 3 *Puppet Show*, p.263
 4 Ibid., pp.264–5
 5 Ibid., pp.265–6
 6 Ibid., p.268
 7 Ibid., pp.268–9
 8 MB, *What I Saw in Russia* (London, 1927), p.13
 9 *What I Saw*, pp.14–15
10 Ibid., p.29
11 *Puppet Show*, p.274
12 *What I Saw*, pp.33–4
13 *Puppet Show*, p.275
14 Ibid., p.278
15 Ibid., p.279
16 *What I Saw*, p.36
17 Ibid., p.39
18 Ibid., pp.46–7
19 Ibid., p.48
20 *Puppet Show*, pp.280–81
21 Ibid., p.281
22 *What I Saw*, p.57
23 Ibid., p.58
24 *Puppet Show*, p.282
25 Ibid., p.283
26 *What I Saw*, pp.149–52
27 *Puppet Show*, pp.284–5
28 *What I Saw*, p.105
29 Ibid., pp.123–4
30 Ibid., p.138
31 Ibid.
32 *Tinker's Leave*, p.182
33 *What I Saw*, p.56
34 Ibid., p.55
35 MB, Letter to Edmund Gosse, 17 July 1904

36 *Puppet Show*, 291, 292
37 *What I Saw*, p.143

Chapter 7

1 Review of *With the Russians in Manchuria, Sunday Times*, 25 June, 1905
2 Review of *With the Russians in Manchuria, Morning Post*, June 1905
3 *What I Saw*, p.168
4 *Puppet Show*, pp.312–13
5 Ibid., p.313
6 *What I Saw*, p.179
7 Ibid.
8 *Puppet Show*, p.319
9 *What I Saw*, p.184
10 Ibid., p.187
11 Ibid., pp.188–9
12 Ibid., p.190
13 Ibid., p.194
14 Ibid., p.200
15 *Puppet Show*, p.314
16 *What I Saw*, p.201
17 Ibid., pp.205–206
18 MB, Letter to Vernon Lee, 7 January 1907
19 *What I Saw*, p.302
20 Ibid., p.206
21 Ibid., p.207
22 Ibid., pp.207–208
23 *Puppet Show*, pp.332–3
24 *What I Saw*, p.223
25 Ibid., p.224
26 Ibid., p.226
27 Vernon Lee, *The Spirit of Rome: leaves from a diary* (London, 1906)
28 *What I Saw*, pp.231–2
29 Ibid., pp.235–6
30 Ibid., pp.236–7
31 Ibid., p.252
32 *Puppet Show*, p.339
33 Ibid., p.342
34 *What I Saw*, p.297
35 Ibid., p.299
36 Ibid., p.311
37 Ibid., p.313
38 *Russian People*, pp.309–311

39 G.K. Chesterton, *Autobiography*, Introduced by Richard Ingrams (London, 1986), p.313

Chapter 8

1 Letter from John Revelstoke to MB, 13 November 1906
2 Letter from the same to the same, 19 December 1906
3 Letters from the same to the same, 15 May 1907 and 23 May 1907
4 *Puppet Show*, p.356
5 Ibid., p.358
6 Ibid., p.361
7 Ibid., p.366
8 Ibid., pp.367–8
9 *What I Saw*, p.319
10 Ibid., p.320
11 *Puppet Show*, p.372
12 Ibid., p.373
13 Ibid., p.376
14 Ibid., p.377
15 Ibid., p.378
16 Ibid., pp.379–80
17 Ibid., p.382
18 Ibid., pp.384–5
19 Ibid., p.386
20 Ibid., pp.386–7
21 Ibid., pp.388–9
22 See 'Pogrom', *Russian Essays and Stories* (London, 1908). A Bobrinsky version of this story is found in *The Other Russia: The Experience of Exile*, edited by Michael Glenny and Norman Stone (London, 1990), pp.74–8
23 *Puppet Show*, p.389
24 Ibid., pp.389–90

Chapter 9

1 See Ziegler, p.275 and Smyth, *Baring*, p.40
2 MB, *The Mainsprings of Russia* (London, 1914), p.318
3 *Mainsprings*, pp.v, vii
4 Ibid., p.44
5 Ibid., pp.151–2
6 Ibid., pp.161–3
7 MB, *Landmarks in Russian Literature* (London, 1910, reprinted 1960), p.xi
8 *Daily Graphic*, 11 March 1910
9 *Landmarks*, p.7
10 Ibid., p.9

11 Ibid., p.24
12 Ibid., p.38
13 Ibid., p.48
14 Ibid., p.64
15 Ibid., p.73
16 See *Quarterly Review*, vol. 211, July 1909, 180–202
17 *Landmarks*, p.74
18 Ibid., p.79
19 Ibid., p.105
20 Ibid., p.119
21 Ibid., p.134
22 Ibid., pp.136, 140
23 Ibid., p.156
24 MB, *An Outline of Russian Literature* (London, 1914), p.222
25 *Landmarks*, p.163
26 Ibid., pp.164–5
27 Ibid., pp.191–3
28 Ibid., p.195
29 Ibid.
30 Ibid., p.196
31 Ibid., pp.199–200
32 Ibid., p.208
33 Ibid., p.209. See also Mirsky's comments as discussed in *Chesterton Review*, p.53; he calls MB 'the author of the only valuable books written in English about Russian literature' and refers to MB's essay prefaced to the *Oxford Book of Russian Verse* as a 'remarkable introduction'.
34 *Outline*, pp.v, vi
35 D.S. Mirsky, *The Intelligentsia of Great Britain*, translated by Alex Brown (London, 1935), p.8
36 Ibid., p.115
37 *Outline*, pp.249–50
38 Review of *Landmarks* in *The Times Literary Supplement*, 24 March 1910
39 'New Books', *The Times Literary Supplement*, 10 March 1910
40 *The Observer*, 13 March 1910
41 *The Outlook*, 19 March 1910
42 *Russian People*, p.x
43 Review of *The Russian People* in *The Times Literary Supplement*, 2 November 1911
44 Review of *With the Russians in Manchuria* in the *Daily Graphic*, 21 June 1905
45 Reviews of *With the Russians in Manchuria* in *The Speaker*, 24 June 1905 and *Vanity Fair*, 15 June 1905

46 *The Outlook*, 17 June 1905
47 Review of *A Year in Russia* in the *New Statesman*, 17 November 1917

Chapter 10
  1 Smyth, *Baring*, p.38
  2 G.K. Chesterton, *Autobiography*, Introduction Richard Ingrams (London, 1986), p.228
  3 Dudley Barker, *G.K. Chesterton* (London, 1973), p.151
  4 *Puppet Show*, p.391
  5 Barker, p.151
  6 *Puppet Show*, pp.392–3
  7 Ibid., pp.394–5
  8 MB, Letter to G.K. Chesterton, 1908
  9 *The New Age*, 15 February 1908, pp.308–309
 10 *Puppet Show*, pp.395–6
 11 Julian Jeffs, 'The Conversion of Maurice Baring', *Chesterton Review XIX* (1988), 83–91
 12 Smyth, *Baring*, p.185
 13 Jeffs, p.86
 14 MB, Letter to Hubert Cornish, 30 December 1900
 15 MB, Letter to George Grahame, *c.* January 1901
 16 Jeffs, p.87
 17 MB, *Passing By* (London, 1921) p.34
 18 Victoria Ingrams, 'Baring's Hidden Holiness', *Chesterton Review XIX* (1988), p.106
 19 MB, Letter to Hilaire Belloc, 7 February 1932
 20 MB, Letter to Ethel Smyth, 16 October 1919
 21 Jeffs, p.87
 22 MB, *Collected Poems* (London, 1925), pp.65–67
 23 MB, Letter to Elodie Belloc, 9 August 1911
 24 MB, Letter to Daphne Baring, 13 December 1923
 25 Jeffs, p.87
 26 Thomson, pp.363–4, 472 n.1
 27 MB, *Letters from the Near East* (London, 1913), pp.13, 25
 28 *Near East*, pp.54–7
 29 Ibid., p.66
 30 Ibid., pp.73–4
 31 Ibid., pp.75–6
 32 Ibid., p.76
 33 Ibid., p.80
 34 Ibid., pp.82–3
 35 Ibid., pp.83–4

36 Ibid., pp.99–100
37 *Puppet Show*, p.405
38 *Near East*, p.101
39 *Puppet Show*, p.406
40 *Near East*, p.110
41 *Puppet Show*, p.412
42 Ibid., p.413
43 Ibid., p.414
44 *Near East*, p.137
45 Ibid., pp.138–139
46 Ibid., p.141
47 Ibid., pp.148–50
48 *Puppet Show*, p.423
49 MB, Letter to Countess Benckendorff, 27 November 1912
50 *Puppet Show*, p.428
51 Letter to Nan Herbert from Lord Lucas, 12 December 1912
52 Letter to MB from G.K Chesterton, [Christmas] 1912
53 Letters to Nan Herbert from Lord Lucas, 12 December 1912; 15 December 1912; 14 December 1912; 26 December 1912
54 *Near East*, pp.154–6
55 Ibid., pp.156–8
56 Extracts from the Diary of Nan Herbert, later Lady Lucas, 13 August 1909
57 Chesterton, p.229
58 Herbert, *Diary*, 13 July 1910
59 Ibid. 30 June 1911, 1 July 1911, 14 July 1911, 10 June 1912, 18 & 19 June 1912
60 MB, *Lost Diaries and Dead Letters* (reprinted London, 1988), p.83
61 Ibid., pp.96–97
62 Ibid., pp.59, 89–94
63 Ibid., p.166
64 *Russian People*, pp.139–40

Chapter 11

1 MB, Letter to Wing Commander Marson, 2 December 1925
2 Andrew Boyle, *Trenchard* (London, 1962), p.142
3 *Puppet Show*, p.438
4 MB, *Cat's Cradle* (London, 1925), p.716
5 H.G. Wells, *Mr Britling Sees it Through* (London, 1916), pp.114, 123
6 Peter Vansittart (ed.), *Voices from the Great War* (Harmondsworth, Middlesex, 1983), p.11
7 Albums of Nan Herbert, later Lady Lucas; letter E. Atkinson, *c.* 3 or 4 August 1904
8 *Puppet Show*, p.292

9 Ethel Anne Priscilla Grenfell [Lady Desborough], *Pages from a Family Journal* (Privately Printed, Eton, 1916), p.452

10 Vansittart, p.22

11 MB, *War Diary, 1914–1918*, p.10 (New York Public Library, Berg Collection); *Flying Corps Headquarters 1914–1918* (London, reprinted 1968), p.8

12 Herbert, *Diary*, 9 August 1914

13 As quoted in Sholto Douglas, *Years of Combat* (London, 1963), p.59

14 Douglas, pp.75, 149

15 Letter from Lady Henderson to Nan Herbert, 22 August (?) 1914

16 *Flying Corps*, p.104

17 Boyle, p.142

18 MB, Letter to G.K. Chesterton, 29 December 1916

19 MB, Letter to Lady Desborough, 8 September 1915

20 *Flying Corps*, p.125

21 Ibid., p.126

22 Boyle, p.146

23 *Flying Corps*, p.169

24 Ibid., pp.178–82

25 Ibid., p.248

26 Boyle, p.375

27 Lady Cynthia Asquith, *Diaries 1915–1918* (London, 1968), p.222

28 MB, Letter to Hilaire Belloc, 5 March 1919

29 A.N. Wilson, *Hilaire Belloc* (London, 1984), p.223

30 MB, *Dear Animated Bust* (Wilton, Salisbury, 1981), p.17

31 Ibid., p.45

32 Ibid., p.43

33 Ibid., pp.20–21

34 MB, Letter to Edward Marsh, April 1917

35 *Dear Animated Bust*, p.154

36 Ibid., p.122

37 William Orpen, *An Onlooker in France 1917–1919* (London, 1924), pp.54–55

38 MB, Letter to Hilaire Belloc, November 1915

39 MB, Letter to Hilaire Belloc, 29 November 1915

40 [John Squire] review of *English Landscape* in the *New Statesman* 22 July 1916

41 MB, Letter to John Squire, 24 July 1916

42 MB, Letter to G.K. Chesterton, May 1915

43 MB, Letter to Edward Marsh, 26 January 1916

44 MB, Letter to Spencer Wilkinson, 23 March 1916; MB, Letter to Desmond MacCarthy, 14 April 1917

45 MB, Letter to Ethel Smyth, 20 September 1916
46 *Flying Corps*, p.227
47 *Flying Corps*, p.94
48 MB, Letter to Lady Desborough, 5 September 1916
49 MB, Letter to Lady Islington, 20 September 1916
50 Letter from Hilaire Belloc to MB, n.d.; Letter from Edmund Gosse to MB as quoted in Evan Charteris, *The Life and Letters of Sir Edmund Gosse* (London, 1931), pp.409–10
51 MB, Letter to Edmund Gosse, 11 November 1916
52 Quoted in F.D. Tredrey's foreword to *Flying Corps*, p.xvii

Chapter 12

1 MB, Letter to G.K. Chesterton, 10 December 1924
2 Letter from John Revelstoke to MB, 5 May 1920
3 MB, Letter to General Trenchard, 21 December 1918
4 MB, Letter to General Trenchard, 23 March 1920
5 MB, Letters to General Trenchard, 22 May 1924; 7 June 1924
6 Review of C. in the *New Statesman*, 31 May 1924
7 Interview with Lady Maclean
8 Smyth, *Baring*, p.320
9 Letter to Laura, Lady Lovat from Commander (S) A.W.B. Messenger, FSA, RN, 16 March 1948
10 Admiral Sir William James, *Admiral Sir William Fisher* (London, 1943), p.53
11 MB, Letter to Edmund Gosse, 12 March 1925
12 MB, Letter to Diana Cooper, 1925
13 MB, Letter to William Fisher, 15 or 16 April 1925
14 MB, Letter to William Fisher, 10 January 1928
15 MB, Letter to William Rothenstein, 11 March 1931; Letter to Lady Fisher, 21 March 1931
16 Nina Lavroukine, 'Maurice Baring and D.S. Mirsky: A Literary Relationship', *The Slavonic and East European Review*, 62, (January 1984)
17 Lavroukine, p.7
18 MB, Letter to Juliet Duff, August 1921
19 *Dear Animated Bust*, p.ix. A.N. Wilson attributes this rhyme to Belloc (*Hilaire Belloc*, p.233)
20 Lavroukine, p.13
21 *The Diary of Virginia Woolf*, III 1925–30, edited by Anne Olivier Bell (Harmondsworth, 1982), p.viii
22 Louise Collis, *Impetuous Heart: The Story of Ethel Smyth* (London, 1984), p.210

23 MB, Letters to Ethel Smyth, 16 October 1919; 24 October 1919; 25 (?) October 1919

24 MB, *Passing By* (London, 1921), p.34

25 MB, Letter to Ethel Smyth, 21 June 1921

26 Letter from Hilaire Belloc to MB, September 1921; letter from Venetia Montagu to MB, (?) July 1921

27 Review of *Flying Corps Headquarters* in the *Daily Telegraph*; Letter from 'GB' at the Air Ministry to MB, 1 May 1920; Letter from Edmund Gosse to MB, 29 April 1920

28 *Flying Corps*, p.147

29 Letter from Blanche Warre Cornish to MB, 23 May (?) 1922; letter from Vernon Lee to MB, n.d.

30 Edmund Gosse, 'Mr Maurice Baring', *The Sunday Times*, 4 June 1922

31 Letter from Walter Durnford to MB, 22 May 1922; letter from M.T. Tatham to MB, 26 September 1922

32 Letter from Donald Tovey to MB, 3 June 1922; letter from Augustus Ralli to MB, 3 June 1922

33 Letter from Hilaire Belloc to MB, September 1921

34 Chesterton, p.228

35 Diana Cooper, *The Light of Common Day* (London, 1959; Century Edition, 1984), pp.34–5

36 Ibid., pp.87–9

37 Diana Cooper, Letter to Conrad Russell, 18 December 1945

38 Cooper, *Common Day*, p.88

39 Letter from John Revelstoke to MB, 1 June 1924; *Spectator*, 12 July 1924; [Maurois] as quoted in L. Chaigne, *Maurice Baring* (Paris, 1935), p.48; Review of C. in the *New Statesman*, 31 May 1924

40 *The Diary of Virginia Woolf*, edited by Anne Olivier Bell (Harmondsworth, 1982), p.104

41 MB, Letter to Vernon Lee, 5 April 1926

42 MB, Letter to Countess Benckendorff, 3 August 1926

43 Letter from Vernon Lee to MB 26 March 1926 [as quoted in Smyth, *Baring*, p.331]; MB, Letter to Vernon Lee 5 April 1926

44 Arnold Bennett, *Journals*, vol. 3 (London, 1932), p.270

45 MB, Letter to Diana Cooper, 16 November 1925

46 MB, Letters to Daphne Baring, 19 June 1925 and 9 June 1925

47 MB, Letter to Daphne Baring, March 1925

48 Quoted in MB, letter to Diana Cooper, 5 October 1925; review of *Cat's Cradle* in *Punch*, 14 October 1925; Edith Somerville to MB, 19 October 1925 (in MB's albums); Letter from André Maurois to MB, 12 October 1925

49 *Puppet Show*, p.167

50 Letter from Vernon Lee to MB, 28 March 1926; MB, Letter to Vernon Lee, 2
    April 1926
51 *Cat's Cradle*, p.720
52 MB, Letter to George Grahame, (?) 1921
53 MB, *Daphne Adeane* (London, 1926), p.155
54 MB, *Darby and Joan* (London, 1936) p.221
55 MB, Letter to Diana Cooper, 13 January 1925
56 MB, Letter to Countess Benckendorff, 1926 (?)
57 Review of *Daphne Adeane* in the *New Statesman*, September 1926
58 Cooper, *Common Day*, p.81
59 *Collected Poems*
60 Ziegler, p.358
61 *Morning Post*, 20 April 1929
62 MB, Letter to Diana Cooper, 22 April 1929

Chapter 13

1 Cooper, *Common Day*, pp.165–66. Personal communication from Lady
    Diana Cooper
2 Gérard Boutelleau, *Reminiscences* (January, 1946)
3 Enid Bagnold, *Autobiography* (London, 1969, new edition 1985), p.209
4 Ibid., p.203
5 Ibid., p.211
6 Ibid., p.212
7 *The Letters of Virginia Woolf*, edited by Nigel Nicolson (London, 1979), V,
    p.22
8 Ibid., p.45
9 Ibid., p.260
10 Ibid., p.144
11 Ibid., pp.320, 321
12 Collis, p.201
13 Ibid.
14 Russell, p.254
15 Collis, p.201
16 Letter from G.K. Chesterton to MB, 13 May 1929
17 MB, *The Coat Without Seam* (London, 1929), p.68
18 Ibid.
19 Ibid., p.194
20 Ibid., p.321
21 Review of *Robert Peckham* in *The Times*, 20 June 1930
22 Comment in Maurice Baring's Albums
23 John Buchan, Review of *In the End is my Beginning* in *The Spectator*, June
    27, 1931

24 Hilaire Belloc, Letter to Mrs Reginald Balfour (as quoted in A.N. Wilson, *Hilaire Belloc* London, 1984, p.158)

25 Edmund Gosse, Review of MB, *Collected Poems* in *The Sunday Times*, 26 April 1925

26 Letter from G.K. Chesterton to MB, 2 July 1924

27 Letter from the same to the same, [?] 1924

28 Review of *Friday's Business* in the *Morning Post*, 8 November 1932

29 Desmond MacCarthy, 'Mr Maurice Baring's Method', *The Sunday Times*, 29 July 1934

30 MB, Letter to André Maurois, 22 February 1929

31 André Maurois, 'Mon Ami Maurice Baring', *Les Nouvelles Littéraires*, February 1938

32 Hugh & Mirabel Cecil, *Clever Hearts: Desmond and Molly MacCarthy. A Biography* (London, 1990), p.270

33 Robert Speaight, 'Maurice Baring the Novelist', *The Tablet*, 29 December 1945

34 *Corréspondance André Gide-Arnold Bennett* (Paris, Librarie Droz, 1964), p.127

35 Frank C. Hanigen, 'The Art of Maurice Baring', *The Bookman* (New York), LXXV (August 1932)

36 J.C. Squire, Review of *Lost Lectures* in *The Sunday Times*, 20 March 1932

37 Comments by Shane Leslie and David English [MB Albums]

38 Review of *Sarah Bernhardt* in the *Times Literary Supplement*, 12 October 1933; Desmond MacCarthy, Review of *Sarah Bernhardt* in *The Sunday Times*, 15 October 1933; MB, Letter to Desmond MacCarthy, 15 October 1933; MB, Letter to Hilaire Belloc, 4 April 1923

39 *Punch*, 11 May 1932

40 MB, 'The Last Cruise of H.M.S. Tiger' (London, privately printed, 1931)

41 G.K. Chesterton, *Collected Nonsense and Light Verse*, selected and arranged by Marie Smith (London, 1988), p.138

42 MB, Letter to Frances Chesterton, 16 June 1936

43 Review of *Darby and Joan* in *The Times*, 17 September 1935

44 Review of *Have You Anything to Declare?* in *The Times*, 24 November 1936

Chapter 14

1 Quoted in Cooper, *Common Day*, p.251

2 MB, Letter to Frances Chesterton, 16 June 1936

3 MB, Letter to Ronald Storrs, 5 June 1937

4 *F. Matthias Alexander, 1969–1955: A Biographical Outline* (London, 1979)

5 *London Music in 1888–1889 as heard by Corno de Bassetto* (later known as Bernard Shaw) with some further autobiographical particulars (London, 1937), pp.17–18

6 See G. Stern, *Parkinson's Disease; the Facts* (London, 1982), pp.18–19

7 MB, Letter to Lady Desborough, 22 October 1937

8 MB, Letter to Edward Marsh, 22 September 1937

9 MB, Letter to William Rothenstein, 13 November 1939

10 MB, Letter to Rupert Hart-Davis, 30 November 1939

11 MB, Letter to Virginia Woolf, 1 October 1937; personal communication with Marjorie Barlow

12 MB, Letter to H.G. Wells, 10 January 1938

13 MB, Letter to H.G. Wells, 6 January 1938

14 MB, Letter to Enid Bagnold, 21 January 1938

15 MB, Letter to Enid Bagnold, 1 February 1938

16 Stern, p.33

17 MB, Letter to Juliet Duff, 6 October 1936

18 MB, Letter to Lady Desborough, 19 November 1938

19 Cooper, *Common Day*, pp.252–3

20 Russell, p.254

21 Diana Cooper, *Trumpets from the Steep* (London, 1984), p.50

22 Ibid., p.54

23 Ibid., p.60

24 Laura Lovat, *Maurice Baring, a Postscript* (London, 1947), p.18

25 Ibid., p.19

26 Bagnold, p.21

27 Cooper, *Trumpets*, pp.159–60

28 Letter from Hilaire Belloc to Lady Lovat, 28 January 1941

29 Lovat, pp.20–21

30 Ibid., p.21

31 Ibid., p.22

32 Letter from Jean Neill to the late Dudley Barker

33 Lovat, p.26

34 Lady Fisher, '18 December 1945'

35 Letter from Molly MacCarthy to Susan Reid, December 1945

36 Letter from M.E. Sabline to Susan Reid, December 1954

37 Letter from Edward Marsh to Susan Reid, December 1945

38 Letter from Viscount Trenchard to Susan Reid, December 1945

39 Russell, p.256

40 Letter from Frank Mildmay to Susan Reid

41 *The Times*, 19 December 1945

Select bibliography

ABDY, JANE AND CHARLOTTE GERE, *The Souls*, Sidgwick and Jackson, 1984

ASQUITH, LADY CYNTHIA, *Diaries 1915–1918*, Hutchinson, 1968

BAGNOLD, ENID, *Autobiography*, Heinemann, 1916; Century 1985

BARKER, DUDLEY, *G.K. Chesterton*, Constable, 1973

BENCKENDORFF, COUNT CONSTANTINE, *Half a Life, Reminiscences of a Russian Gentleman*, Richards Press, 1954

BENNETT, ARNOLD, *Journals*, II and III, Cassell, 1932

BLAKISTON, GEORGIANA (ED.), *The Letters of Conrad Russell*, John Murray, 1987

BOYLE, ANDREW, *Trenchard*, Collins, 1962

BUCHAN, JOHN, *Memory-Hold-The-Door*, Hodder & Stoughton, 1940

CECIL, HUGH AND MIRABEL, *Clever Hearts: Desmond and Molly MacCarthy. A Biography* Gollancz, 1990

CHAIGNE, L. *Maurice Baring*, J. de Gigard, Paris. 1935

CHARTERIS, EVAN, *The Life and Letters of Sir Edmund Gosse*, Heinemann, 1931

CHESTERTON, G.K., *Autobiography*, intro. Richard Ingrams, Hamish Hamilton, 1986

Chesterton Review, *Maurice Baring Special Issue*, Vol. XIX, No. 1 (February 1988)

COLLIS, LOUISE, *Impetuous Heart: The Story of Ethel Smyth*, William Kimber, 1984

COOPER, LADY DIANA, *The Light of Common Day*, Hart-Davis, 1959; Century 1984

–*The Rainbow Comes and Goes*, Hart-Davis, 1958; Century, 1984

–*Trumpets from the Steep*, Hart-Davis, 1958; Century, 1984

DESBOROUGH, LADY ETHEL ANNE PRISCILLA, *Pages from a Family Journal*, Privately printed, 1916

DOUGLAS, SHOLTO, *Years of Combat*. Collins, 1963

GIDE, ANDRÉ, BENNETT, ARNOLD, *Correspondance*, Librarie Droz, Paris, 1964

GUNN, PETER, *Vernon Lee*, Oxford University Press, 1964

HASSALL, CHRISTOPHER, *Edward Marsh*, Longmans, Green, 1959

HORGAN, PAUL, *Maurice Baring Restored*. Heinemann, 1970

JOLLIFFE, JOHN, *Raymond Asquith, Life and Letters*, Collins, 1980

LAVROUKINE, NINA, 'Maurice Baring & D.S. Mirsky: A Literary Relationship.' –*The Slavonic & East European Review* 62 (January 1984), pp.25–35

LOVAT, LAURA LADY, *Maurice Baring, a Postscript*, Hollis and Carter, 1947

MACCARTHY, MARY, *A Nineteenth Century Childhood*, Heinemann, 1924

MARSH, EDWARD, *A Number of People*, Heinemann, 1939

MIRSKY, D.S., *The Intelligentsia of Great Britain*, trans. Alex. Brown, 1935

MOSLEY, NICHOLAS, *Julian Grenfell*, Weidenfeld and Nicolson, 1976

NICOLSON, NIGEL (ED.), *The Letters of Virginia Woolf*, Hogarth, 1979

ORPEN, WILLIAM, *An Onlooker in France 1917–1919*, Williams and Norgate, 1924

PARES, BERNARD, *My Russian Memoirs*, Jonathan Cape, 1931

POLLEN, DAPHNE, *I Remember, I Remember*, privately printed, 1983

PONSONBY, MAGDALEN, (ED.), *Mary Ponsonby: A Memoir, Some Letters and a Journal*, John Murray, 1927

REID, MICHAELA, *Ask Sir James*, Hodder and Stoughton, 1987

SMYTH, ETHEL, *The Memoirs of Ethel Smyth*, abridged and introduced by Ronald Crichton, Viking, 1987

–*Maurice Baring*, Heinemann, 1938

–*Streaks of Life*, Longmans, Green, 1921

–*What Happened Next*, Longmans, Green, 1940

THWAITE, ANN, *Edmund Gosse*, Secker and Warburg, 1984

WILSON, A.N., *Hilaire Belloc*, Hamish Hamilton, 1984

WILSON, EDMUND, *How not to be bored by Maurice Baring*, The New Yorker, September 1 1971

WOOLF, VIRGINIA, *Diary*, III, ed. Anne Olivier Bell, Penguin, 1982

ZIEGLER, PHILIP, *Lady Diana Cooper*, Hamish Hamilton, 1981

–*The Sixth Great Power: Barings 1762–1912*, Collins, 1988

Principal books by Maurice Baring

Algae (1928)
Algae (second series) (1928)

The Black Prince and Other Poems
(1902)

C. (1924)
Cat's Cradle (1925)
The Coat Without Seam (1929)
Collected Poems (1911)
Collected Poems (1925)
Comfortless Memory (1928)

Daphne Adeane (1926)
Darby and Joan (1925)
Dead Letters (1910)
Desidero (1906)
Diminutive Dramas (1911)
The Double Game (1912)

English Landscape (Ed) (1916)

Fantasio (translation) (1929)
Flying Corps Headquarters 1914–
1918 [R.F.C. H.Q. 1914–1918]
(1920)
French Literature (1927)
Friday's Business (1933)

Gaston de Foix and Other Plays (1903)
The Glass Mender and Other Stories
(1910)
The Green Elephant (1911)
The Grey Stocking and Other Plays
(1912)

Half a Minute's Silence and Other
Stories (1925)
Have You Anything to Declare?
(1936)
Hildesheim: Quatre Pastiches (1899)
His Majesty's Embassy (1923)

In the End is my Beginning (1931)

Landmarks in Russian Literature
(1910)
Last Days of Tsarskoe Selo
(translation) (1926)
Letters from the Near East 1909 and
1912 (1913)
The Lonely Lady of Dulwich (1934)
Lost Diaries (1913)
Lost Lectures (1932)

Mahasena (1905)
The Mainsprings of Russia (1914)
Manfroy (1920)

Orpheus in Mayfair and Other
Stories and Sketches (1909)
Outline of Russian Literature (1914)
Overlooked (1922)
Oxford Book of Russian Verse
(Chosen by Maurice Baring)
(1924)

Palamon and Arcite (1913)
Passing By (1921)
Poems 1914–19 (1921)
Proserpine (1908)

Punch and Judy and Other Essays
(1924)
The Puppet Show of Memory (1922)

Robert Peckham (1930)
Round the World in any Number of
Days (1914)
Russian Essays and Stories (1908)
Russian Lyrics (1943)
The Russian People (1911)

Sonnets and Short Poems (1906)
The Story of Forget-me-not and Lily
of the Valley (1909)

Thoughts on Art and Life of
Leonardo da Vinci (translation)
(1906)
Tinker's Leave (1927)
Translations Ancient and Modern
(with originals) (1925)
Translations (Found in a
Commonplace Book) (1916)
A Triangle (1923)

What I Saw in Russia (1913)
With the Russians in Manchuria
(1905)

A Year in Russia (1907)

Index

Note: Maurice Baring's own works appear directly under title; works by others under authors' names

with Marsh, 47; takes Diplomatic
exam, 48–9, 54; travels to Egypt,
49–50; studies at Oxford, 51–3;
parodies, 51; at Foreign Office, 54–5;
at Paris Embassy, 55, 59–62, 71;
practical jokes and exploits, 60–1,
191–2; cuts out poems from books, 62;
social and literary life in Paris, 64–6;
enthusiasm for theatre, 65–7;
admiration for Bernhardt, 65–9;
depression (*ridges*), 69–70; interest in
Catholicism, 70–1, 82; on Diplomatic
career, 71–2; post in Copenhagen, 72,
73–7; poetical dramas, 77–9; first visit
to Russia (1901), 79–81; learns
Russian, 81–3; posted to Rome, 82–4;
leaves Foreign Office, 84–5; moves to
Russia, 84–5, 89–91; reports Russo-
Japanese War, 91–101, 136; returns to
Manchuria, 103–4; journalism, 103,
108, 112, 115; in 1905 Russian
revolution, 104–10, 112–14; prophesies
1917 revolution in Russia, 111; treated
by Wise Woman, 104; finances and
extravagance, 115–16, 189; travels and
experiences in Russia, 116–24;
baldness, 119, 176; negotiates financial
deal in St Petersburg, 125; writings on
Russia and Russian literature, 125–37;
in Near East, 137; converts to Roman
Catholicism, 141–5, 196; in Turkey,
145–9; reports Balkan War, 150–6;
operation for abscess, 156; stays with
Bron and Nan Herbert, 157–9; social
life in London, 158–9, 203–4; trip to
New Zealand, 159; with Trenchard's
RFC in France in Great War, 165–6,
172–5; and outbreak of war, 167–72;
correspondence with Lady Juliet Duff,
176–80, 195; view of women, 177, 196;
wartime patriotic stance, 181–3; on
death of Auberon Herbert, 184;
awarded OBE, 185; turns to full-time
writing, 185, 189–90; declines post-war
offers from Trenchard, 189–90; at
Lovats in Scotland, 191–2; on naval
exercises, 192–4, 210, 223; audience
with Pope, 193; 50th birthday,
199–200; and Diana Cooper, 200–1;
anti-modernism, 202; made Honorary

Wing Commander, 203; bachelorhood,
207–8; scrapbooks, 208; concert and
theatre-going, 209–10; financial
improvement, 213; house at
Rottingdean (Half Way House),
213–14; illness (Parkinson's Disease),
214, 216, 227–34; relations with
women, 216; Ethel Smyth's biography
of, 216–17; literary reputation,
215–223; reputation in France, 220–1;
moves to Scotland in Second War,
232–5; death and obsequies, 233, 235–7
Baring, Susan (MB's sister) *see* Reid,
Susan, Lady
Baring, Thomas (Uncle Tom), 71, 142
Baring, Thomas George *see* Northbrook,
T.G. Baring, 1st Earl
Baring, Lady Ulrica (*née* Duncombe;
Everard's wife), 21
Baumann (vet), 105
Béarn, Martine de, 64, 82–3
Beaton, Cecil, 214
Beaufort (Scotland), 191, 196, 203, 210,
232–5
Beaverbrook, William Maxwell Aitken,
1st Baron, 181, 204
Beerbohm, Max, 44, 209, 231
bell-casting (Russia), 120–2
Belloc, Elodie (*née* Hogan), 51, 144;
death, 177
Belloc, Hilaire: friendship with MB,
51–2, 69, 140–1, 158–9, 223; on French
usage, 69; and MB's interest in
Catholicism, 82, 141–2; reviews MB,
136–7; in North Street, 138; co-edits
North Street Gazette, 139; edits *Eye
Witness*, 140; attacked by Shaw, 140;
on MB as wanderer, 157; and Lady
Juliet Duff, 177; helps with MB's
English Landscape, 180; praises MB
poem, 184; praises *Passing By*, 197; at
MB's 50th birthday party, 200; praises
Cat's Cradle, 206; on MB's
truthfulness, 219; and Sarah Bernhardt,
223; and MB's last illness in Scotland,
233; *The Life of Danton*, 69
Benckendorff, Count Alexander
Konstantinovich, 74–5, 79, 84, 91,
166–7
Benckendorff, Constantine, 74